TOURS

OF HELL

An Apocalyptic Form in Jewish and
Christian Literature

Martha Himmelfarb

FORTRESS PRESS
Philadelphia

Library of Congress Cataloging in Publication Data

Himmelfarb, Martha, 1952–
   Tours of hell.

   Based on the author's thesis, University of Pennsylvania.
   Bibliography: p.
   Includes index.
   1. Apocalyptic literature—History and criticism.
   2. Future punishment in literature. 3. Hell in literature.
   I. Title.
   [BL501.H56 1985]   236'.25   84–48729
   ISBN 0-8006-1845-9 (pbk.)

1412K84   Printed in the United States of America   1–1845

CONTENTS

ACKNOWLEDGMENTS

It is a pleasure to remember the many people for whose assistance in the writing of this book I am grateful. The book grows out of a dissertation for the Department of Religious Studies of the University of Pennsylvania. My adviser, Robert A. Kraft, has had a profound influence on my approach to the study of texts. E. Ann Matter, of the same department, offered many helpful comments on the final draft of the dissertation. It was my great good luck that Michael E. Stone, who introduced me to the study of apocalyptic literature years ago at the Hebrew University of Jerusalem, began his regular visits to the department at the University of Pennsylvania in 1977–78, just as I began work on my dissertation. The importance of his ideas for my work goes far beyond what can be footnoted.

At a later stage in its development, my manuscript benefited from the comments of Chancellor Gerson D. Cohen of the Jewish Theological Seminary and George W. E. Nickelsburg of the University of Iowa. John G. Gager, my colleague in the Department of Religion at Princeton University, read the manuscript and was always available for advice and encouragement.

My father, Milton Himmelfarb, took an active interest in the project from the beginning, and his comments on broad issues and technical points have improved the final product in many ways. My husband, Steven Weiss, read and criticized draft after draft of the manuscript; his encouragement and enthusiasm were unfailing.

Lorraine Fuhrmann and Bernice Leichter of the Department of Religion at Princeton typed the manuscript, parts of it several times, expertly and uncomplainingly. In addition, the Council on Research in the Humanities and Social Sciences of Princeton University provided funds for some outside help with typing and a generous grant toward the cost of publication.

Finally, I hope that it does not seem inappropriate to dedicate a book about hell to the memories of two women who surely now shine like the brightness of the firmament, my grandmother, Minnie Siskind, and our beloved friend, Margaret Gaffney.

GENERAL ABBREVIATIONS

ANET	J. Pritchard, *Ancient Near Eastern Texts Relating to the Old Testament*
ApNT	M. R. James, *The Apocryphal New Testament*
APOT	R. H. Charles, *The Apocrypha and Pseudepigrapha of the Old Testament*
Danby	H. Danby, *The Mishnah*
EJ	*Encyclopedia Judaica*
FRLANT	Forschungen zur Religion und Literatur des Alten und Neuen Testaments
GCS	Die griechischen christlichen Schriftsteller der ersten drei Jahrhundert
HSW	E. Hennecke, *New Testament Apocrypha* (Ed. W. Schneemelcher; English translation ed. R. McL. Wilson)
HUCA	*Hebrew Union College Annual*
JE	*Jewish Encyclopedia*
JTS	*Journal of Theological Studies*
LAOT	M. R. James, *Lost Apocrypha of the Old Testament*
LXX	Septuagint
PVTG	Pseudepigrapha Veteris Testamenti Graece
PW	Pauly-Wissowa, *Realencyklopadie der classischen Altertumswissenschaft*
1QH	Thanksgiving Psalms from Qumran
1QS	Manual of Discipline from Qumran
RSV	Revised Standard Version of the Bible
SCS	Septuagint and Cognate Studies
SVTP	Studia in Veteris Testamenti Pseudepigrapha
TNDT	*Theological Dictionary of the New Testament*
TU	Texte und Untersuchungen

ABBREVIATIONS FOR THE TOURS OF HELL

Acts Th.	Acts of Thomas
Apoc. Ezra	Apocalypse of Ezra
Apoc. Gorg.	Apocalypse of Gorgorios
Apoc. Paul	Apocalypse of Paul
Apoc. Pet.	Apocalypse of Peter
Apoc. Zeph.	Apocalypse of Zephaniah
Dar. Tesh.	midrash from *Darkhei Teshuvah*
Elij. frag.	Elijah fragment
Eth. Apoc. Bar.	Ethiopic Apocalypse of Baruch
Eth. Apoc. Mary	Ethiopic Apocalypse of Mary
Ged. Mosh.	*Gedulat Moshe*
Gk. Apoc. Mary	Greek Apocalypse of Mary
Isa. frag.	Isaiah fragment
Josh. frag.	Joshua b. Levi fragment
L. Pach.	vision from the Life of Pachomios
T. Isaac	Testament of Isaac
Vis. Ezra	Vision of Ezra

INTRODUCTION
The Tradition of Tours of Hell

From the ancient Egyptian Book of the Dead to Dante's *Divine Comedy*, the living have attempted to describe the world of the dead. This study is concerned with one form that attempt took, the tours of hell in Jewish and Christian writings of late antiquity (from the turn of the era to perhaps the fifth century), their background, and the tradition to which they gave rise. The popularity of this mode of speculation about the fate of the dead with its opportunity for moralizing instruction was long-lived; indeed, among the sources on which Dantologists believe the master drew are descendants of tours from the beginning of the era.

The seventeen tours of hell examined below are preserved in five languages and span perhaps a thousand years. They appear in a variety of contexts. Some of the texts consist only of a tour of hell; others place the tour in a narrative. Some tours include paradise as well as hell. Others add predictions about the end time, collective eschatology, to the individual eschatology of the tour. The texts have in common such features as the tour form, a hero (or a single heroine, the Virgin Mary) drawn from Jewish or Christian scripture (or occasionally a later holy man), a heavenly revealer, and descriptions of the punishments awaiting the wicked in hell.

The presence of any one of these features alone does not necessarily indicate a relationship among the works in which it appears; even the presence of all of them together might mean no more than common religious assumptions and shared canonical texts. But the consistent appearance of explanations of the sights of hell which employ demonstrative pronouns or adjectives in a characteristic manner (Chapter 2) and the recurrence of specific punishments and groups of punishments in various subgroups of the texts (Chapters 3 and 4), taken together with those broad similarities, strongly suggest some kind of continuity among the tours of hell.

This does not mean that the link between two related texts is always or even usually one of literary dependence. The possible (and actual) types of relationship between texts can be placed on a continuum with literary borrowing at one end and nonliterary influence at the other. In between are the use of common sources, written and otherwise, common models, and nonliterary borrowing. The nature of the relationship between two tours of hell can be determined only by a careful reading of both texts in the context of the tours of hell as a group; without that context it is impossible to judge whether a parallel indicates relationship or whether it is a cliché. One text may engage in literary borrowing from a second text, share a common source with a third text, and show the influence of a fourth text without any literary link.

It is this uneven web of relationships among the texts that leads me to speak of them as constituting a tradition. I use "tradition" to suggest historical continuity, while leaving open the precise nature of the connection between particular texts.[1]

The decision to treat the tours of hell but to give relatively little attention to the tours of paradise that accompany some of them requires a word of explanation. While other tours contain glimpses of paradise, a real tour of paradise appears only in the Apocalypse of Paul and its Ethiopic descendants. Thus paradise is of less interest than hell for the development of these tours.

The goal of this study is to reconstruct as far as possible the history of the development of the tradition of tours of hell. It will be argued in Chapter 2 that the prehistory of this tradition goes back as far as the Book of the Watchers, the work preserved as chapters 1–36 of 1 Enoch, the first place the characteristic explanations with demonstratives of the tour apocalypses appear.

J. T. Milik's publication of the Aramaic fragments of 1 Enoch from Qumran[2] has shown that the Book of the Watchers is much older than previously realized. It goes back to some time in the third century B.C.E., while another section of 1 Enoch, chapters 72–82, the Book of the Heavenly Luminaries, appears to be even older. The Qumran fragments, then, place these two Enochic works among the earliest surviving extrabiblical Jewish texts and make them the earliest apocalypses. Both works are tours,

---

1. To avoid confusion, it should be noted that "tradition" is used in a second way in the course of this study, as more or less synonymous with "lore." A story or motif that cannot be attributed to a single author or text, probably oral in origin and transmitted orally for some time, is a tradition.

2. J. T. Milik, in collaboration with M. Black, *The Books of Enoch: Aramaic Fragments of Qumran Cave 4* (Oxford: Oxford University, 1976).

concerned primarily with the sights that the visionary sees in the course of a journey through the cosmos, rather than with collective eschatology. Thus the tour apocalypse emerges as the earliest form of apocalypse and takes a central place in the discussion of the development of the apocalypse as a literary genre.

The view that the tours of hell find their proper context in Jewish and Christian apocalyptic literature is not shared by what is probably the most influential work about a tour of hell, A. Dieterich's *Nekyia*.[3] This book is a study of the Apocalypse of Peter, the earliest tour of hell that can be dated with any certainty, generally regarded as the fountainhead of the tradition. Dieterich considers the Apocalypse of Peter to be the successor to archaic and classical Greek descents into Hades, far removed from Jewish literature. The claim of indebtedness to these Greek descents is repeated in much of the secondary literature, and it will be discussed in Chapters 2, 3, and 4.

Unfortunately for the historian who turns from the prehistory to the development of the tradition, it is extremely difficult to date most of the tours of hell or to place them geographically or culturally. While several of the texts can be dated within certain limits on the basis of patristic references or similar evidence, for most the dating is guesswork. In many instances the only evidence about the date is the manuscripts. Thus for some tours of hell the only firm *terminus ad quem* is the seventeenth century, although the works are surely earlier.

For many of the tours of hell, language is one of the few clues to an historical setting. Even when the language in which it is preserved is not the language in which it was composed, the presence of a text in a particular language indicates sufficient interest on the part of some group of speakers of that language to translate and copy the text at some point in its career. When the language is that of the original or when the translator was also a reviser, the text is linked more securely to the history of the linguistic group, although it often remains impossible to identify a specific historical context.

Three Ethiopic texts, for example, are among the tours of hell discussed below. All contain references that indicate that at least in their present form they are not simply translations, but the work of either Ethiopian Christians or of Falashas, the nonrabbinic Jews of Ethiopia. Yet the study of the Ethiopic church, as of the other oriental churches, is not yet at a stage where the resources are available to place these texts more precisely in time

---

3. A. Dieterich, *Nekyia: Beiträge zur Erklärung der neuentdeckten Petrusapokalypse*, 2d ed., annotated by R. Wünsch (Leipzig and Berlin: Teubner, 1913; 1st ed., 1893).

or in relation to developments in thought.[4] Much of what has been written about Ethiopic Christianity concentrates on what is unique to it rather than on popular or monastic concerns that it shares with other varieties of medieval Christianity. Research on the history of the Falashas is in an even more primitive state.[5] Nevertheless, with careful study, despite the inherent problems in using the tours of hell as a source for social history (see below, pp. 73–75), an expert in the religious history of Ethiopia might be able to begin to place these texts in historical context.

The same lament about the absence of resources for the historian can be repeated in relation to the Coptic church and the Coptic texts considered below.[6] While the discovery of the Nag Hammadi codices has given new momentum to research on the early period, results that are relevant to this study are still many years away.

Even for the Latin and Greek churches, which have certainly not suffered from lack of attention, it is in general high theology rather than popular religiosity that has been the focus of investigation.[7] Further, when a text cannot be assigned to a particular century or to a 500-mile radius, outstanding subtlety and learning are required to bring it into relation to specific movements or events.

In the case of the Hebrew tours of hell, the problem is if anything more acute. Since Hebrew was used for religious literature by chronologically and geographically diverse Jewish communities, the Hebrew texts, with the exception of one tour of hell transmitted by an identifiable figure, are particularly difficult to link to specific periods, locations, or movements at

---

4. The history of the Ethiopic church as it has been written is primarily institutional history, of relatively little use for this study. An indication of the present state of study of the Ethiopic church is the bibliography to the article "Ethiopian (Abyssinian) Church" in F. L. Cross and E. A. Livingstone, *The Oxford Dictionary of the Christian Church*, 2d ed. (London: Oxford University, 1974), in which there appear relatively few twentieth-century works, many broad surveys of the Eastern churches in general, a few works on subjects like the liturgy of the Ethiopic church, and no history of thought.

5. For a summary of what is known about the Falashas, see M. Wurmbrand, "Falashas," *EJ*. Little more is known about the origins of the Falashas than the legends. The relationship of the Falashas to Ethiopian Christians in different periods and its bearing on the literature of the two groups have not been studied in detail.

6. The institutional history of the Coptic church, at least from the sixth century, is relatively well documented, but again, as a glance at "Coptic Church" in *The Oxford Dictionary of the Christian Church* indicates, much of the work is not from this century, and there is no history of thought.

7. Even J. Pelikan's new history of Christian thought (*The Christian Tradition: A History of the Development of Doctrine*, 3 vols. to date [Chicago and London: University of Chicago, 1971–]), with its emphasis on doctrine rather than dogma, shows no interest in texts of the kind discussed here.

any stage of their transmission. While it seems likely that the Christian texts could be integrated into the wider history of Christian thought if only more were known about popular religion or monastic literary activity, the Jewish texts considered here describe hell in terms quite different from those of the standard rabbinic sources and even of the more popular midrashim. As with the various ethnic Christian churches (Coptic, Ethiopic, etc.), the popular literature has received little scholarly attention.[8]

The vacuum surrounding most of the texts discussed here makes a truly historical account of their emergence and development, relating them to specific trends in Jewish and Christian thought and movements in Jewish and Christian history, impossible. At this stage, any study of the tours of hell must be almost exclusively literary.

Significant similarities of language and imagery are thus the primary evidence for relationships between texts. While it is clear that the temptation to view every such similarity as significant is a danger to be avoided, the determination of which parallels do suggest a relationship between two texts is one of those matters of judgment for which few clear-cut criteria exist. A critic must consider all relevant factors, different in each case, in order to arrive at a conclusion that is inevitably subjective.

In the texts considered below, for example, many parallels consist of the use of biblical language or biblical motifs. Such parallels in themselves prove little about the relationship between two texts, because the authors of all the texts undoubtedly had access to the Bible. Thus the presence of adulterers and adulteresses in hell in several of the texts in itself indicates nothing about the relationship of those texts. The combination of adultery with a specific punishment that has no biblical or other obvious precedent (hanging by the genitals for men, by the hair or breasts for women), on the other hand, strongly suggests some relationship among the texts in which it appears, although not necessarily a literary relationship or a relationship of direct dependence.

The background of the sins and punishments of hell, their relation to earlier Jewish and Greek beliefs and motifs, then, is important not only for the question of the prehistory of the tours of hell and Dieterich's view of the Apocalypse of Peter as a Christianized version of a Greek descent. It is this background that allows one to determine whether a motif was widely known or appeared in a work to which the author of the tour in question is likely to have had access.

---

8. This is made clear by the discussions in H. L. Strack, *Introduction to the Talmud and Midrash* (Philadelphia: Jewish Publication Society, 1931), L. Zunz and H. Albeck, *HaDerashot B'Yisrael* (Jerusalem: Mosad Bialik, 1947), or most recently, M. D. Herr, "Midrashim, Smaller," *EJ*.

In order to arrive at the most balanced evaluation of textual parallels, the widest possible range of evidence must be considered. To cite an example discussed below in considerable detail (see the discussion of punishment for abortion and infanticide in chap. 3), scholars since M. R. James have viewed the punishment for abortion/infanticide in the Apocalypse of Paul as one piece of evidence for its direct dependence on the Apocalypse of Peter. Yet if these two punishments are placed on a continuum that includes the punishments for the same sins in other tours of hell, these two instances turn out to be relatively distant. Thus, while the similarity between the punishments in the two texts cannot be denied, this particular parallel should not be presented as evidence of direct literary dependence.

What is required, then, is a careful examination of the contents of the tours of hell. While the presence of demonstrative explanations in a tour of hell may be sufficient to mark it as belonging to the tradition discussed here, the determination of precisely which sins and punishments each text shares with others is crucial for clarification of the nature of the relationships among the various texts.

As families of sin-and-punishment combinations emerge, they begin to point to common sources and lines of influence. Different degrees of similarity suggest different types of relationship. Sometimes a common detail is so striking that it suggests direct literary dependence. More often common sources, texts or traditions not confined to a single text or group of texts, provide a more plausible explanation of parallels. Sometimes the similarities are so vague that one can speak only of the influence of other tours in the most general way rather than of common sources.

Under close scrutiny the patterns of distribution of sins and punishments yield a picture not of linear development based on direct literary dependence but of a far more complex course of development. (These patterns are discussed in Chapters 3 and 4; they provide the basis for the view of the history of the texts set forth in Chapter 5).

In light of the difficulty of giving them a conscientious historical treatment, it is not surprising that relatively little has been written about the tours of hell. *Nekyia*, published almost a century ago, remains the only full-length treatment of one of the early texts, and in the absence of competition it continues to exert its influence on the major sources of information about the other tours of hell, the introductions to individual texts and the dictionary and encyclopedia articles.[9]

These short treatments by their very nature are fragmented, concerned

---

9. See, e.g., the introductions to the Apocalypse of Peter and the Apocalypse of Paul in HSW.

not with the whole picture but with single texts. Perhaps as a result of this narrow focus they have a tendency to understand the history of the tours of hell as one of linear development. The Apocalypse of Paul, for example, is seen as a direct descendant of the Apocalypse of Peter because of the parallels between the two works; almost any parallel is treated as suggesting direct dependence. Little attempt is made to achieve a more comprehensive view of the possible types of relationship between two texts or a more sensitive understanding of the meaning of parallels.

Another angle of approach to the tours of hell appears in the work of medievalists and students of Dante.[10] In linking the early texts to the medieval visions with which they are especially concerned, these scholars are misled by their ignorance of the existence of less well-known writings that may have served as intermediaries in the transmission process. T. Silverstein's *Visio Sancti Pauli*,[11] a detailed history of the transmission of the Apocalypse of Paul in western Europe in the Middle Ages, is an exception; I have drawn on it extensively.

One more study is particularly worthy of mention. S. Lieberman's "On Sins and Their Punishments"[12] treats the history of the Hebrew texts. Although its conclusions are disputed below (see Lieberman's reconstruction of the development of the Jewish tours of hell in chap. 5), it has been of great importance for shaping the views put forward in opposition to it.

---

10. For literature on the medieval visions, see the bibliography of T. Silverstein, *Visio Sancti Pauli*, Studies and Documents 4 (London: Christophers, 1935). For the literature on Dante, see the references and discussion in Silverstein, "Dante and the Legend of the *Mi'rāj*: The Problem of Islamic Influence on the Christian Literature of the Other World," *Journal of Near Eastern Studies* 11(1952): 91–93.

11. See note 10 above.

12. S. Lieberman, "On Sins and Their Punishments," in *Texts and Studies* (New York: KTAV, 1974); Eng. trans. of "On Sins and Their Punishments" [Hebr.], in *Louis Ginzberg Jubilee Volume*, Hebrew section (New York: American Academy of Jewish Research, 1945).

Chapter 1

THE TEXTS

The purpose of this chapter is to provide an introduction to the texts considered in this study through brief discussions of their historical settings, as far as they are known, and of their contents. Technical matters are treated in appendixes to these discussions. Information about editions, translations, and bibliographical sources for each of the texts is provided in the first part of the Bibliography at the end of the book, "Select Bibliography of the Tours of Hell."

The texts are arranged in roughly chronological order with the exception of the Apocalypse of Paul family, which is treated immediately after its ancestor, and of the Hebrew texts and the Latin Elijah fragment, which are reserved until after the other texts. Grouping the Hebrew texts together makes it easier to discuss certain common features and influences. The Elijah fragment is treated with the Hebrew texts because of the indications that it is related to some of them. Finally several groups of texts related to those that form the subject of this study are discussed very briefly.

THE APOCALYPSE OF PETER

The earliest of the tours of hell that can be dated with any certainty is the Apocalypse of Peter. Citations by Clement of Alexandria (*Eclogues* 41 and 48) place it no later than the middle of the second century.[1] Before the

---

1. C. Maurer, "Apocalypse of Peter," HSW 2:664, argues for a *terminus a quo* in 4 Ezra, about 100 C.E. But Peter's lament over the sinners and Jesus' answer do not seem to imply literary dependence on 4 Ezra. Maurer also puts forward H. Weinel's suggestion of an allusion to Bar Kokhba in the parable of the fig tree (chap. 2). This would give a date about 135 C.E. F. Spitta argued for the dependence of the Apocalypse of Peter on 2 Peter ("Die Petrusapokalypse und der zweite Petrusbrief," *Zeitschrift für die neutestamentliche Wissenschaft* 12[1911]:237–42). Even if he is correct (he knew only the Akhmim text), the date of 2 Peter is too controversial to be of much help.

discovery in 1887 of a Greek manuscript of the eighth or ninth century in the grave of a monk at Akhmim in Upper Egypt, it had been known only from patristic allusions and mentions in canon lists. In the first decade of the twentieth century a longer Ethiopic version came to light in the d'Abbadie manuscript collection.

From the beginning, M. R. James argued that the Ethiopic text was closer to the lost original of the Apocalypse of Peter than was the Greek from Akhmim. In this he was supported by K. Prümm, and their view has been widely accepted.[2]

For Clement and the Muratorian Canon, the Apocalypse of Peter is scripture, although the Canon knows that some reject it. It is quoted both in the East and in the West until the beginning of the fifth century. Its last appearance in patristic literature comes in Sozomen's report in the early fifth century of public readings in Palestine during holy week (*Ecclesiastical History* 7.19).[3] The text from Akhmim indicates knowledge of the Apocalypse of Peter in eighth- or ninth-century Egypt, if only in a revised form. This and the existence of an Ethiopic translation suggest that it circulated in the East longer than in the West.[4]

In the Ethiopic, the Apocalypse of Peter is a revelation made by Jesus to his disciples, and Peter in particular. It begins with the disciples' request that Jesus, seated on the Mount of Olives, reveal to them the signs of the end. This setting and the contents of the first several chapters are closely related to Matthew 24 and parallels. Jesus warns the disciples against the deceiving Christs who will arise, causing many to be martyred (chaps. 1–2).[5] Then Jesus shows Peter "on the palm of his right hand the image of that which shall be fulfilled at the last day" (chap. 3). Hell will open and a general resurrection will take place (chap. 4). The earth will be consumed by fire and covered with darkness (chap. 5). Jesus will come on a cloud, and the eternal punishment of the sinners will begin (chap. 6).

The description of their punishment follows (chaps. 7–12). Some sin-

2. M. R. James, "A New Text of the Apocalypse of Peter," *JTS* 12(1910–11):36–54, 157, 362–83, 573–83; idem, "The Recovery of the Apocalypse of Peter," *Church Quarterly Review* 159(1915):1–36; idem, "The Rainer Fragment of the Apocalypse of Peter," *JTS* 32(1931): 270–79. K. Prümm, "De Genuino Apocalypsis Petri Textu," *Biblica* 10(1929):62–80. Maurer, HSW 2:663–68.

3. On knowledge of the Apocalypse of Peter in the early Middle Ages, A. von Harnack, *Die Petrusapokalypse in der alten abendländischen Kirche*, TU 13.1, 71–73; (Leipzig: J. C. Hinrichs, 1895); James, "New Text," 380–83; Maurer, HSW 2:664.

4. S. Grébaut, who first summarized the Ethiopic Apocalypse of Peter ("Littérature éthiopienne pseudo-clémentine," *Revue de l'orient chrétien* 12[1907]:139–45) and then published and translated it ("Littérature éthiopienne pseudo-clémentine," *Revue de l'orient chrétien* 15[1910]:198–214, 307–23), does not provide any information about the date of the MS.

5. References to chapters in the body of the text refer to the translation of H. Duensing in HSW.

ners hang by the limb that sinned. Others are immersed in fiery pits and are tortured by cruel beasts. Still others have fire applied to the sinful limb. It is clear from chapters 1–6 that the Apocalypse of Peter views the punishments as beginning only at the last judgment unlike most of the other texts to be discussed here, which understand themselves to describe what is actually taking place in hell at the moment of the revelation.

Finally Peter is given a glimpse of the future bliss of the righteous. They will witness the punishment of the sinners (chap. 13), and they will be transported to Acherusia, elsewhere a lake but here identified with the Elysian fields (chap. 14).

The scene shifts to Jesus and the disciples at the "holy mountain." The disciples see two men of wonderful appearance (chap. 15), identified by Jesus as Moses and Elijah. Peter sees the beautiful garden, now the abode of the patriarchs, soon to be the place of the persecuted righteous (chap. 16). The conclusion of the Apocalypse of Peter is a version of the transfiguration narrative of the Gospels (chaps. 16–17).

APPENDIX: THE RELATIONSHIP OF THE GREEK AND ETHIOPIC TEXTS

M. R. James is responsible for establishing the view that the Ethiopic version stands closer to the original Greek of the Apocalypse of Peter than does the Greek of the Akhmim manuscript. He argued that (1) the length of the Ethiopic version corresponds better to the length of the Apocalypse of Peter according to the ancient lists;[6] (2) all the certain patristic references correspond to the Ethiopic version;[7] (3) the order of the Ethiopic text is paralleled by Sib. Or. 2:238–338, which follows the Apocalypse of Peter very closely;[8] (4) the future and present tenses of the Ethiopic are attested in Clement, Methodius, and the Bodleian fragment;[9] (5) the Bodleian and Rainer fragments, the earliest of all manuscripts of the Apocalypse of Peter, correspond better to the Ethiopic than to the Akhmim text.[10]

James also suggested an explanation for the form of the Akhmim text: the Apocalypse of Peter has been adapted to serve as part of the Gospel of Peter, another

---

6. James, "New Text," 583.

7. Ibid., 369–75; James, "Recovery," 19–20. Maurer points out that the passages cited appear in chaps. 4, 5, 8, 10, 12, and 14, thus vouching for the work as a whole, not just a single section (HSW 2:665–66).

8. James, "New Text," 576.

9. Ibid., 369; James, "Recovery," 17–19.

10. James, "New Text," 367–69; idem, "Rainer Fragment," 270–75. James argues in "Rainer Fragment" (278–79) that the Bodleian fragment and the Rainer fragment come from a single MS. He attributes the discrepancy in the dates assigned the fragments (the Bodleian was assigned to the fifth century, the Rainer to the third or fourth century) to their poor condition, but does not offer an opinion on the correct date.

long-lost text that came to light in the same codex from the grave at Akhmim. James attributed this adaptation to the author of the Gospel of Peter.[11]

James operated on the assumption that the Ethiopic version was a direct translation from Greek. But it is more usual during the Middle Ages for Greek texts to reach Ethiopic through the intermediary of Arabic translations.[12] Further, the Ethiopic Apocalypse of Peter is attached to a discourse of Peter to Clement, "his son."[13] Much of the Ethiopic pseudo-Clementine literature is known to have been translated from Arabic.[14] Prümm alludes to the possibility of an intermediate Arabic translation,[15] but to the best of my knowledge no one has systematically addressed the question of whether such a translation lies between the original Greek form of the Apocalypse of Peter and the Ethiopic version.

THE ACTS OF THOMAS

The Acts of Thomas has come down to us in two major versions, Greek and Syriac. The earliest form is usually dated to the first half of the third century. There is widespread agreement that its original language was Syriac but that the Greek was translated from a form of the Syriac earlier than the one extant.[16] Yet, as G. Bornkamm cautions, each case must be judged

---

11. James, "Recovery," 21–23.

12. E. Ullendorf, *Ethiopia and the Bible* (London: British Academy, 1968), 57–59. M. Chaîne ("Apocalypsis seu Visio Mariae Virginis," in *Apocrypha de B. Mariae Virginis*, Corpus Scriptorum Christianorum Orientalium, Scriptores Aethiopici 1/7 [1909] Latin section, 43) thinks that the Ethiopic Apocalypse of Mary is translated from Arabic. (He is wrong about the Greek works that he assumes are the originals of that Arabic. They are considerably shorter works concerned only with punishments. The Greek Apocalypse of Mary, discussed below, is one of them. Thus, while the Ethiopic Apocalypse of Mary may derive from a Greek original, none of these texts is that original.) On the subject of translation into Ethiopic, see also the brief remarks of W. Leslau, *Falasha Anthology*, Yale Judaica Series 6 (New Haven: Yale University, 1951), 63, and Grébaut, "Littérature éthiopienne" (1907), 285.

13. The Ethiopic Apocalypse of Peter is the first part of an apocryphon that concludes with a discourse by Peter to Clement. The apocalypse is not separated from the discourse. The work as a whole is entitled "Second Coming of Christ and Resurrection of the Dead." It is found in MS d'Abbadie 51, together with several other short apocrypha.

14. Grébaut, "Littérature éthiopienne" (1907), 140–41. The Ethiopic Apocalypse of Peter does not, however, correspond to the Arabic Apocalypse of Peter translated by A. Mingana (*The Apocalypse of Peter, Edited and Translated*, Woodbrooke Studies 3.2 [Cambridge, Eng.: W. Heffer & Sons, 1931]). This is why Maurer feels it necessary to make the otherwise odd statement "There is no point of contact with the so-called Apocalypse of Peter translated from the Arabic" (HSW 2:664). Leslau seems to have made the mistake of identifying the Arabic apocalypse with the Ethiopic (*Falasha Anthology*, 63).

15. Prümm, "De Genuino," 64, 76–78.

16. The major differences between the Greek and the Syriac consist largely of passages in which the Syriac is more "orthodox" than the Greek. This is usually taken as a sign of the Greek's relative earliness.

on its own merits,[17] and the passage containing the vision of hell turns out to be particularly difficult from this point of view.

Among the many conversions effected by the preaching of the apostle in the Acts of Thomas is one that requires a tour of hell to persuade the sinner to repent. In both versions of Act 6, a young man tries, after hearing Thomas preach, to convince his beloved to join him in a life of chastity. She refuses, and he kills her. When she is brought back to life by Thomas's prayers, she describes the tour of hell on which she was taken while dead. The moral of the story is that one should give up the sins of one's old life and follow Jesus.

While the frame of the tour is the same in both versions, the descriptions of hell differ considerably. The Syriac version is concerned exclusively with sexual sins, and the punishments consist mainly of confinement in fiery pits and dark caves. The Greek version includes other types of sins, hanging punishments, and a punishment for abortion similar to the two such punishments found in the Apocalypse of Peter.

The relationship between the Greek and Syriac of this passage is difficult to clarify. Is one the original, the other a reworking? Are both reworkings of some earlier form? For the purposes of this study, it is the Greek version that is important, whether it is original or not, because of its similarities to the Apocalypse of Peter and the Jewish texts.[18]

The meaning of these similarities can be analyzed more easily after a full discussion of the sins and punishments of all the tours of hell, and so I shall postpone the analysis to Chapter 5. Yet one point needs to be made at the outset. Both James and Bornkamm interpret the similarities between the tours of hell in the Greek version of the Acts of Thomas and the Apocalypse of Peter as evidence that the Acts borrowed from the apocalypse. In their view the Acts of Thomas is not an independent witness to an early tradition of punishments in hell.[19] For the purpose of the discussion in the intervening chapters, let me anticipate my conclusions: there are no grounds for viewing the Acts of Thomas as dependent on the Apocalypse

---

17. G. Bornkamm, "The Acts of Thomas," HSW 2:428.

18. Similarity to the Jewish texts can be used as an argument for or against the originality of the Greek. Someone like A. F. J. Klijn (*The Acts of Thomas*, Novum Testamentum Supplements 5 [Leiden: Brill, 1962], 251–53), who claims that the Syriac is original, could argue that the Greek represents a reworking under the influence of Jewish traditions. (Klijn's argument is not clear, but he appears to think that the Syriac is as indebted to Jewish traditions as is the Greek.) But one could also argue that the Greek version reflects contemporary Jewish and Greek traditions while the Syriac has been reworked by someone with ascetic interests.

19. M. R. James (*ApNT*, 390, n. 1) offers no arguments for his claim, which appears in a one-sentence note to his translation of the Acts of Thomas. G. Bornkamm (*Mythos und Legende in der apokryphen Thomas-Akten*, FRLANT, n.s. 31 [Göttingen: Vandenhoeck & Ruprecht, 1933], 46–48) prints the parallel passages from the Acts of Thomas and the Apoc-

of Peter; rather, both texts drew on the same early traditions as the later Hebrew texts and the Latin Elijah fragment.

THE APOCALYPSE OF ZEPHANIAH

Although it is clearly related to them, the Apocalypse of Zephaniah stands apart from the other texts discussed here. The fate of souls after death is the dominant interest of the work, but only a small part of the tour is concerned with hell itself.

The Apocalypse of Zephaniah comes down to us in a single Akhmimic manuscript. G. Steindorff inclines toward a fourth- or early fifth-century date for the manuscript and believes that it was translated from Greek.[20] The passage cited by Clement of Alexandria from an Apocalypse of Zephaniah (*Stromateis* 5.11.77) does not correspond to the Akhmimic, and although the Akhmimic text breaks off before its completion, it is difficult to imagine how the description of the fifth heaven quoted by Clement could be integrated into a text that does not show any traces of a belief in a multiplicity of heavens.

The fact that the text is preserved in a Coptic dialect indicates that in the form in which it has reached us it is the property of Christians. There is nothing in the contents of the work that marks it clearly as Christian, however, and some of the features of the Apocalypse of Zephaniah to be discussed later (see the discussion of the Apocalypse of Zephaniah and the Book of the Watchers in chap. 5) may suggest that it is a relatively early Jewish work.

The Apocalypse of Zephaniah begins in the middle of what seems to be the account of a death (1).[21] An angel takes Zephaniah to the place of the righteous dead, which is full of light (2). Zephaniah sees also the punishment of wicked souls and gets an account of the role of the angels who record men's deeds (2–4). Then he comes on a host of terrifying angels whose job it is to punish sinners. His guide assures him that his righteousness will protect him from harm (4–6).

Now Zephaniah follows his guide through brass gates into a beautiful

---

alypse of Peter in two columns, side-by-side, but he does not consider other sources on which the Acts of Thomas might have drawn. The reasoning of both scholars seems to be that given the parallels and the earlier date of the Apocalypse of Peter, the Acts of Thomas depends on the apocalypse.

20. G. Steindorff, *Die Apokalypse des Elias, eine unbekannte Apokalypse und Bruchstücke der Sophonias-Apokalypse*, TU, n.s., 2.3a (Leipzig: J. C. Hinrichs, 1899), introduction, 5–6, 16.

21. References in the body of the text refer to the pages of the Akhmimic MS, published by Steindorff.

city. Suddenly the gates become fiery, a sea of fire and slime appears, and its waves rush at Zephaniah. He thinks that God has come to save him and cries out to him, but, looking up, he discovers a terrible angel about to destroy him. A description of the angel's frightening appearance follows (6–8).

Now Zephaniah prays to God. When he looks up, he sees a magnificent angel, whom he takes to be God. The angel rebukes him for the mistake and introduces himself as Eremiel, the archangel in charge of the dead. He tells Zephaniah that he is now in Amente [22] and that the frightening angel who first appeared to him was none other than the accuser (8–10)!

In his hand the magnificent angel holds a scroll on which Zephaniah finds written in his own language all the sins he had ever committed. He prays to God for forgiveness. A tall angel arrives to lead Zephaniah to paradise. The angel brings him another scroll, also in his own language (10–12). Unfortunately, the text breaks off here.

When we rejoin our hero, he is being helped into a boat while a host of angels sings before him. He puts on an angel's robe and begins to pray and converse with the angels. In paradise are the righteous heroes of the Hebrew Bible (13–14).

Another vision of punishments follows. Abraham, Isaac, and Jacob, along with the other righteous, beseech God on behalf of the sinners once a day (14–17).

Zephaniah is then denied permission to see something—it is not clear from the text exactly what—until the day of judgment, of which he offers a frightening description. In the midst of the description the text breaks off (17–18).

APPENDIX: THE TITLE OF THE APOCALYPSE

Steindorff cautiously refers to this text as an anonymous apocalypse. Others, however, identify it as the Apocalypse of Zephaniah on the evidence of a Sahidic fragment found with the Akhmimic text, in which the seer speaks of himself as Zephaniah.

A Sahidic version of the Apocalypse of Elijah makes up the bulk of the Sahidic manuscript of which this Zephaniah fragment is a part. An Akhmimic version of the Apocalypse of Elijah follows the anonymous apocalypse in the Akhmimic manuscript. Both manuscripts, then, contain the Apocalypse of Elijah. Why not assume that the first text in the Akhmimic manuscript also matches the Sahidic?

Despite the fact that almost every individual sentence in the Sahidic Apocalypse

---

22. Amente is the ancient Egyptian word for the land of the dead, which survives in Coptic.

of Zephaniah has a parallel in the Akhmimic text, the *incident* related in the Sahidic fragment is not found in the Akhmimic. Against the identification of the anonymous apocalypse with the Sahidic Apocalypse of Zephaniah, Steindorff argues that the Sahidic fragment would not make sense in any of the lacunae of the Akhmimic text.[23] Neither the Sahidic nor the Akhmimic manuscript contains the passage quoted by Clement of Alexandria from an Apocalypse of Zephaniah known to him, nor does Clement's passage with its "fifth heaven" seem likely to fit the Akhmimic text. So little is known about an Apocalypse of Zephaniah that it does not add to the understanding of the Akhmimic text to label it "Apocalypse of Zephaniah" even if the title is correct.

Despite these reservations, I have decided to follow the practice of the majority and to refer to the work as the Apocalypse of Zephaniah for ease of reference. Since it appears under that name in the Doubleday edition of the pseudepigrapha, the name is likely to become even better established.

APPENDIX: JEWISH OR CHRISTIAN PROVENANCE?

Steindorff considered the Apocalypse of Zephaniah a Jewish text. In favor of this contention is the absence of any indisputably Christian material; there is no need for surgery to recover a *"jüdische Grundschrift"* as there is in the case of the Apocalypse of Elijah, found in the same codex as the Apocalypse of Zephaniah, or of the Ezra apocalypses.[24]

Harnack, on the other hand, claimed Christian reworking of an originally Jewish text. His argument, which is not spelled out as clearly as it might be, seems to be that Clement's citation of an Apocalypse of Zephaniah proves the existence of a Jewish Apocalypse of Zephaniah, while the absence from the Coptic text of the passage cited by Clement suggests that the Coptic is a revision of the Jewish text. To demonstrate that the reworking is Christian, Harnack alludes to parallels to the Revelation of John and the Gospel of John, which he does not specify, as well as to clearly Christian passages.[25]

Unfortunately, Harnack wrote before Steindorff's edition of the text and relied on L. Stern's 1886 publication, which treated both the Apocalypse of Elijah and the Apocalypse of Zephaniah as the Apocalypse of Zephaniah.[26] The passages cited by

---

23. Steindorff, *Apokalypse*, introduction, 14–16.

24. Steindorff (ibid., introduction, 18) goes so far as to claim that the sins written on the angel's roll—not visiting the sick, widows, and orphans; not fasting; not praying at the time of prayer; not "turning myself back to the children of Israel" (text, 11–12)—are typically Pharisaic. Yet these misdeeds would certainly be considered sins not only by Jews, including many non-Pharisees, but also by Christians, especially monks.

25. A. Harnack, *Geschichte der altchristlichen Literatur bis Eusebius*, 2d ed., introduction by K. Aland (Leipzig: J. C. Hinrichs, 1958; 1st ed., 1893–1904), pt. 2.1, 572–73.

26. L. Stern, "Die koptische Apokalypse des Sophonias," *Zeitschrift für ägyptische Sprache und Altertumskunde* 24(1886): 115–35.

Harnack as clearly Christian come from the Apocalypse of Elijah, and I suspect that the parallels to the Gospel of John must also be referred to it. The parallels between the Apocalypse of Zephaniah and Revelation, to the best of my ability to discern them, consist of similar but not identical descriptions of angels. Unless there are other grounds for believing that the Apocalypse of Zephaniah drew on Revelation, this hardly constitutes proof of Christian elements. Steindorff reports that Harnack told him that the term "catechumen" (16, line 1) need not be Christian.[27]

What is certain is that the preserved manuscript of the Apocalypse of Zephaniah is not a Jewish text, plain and simple. It is found in a codex that contains another text indisputably Christian in its present form, and there is at present no evidence that Jews translated their literature into Coptic. Just as the King James Version of the Hebrew Bible is on one level a Christian text, so too is the Apocalypse of Zephaniah.

THE APOCALYPSE OF PAUL

The Apocalypse of Paul is the longest lived and most influential of the tours of hell. The original Greek is preserved best in the long Latin version, translated from the Greek between the end of the fourth century and the beginning of the sixth, and it is to this version that all comments refer unless otherwise indicated. The apocalypse is preserved also in Armenian, Old Russian, Syriac, Coptic, and a Greek abridgment.[28] In addition the Apocalypse of Paul gave rise to several medieval Latin redactions, discussed briefly under related texts, below, and to a number of other apocalypses with different heroes, whose debt to the Apocalypse of Paul is nevertheless unmistakable, considered below as descendants of the Apocalypse of Paul (see the following five sections, this chapter).

The date of the earliest version of the Apocalypse of Paul is especially difficult to determine. There is some evidence that Origen knew the work, and this would agree with the early third-century date that the content of the body of the work suggests; but such a date is in conflict with the precise date, 388 C.E., given in the so-called Tarsus introduction, an account of the discovery of the work found in several of the most important versions. I am inclined to follow R. Casey in viewing the body of the work as dating from the early third century;[29] a fuller discussion of this problem is re-

---

27. Steindorff, *Apokalypse*, introduction, 18, n. 1.

28. Silverstein, *Visio*, offers the most complete discussion of the ancestry of the various versions, and especially of the Latin, including a stemma (20–39). His picture of the development of the medieval Latin redactions is revised in the light of new evidence in "The Vision of St. Paul: New Links and Patterns in the Western Tradition," *Archives d'histoire doctrinale et littéraire du moyen âge* 34(1959):199–248.

29. R. Casey, "The Apocalypse of Paul," *JTS* 34(1933):28, 31.

served for the appendix to this section. The Apocalypse's interest in and praise of ascetics suggests that its author was an ascetic.[30]

Like the Apocalypse of Peter, the Apocalypse of Paul is linked to a passage from the New Testament, in this case 2 Cor. 12:2–4, in which Paul mentions his journey to the third heaven, where he saw unspeakable mysteries. The Tarsus introduction (chaps. 1–2) is followed by nature's complaint to God about the evil ways of the human race and the angels' report on the troubles of the righteous (chaps. 3–10). Paul is caught up to the third heaven (chap. 11), where he sees the departure of both righteous and wicked souls from the body at death (chaps. 11–18). The righteous soul is greeted joyfully by a chorus of good angels, while the wicked soul falls into the hands of the wicked angels.

Next Paul visits paradise, located in the third heaven, where he is greeted by Enoch and Elijah (chaps. 19–20). At this point, it seems that Paul and his angelic guide leave the heavens for their visit to the land of promise, where the righteous will dwell during the millennium. Its beauty and fertility are described (chaps. 21–22). Next Paul sees Lake Acherusia, and he travels in a golden boat to the city of Christ on its shores (chaps. 22–23). Inside the city ascetics who were otherwise righteous but sinned with pride are being punished (chap. 24).

Now Paul tours the four rivers of the city of Christ and meets the righteous who are gathered along them, including heroes of the Hebrew Bible (chaps. 25–28). This tour is followed by a description of the city of Christ and the altar in its midst at which David sings (chaps. 29–30).

Then Paul and his guide turn to the place of punishment (chaps. 31–42). The hell of the Apocalypse of Paul is described in greater detail than the hell of the Apocalypse of Peter. There are more groups of sinners. In addition to pits it contains rivers of fire. It offers worms, beasts, and angels of torment in greater numbers than the Apocalypse of Peter. Hanging is less prominent than it was in the Apocalypse of Peter, although not altogether absent.

By the end of the tour Paul weeps and sighs, "It would be better for us if we who are all sinners had never been born." Paul and the archangel Michael join the sinners in beseeching God for mercy (chap. 43). Finally Christ appears and rebukes the sinners, but grants them Sunday respite.[31] Now Paul returns to paradise (chaps. 45–51). He is met by the righteous,

---

30. Ibid., 8.

31. I. Lévi ("Le repos sabbatique des âmes damnées," *Revue des études juives* 25[1892]:1–13) argues that the Apocalypse of Paul takes this motif from rabbinic tradition. Silverstein (*Visio*, 79, 124, n. 96) accepts his conclusion, as does Lieberman ("Sins," 32), although he objects to some of Lévi's other arguments.

including the Virgin Mary, the patriarchs, Moses, the prophets, John the Baptist, and Adam. The Coptic text goes on to describe still another visit to paradise and finally places Paul on the Mount of Olives with the disciples, like Peter in the Apocalypse of Peter.

APPENDIX: THE DATE AND PROVENANCE OF THE APOCALYPSE OF PAUL

The Apocalypse of Paul presents special problems for dating. The Greek, Latin, and Syriac versions contain an introduction or postscript which claims that the book was discovered under a house in Tarsus in 388 C.E. Yet according to Bar Hebraeus (*Nomocanon* 7.9), Origen, who died in the mid-third century, mentions the Apocalypse of Paul as a work accepted by the church. Origen's *Homily 5 on Psalms* contains a description of the fate of the soul after death very similar to the description in the Apocalypse of Paul, but it does not mention the Apocalypse of Paul by name.[32]

The contradiction between the date in the introduction to the Apocalypse of Paul and the evidence from Origen has led some to amend the text of Bar Hebraeus.[33] Casey argues instead that the Tarsus introduction is not an integral part of the text, as shown by its absence from the Coptic and its position at the end, rather than the beginning, of the Syriac version.[34] If the Tarsus introduction is secondary and Origen's knowledge of the text is accepted, the original form of the Apocalypse of Paul dates back to the early third century.

In support of this date, Casey argues that the heretics found in the apocalypse's hell are more appropriate to the early third century than to the fourth. He has to admit, however, that the monastic flavor of the Apocalypse of Paul is problematic for this early date. He tries to resolve the problem by arguing that none of the passages that are monastic in tone need reflect institutionalized monasticism.[35] Rather, the Apocalypse of Paul is the work of a pious ascetic of the period before the rise of institutionalized monasticism.

Casey does not work out the details of his claim, although he does point out that the Apocalypse of Paul alludes less to monasticism than to ascetic life in the desert. The most noticeably "monastic" passages are found in chapters 9, 24, 26, 39, and 40. Of these, only chapters 24 and 40 give any indication of representing more than ascetic piety. Chapter 24 in the ninth-century St. Gall manuscript speaks of a monastery, but in the Paris manuscript, the oldest of the witnesses, the word does

---

32. For a full presentation of the patristic evidence, see Casey, "Apocalypse of Paul," 26–31. See also Silverstein, *Visio*, 3–4, especially n. 2, and Duensing, "Apocalypse of Paul," HSW 2:755.

33. Casey, "Apocalypse of Paul," 28, n. 5.

34. Ibid., 28.

35. Casey's use of terms is confusing. Despite his view that the Apocalypse of Paul reflects the period before the institutionalization of monasticism, he calls the author a monk (8, 31).

not appear.[36] Thus it does not seem unfair to suggest that the reading of the St. Gall manuscript is the result of the intervention of a monk-copyist.

Chapter 40 shows, among other tortures, the punishment of those who "seemed to renounce the world, wearing our garb" (*ApNT*). This "garb" could be understood as some kind of monastic dress, but it is also possible to read the passage as referring to the simple clothing of the ascetic. After all, philosophers in the ancient world were supposed to be recognizable by their dress in the absence of any institutional definition. (See, e.g., Justin, *Dialogue with Trypho* 1.2; Lucian, *Nigrinus* 24, *Timon* 54, *Dialogues of the Dead* 1.2, 20.5.)

In favor of this argument it should be noted that demonstrably later texts like the Ethiopic Apocalypse of Mary, the Greek Apocalypse of Mary, and the Life of Pachomios allow no mistake about their monastic background. Nuns and monks are frequently mentioned.

INTRODUCTION TO THE APOCALYPSE OF PAUL FAMILY

In general the discussion of the relationships among the works that form the subject of this study will be deferred to Chapter 5, after the presentation of the evidence provided by the distribution of various sins and punishments (Chapters 3 and 4). The recognition of the links between the Apocalypse of Paul and the texts here claimed as its descendants, however, relies not on these elements but on features more or less specific to these texts. The evidence of the sins and punishments (see the discussion of the sins and punishments of the Apocalypse of Paul Family in chap. 4) supports the view put forward here. Since it is not necessary for that view, it seems worthwhile to establish the existence of a group of descendants of the Apocalypse of Paul with some internal ties before examining the sins and punishments as a whole, so as to enter into the discussion of the distribution of the sins and punishments with some perspective on the meaning of the presence of common elements in these texts.

THE ETHIOPIC APOCALYPSE OF MARY

The descendant of the Apocalypse of Paul most obviously modeled on it is the Ethiopic Apocalypse of Mary, which was edited and translated into Latin from a single manuscript by M. Chaîne.[37] Chaîne believes that the

---

36. Duensing's translation follows the St. Gall MS at this point (HSW 2:775).

37. See n. 12 above. Numbers in parentheses in the body of the text refer to the pages of Chaîne's translation.

Ethiopic Apocalypse of Mary was translated from an Arabic text, which in turn was translated from a Greek original. He mistakenly identifies the Greek original with the Greek Apocalypse of Mary, which will be discussed below, and its unpublished sisters. As Chaîne notes, the only indication of date that the text offers is a mention of "Mohammedans" (66). The earliest of the manuscripts, according to Chaîne, dates to the seventeenth century.[38]

The Ethiopic Apocalypse of Mary follows the Apocalypse of Paul very closely. After a brief introduction describing the circumstances of the revelation, Mary is taken up to heaven. She sees righteous souls and wicked souls departing the body (46–51, parallel to Apoc. Paul 11–18). Then Mary is taken to paradise, where she sees more or less the same sights Paul saw, although in a slightly different order and with some additions and subtractions (55–61, parallel to Apoc. Paul 19–30). The same is true in her tour of hell (61–68, parallel to Apoc. Paul 31–42). The text ends with Mary's successful intervention on behalf of all sinners, who are given a long weekend of respite, from the evening of the sixth day to the morning of the second, in keeping with the Sabbath customs of the Ethiopic church (68, parallel to Apoc. Paul 43–44).[39] Throughout descriptions are embellished with passages from the Hebrew Bible and the New Testament.

To indicate more clearly the nature of the relationship of the Apocalypse of Paul and the Ethiopic Apocalypse of Mary, the accounts of the first entrance into paradise of the two travelers may be compared. In Apoc. Paul 19, Paul is about to pass through the golden gate of paradise, where he sees golden tablets above golden columns on which letters are inscribed. He asks the reason for the letters and is told that they are the names of the righteous. Paul then discovers that not only the names but even the faces of the righteous are inscribed on these columns while they are still alive.

In chapter 20 Paul meets an old man with a shining face. He turns out to be Enoch, "the scribe of righteousness." He weeps over the suffering and evil of men. Then Elijah greets the apostle.

In Eth. Apoc. Mary (51–52), the order of the incidents is reversed. On entering paradise Mary first meets Enoch and Elijah. Enoch's face is not described as shining, nor is he called "scribe of righteousness." Then Mary sees a single golden column. The column itself is inscribed; Mary discovers that the writing is the names of the righteous and that their faces too are inscribed on it. The writing has been there since before the time of the

---

38. Greek original: Latin section, 43. Date of MS: Ethiopic section, 51–52.

39. For a brief discussion of Sabbath observance in Ethiopia, see Ullendorf, *Ethiopia and the Bible*, 109–13.

creation of Adam and Eve. Then Mary inquires about the column of fire that she sees. It is inscribed with the names of sinners.

THE ETHIOPIC APOCALYPSE OF BARUCH

A second descendant of the Apocalypse of Paul, the Ethiopic Apocalypse of Baruch, is often referred to as the Falasha Apocalypse of Baruch, but the designation is misleading. The Falashas are Ethiopians who practice a non-rabbinic Judaism. Their holy scripture is the Hebrew Bible in Geez translation, together with some of the apocrypha, and, as for Ethiopian Christians, Jubilees and 1 Enoch. They claim ancestry from the Jerusalemites who they say accompanied the son of King Solomon and the Queen of Sheba back to Ethiopia. Scholarly opinion tends to view them as heirs to the Judaism known in Ethiopia before the introduction of Christianity in the fourth century.[40]

Unlike the Apocalypse of Gorgorios, which will be considered next, the Ethiopic Apocalypse of Baruch does not appear to be a Falasha composition. Rather, it is a Falasha copy of a Christian text extant in three unpublished manuscripts.[41]

The predictions with which the Ethiopic Apocalypse of Baruch concludes contain historical references that provide a *terminus a quo* of 550 C.E.[42] Of course this date does not necessarily tell us anything about the tour, which is connected only loosely to the predictions. Leslau suggests a date in the seventh century, but does not explain why.[43] The condition of the text is rather confused.[44]

---

40. For an introduction and bibliography, see Wurmbrand, "Falashas."

41. Leslau, *Falasha Anthology*, 164, n. 17. According to Leslau (62–63), the Falasha method of naturalizing a Christian text is simply to omit all blatantly Christian language. "Thus, for example, the initial formula of any Ethiopic text, 'In the name of the Father, the Son, and the Holy Spirit,' is replaced by the Falasha formula, 'Blessed be God, the Lord of Israel. . . .'" "Christ" becomes "God"; "church," "sanctuary"; and all church officials are replaced with priests. Occasionally, however, the copyist slipped. In this text, for example, the cross remains (76).

42. Ibid., 64.

43. Ibid.

44. Leslau notes that one long paragraph found in the middle of the tour of paradise belongs in the concluding predictions (ibid., 67; 167, n. 65). Several motifs appear twice. At the beginning of his tour, Baruch sees a golden column inscribed with the names of the just in the heavenly Jerusalem (65). Later he sees Enoch and Elijah "writing down the deeds of the just on earth" in front of a heavenly city (67). Still later Baruch sees an inscribed golden column near another city, inquires, and discovers that the names of the just are written on the

The Ethiopic Apocalypse of Baruch is presented as a revelation to Baruch at the time of the fall of Jerusalem (64–65).[45] The angel Sutu'el takes Baruch on a tour of heaven. He sees paradise (65–69) and hell (70–74). The apocalypse concludes with predictions about good years and bad, righteous monarchs and slothful teachers, the false messiah (whose description, while differing in details, is of the same genre as that of the antichrist of the Apocalypse of Ezra), and finally, the millennium and resurrection (74–76).

As the brief summary indicates, the Ethiopic Apocalypse of Baruch is not as close to the Apocalypse of Paul as is the Ethiopic Apocalypse of Mary.[46] Of the material found in the Apocalypse of Paul, it contains only the tours of paradise and hell. Even in those sections it is considerably shorter. Fewer sights are described, and their description is not as detailed.

Leslau claims that the text "goes back to the Ethiopic Apocalypse of the Virgin, or in many places may even be a copy of it."[47] This is not accurate. It seems clear that the Ethiopic Apocalypse of Mary and the Ethiopic Apocalypse of Baruch at the very least have a source in common. The column of fire appears in both and is not found in the Apocalypse of Paul. But Baruch is far from a copy of Mary. The biblical passages so characteristic of Mary are absent in Baruch. Since many of these passages come from the Hebrew Bible, this is not simply the result of Falasha revision. Further, there are some signs that the author of Baruch knew the Apocalypse of Paul as well. For example, he has Enoch and Elijah recording the deeds of men. The Apocalypse of Paul calls Enoch "the scribe of righteousness," but Mary lacks the phrase. By the river of wine in Baruch are found "those . . . who were given to hospitality" (68). In the Apocalypse of Paul the patriarchs and other saints who have been hospitable are found by this river (chap. 27). Mary has the patriarchs by the river of wine, but makes no mention of hospitality. Line-by-line analysis would surely yield more such examples.

---

golden column with a golden pen, while the deeds of sinners are inscribed with an iron pen. Enoch and Elijah, "who write God's commandments," are the inhabitants of this city (68). Finally, at the beginning of the tour of hell, Baruch sees a column of fire on which the names of sinners are written with a pen of fire (69–70).

45. Numbers in parentheses in the body of the text refer to the pages of Leslau's translation, *Falasha Anthology*.

46. The description of the departure of souls from the body, lacking in the Ethiopic Apocalypse of Baruch, is found, with different details and a concluding exhortation on righteousness, in the "Book of the Angels" (ibid., 50–56). Leslau suggests that the "Book of the Angels" and Baruch may once have formed a single work. There is no MS evidence to support this suggestion, however, and Leslau's own claim that the Falashas borrowed Baruch from the Christians argues against this theory.

47. Ibid., 63.

It appears, then, that the Ethiopic Apocalypse of Baruch knew the Apocalypse of Paul in addition to the Ethiopic Apocalypse of Mary, or a form of the Ethiopic Apocalypse of Mary different from the one that has reached us, or some other text intermediate between the Apocalypse of Paul and Mary.

THE APOCALYPSE OF GORGORIOS

The Apocalypse of Gorgorios is truly a Falasha creation. Gorgorios is a hero of Falasha tradition. While this apocalypse seems to draw on the Apocalypse of Paul or texts related to it, Leslau judges that the author of the text has successfully eliminated any obviously Christian elements. The text survives in several manuscripts. Leslau's fourteenth-century date is a guess.[48]

The Apocalypse of Gorgorios consists of the main elements of the Ethiopic Apocalypse of Mary: a vision of the departure of souls of the righteous and the wicked from the body, and tours of paradise and hell. It concludes with its most obviously Falasha component, Gorgorios' prayers and conversation with the angels. None of the elements that seem to go back ultimately to the Apocalypse of Paul shows any precise contacts with the Apocalypse of Paul, the Ethiopic Apocalypse of Mary, the Ethiopic Apocalypse of Baruch, or the "Book of the Angels," the Falasha work that describes the departure of souls from the body in the manner of the Apocalypse of Paul. The Apocalypse of Gorgorios gives the impression of having been written by someone who was familiar with the contents of some or all of those other texts, but who sat down to write his own work without any of them in front of him and perhaps even without having read any of them recently.

THE GREEK APOCALYPSE OF MARY

No less an authority than M. R. James called the Greek Apocalypse of Mary "a late and dreary production."[49] "I will concede to any critic that it is extremely monotonous, quite comtemptible as literature, and even positively repulsive in some parts."[50]

---

48. Ibid., 80–81.

49. M. R. James, *ApNT*, 563.

50. M. R. James, "Introduction to the Apocalypse of the Virgin," *Apocrypha Anecdota*, Texts and Studies 2.3 (Cambridge: Cambridge University, 1893), iii.

James published the oldest manuscript of the text he could find; he dates the manuscript to the eleventh century.[51] It is one of many similar texts in other languages,[52] and many other copies of the Greek are known.

James is cautious about the date of the text itself. The only hint he gives is his suggestion that the Greek Apocalypse of Mary is a source for the Apocalypse of Ezra, which he places in the ninth century, again cautiously.[53] He does not explain why he views the influence as working in that direction.

As its title, "The Apocalypse of the Holy God-Bearer About the Punishments," indicates, the Greek Apocalypse of Mary is concerned only with hell. Thus it does not exhibit the structural similarities to the Apocalypse of Paul found in the Ethiopic apocalypses related to it.

The text opens with Mary on the Mount of Olives praying for an angelic revelation about the punishments of sinners. Michael arrives (chaps. 1–2) and leads her on a tour of hell (chaps. 3–24). Mary pleads for the sinners (chaps. 25–26), and she is joined in her pleading by the angels and heroes of the Hebrew Bible and of Christianity (chaps. 27–28). Mary's efforts meet with some success, and the sinners are given respite from their suffering for the period of Pentecost (chap. 29). The work concludes with the angels and all the righteous praising God (chap. 30).

Mary's pleading for the sinners is one point of contact with the Apocalypse of Paul. Jesus' indictment of the sinners when Mary intercedes for them (chap. 29) is at some points very close in its wording to Apoc. Paul 44. Without the evidence of the sins and punishments, however, it would be difficult to make a strong case that this text should be considered part of the Apocalypse of Paul family.

THE EZRA APOCALYPSES

By the time of 4 Ezra, written in the wake of the second destruction, the biblical scribe, hero of the restoration of the Temple after its first destruction, had become a seer.[54] Two texts relate tours of hell of which Ezra is the protagonist. The language of the Apocalypse of Ezra is Greek; the Vision

51. Ibid., 109.

52. W. Schneemelcher, "Later Apocalypses," HSW 2:753. M. E. Stone has pointed out to me listings in the New Julfa catalog of Armenian MSS that seem to represent texts of the same sort: two "Visions of the Theotokos on the Mt. of Olives," vol. 1, no. 223 (p. 307) and no. 228 (p. 320), and a "Vision of the Virgin," vol. 1, no. 442 (p. 684).

53. James, "Introduction Virgin," 112–13.

54. On the figure of Ezra in Judaism and Christianity, see R. A. Kraft, "'Ezra' Materials in Judaism and Christianity," in *Aufstieg und Niedergang der römischen Welt* II.19.1 (119–36).

of Ezra is preserved in Latin, but seems to have been translated from Greek.[55]

It is extremely difficult to date the Ezra apocalypses. None of the manuscripts of the Vision of Ezra is earlier than the tenth century, while the earlier of the two manuscripts of the Apocalypse of Ezra dates to the fifteenth century.[56] M. R. James cites a reference to an apocalypse of Ezra in the canon of Nicephorus Homologeta (c. 850 C.E.), which he believes to be this Apocalypse of Ezra.[57] The use of the Vision of Ezra by the author of the Vision of Alberic does not push the date of the Vision of Ezra back any further than does the oldest manuscript.[58]

The Apocalypse of Ezra begins with Ezra's lengthy argument before God on behalf of the sinners (1:1–4:4), an argument much indebted to 4 Ezra. Then Ezra takes a tour of hell (4:5–5:6) in which he sees several punishments, including that of the antichrist, whose appearance he describes in some detail (4:25–42). After the tour of hell, Ezra resumes his argument with God (5:7–19). Then in rapid succession he sees paradise (5:20–22), cosmological wonders (5:23), more punishments, and the depths of Tartarus (5:23–28). God announces to Ezra that the time has come for him to die. Ezra resists, claiming that all the exits of his body are too holy to allow the soul to depart through them (chap. 6). Finally, after striking a bargain with God that all who copy his book and remember his name will receive a place in paradise, Ezra gives up his soul.

The Vision of Ezra consists mainly of a tour of hell in which Ezra at each sight prays, "Lord, spare the sinners." At the end of the text (vv. 59–59e),

---

55. In what follows, Apocalypse of Ezra refers to the Greek Apocalypse of Ezra; Vision of Ezra, to the Latin Vision of Ezra; and Ezra apocalypses, in the plural, to both texts. The suggestion that the Vision of Ezra is a translation from Greek has been made from the start; G. Mercati, who first published the text, noted several instances of language that appears to reflect a Greek original, although he was too cautious to come to a firm conclusion ("Anecdota apocrypha latina. Una 'Visio' ed una 'Revelatio' d'Esdra con un decreto di Clemente Romano," in *Note di letteratura biblica e christiana antica*, Studi e Testi 5 [Rome: Vatican, 1901], 68).

56. O. Wahl, *Apocalypsis Esdrae. Apocalypsis Sedrach. Visio Beati Esdrae*, PVTG 4 (Leiden: Brill, 1977), 14–15, 22–23 (Vision of Ezra); 11–12 (Apocalypse of Ezra). Since the publication of *Apocalypsis Esdrae*, Wahl has announced four new MSS of the Vision of Ezra ("Vier neue Textzeugen der 'Visio Beati Esdrae,'" *Salesianum* 40[1978]:583–89). None is earlier than the twelfth century.

57. Introduction to R. L. Bensly, *The Fourth Book of Ezra*, Texts and Studies 3.2 (Cambridge: Cambridge University, 1895), lxxxvii.

58. P. Dinzelbacher, "Die Vision Alberichs und die Esdras-Apokryphe," *Studien und Mitteilungen zur Geschichte des Benediktiner-Ordens und seiner Zweige* 87(1976):440, points out that the relationship to the Vision of Alberic is useful for providing a *terminus ante quem* of IIII for the version of the Vision of Ezra found in the Magnum Legendarium Austriacum, MS H in Wahl's edition.

Ezra takes a glance at paradise and is escorted to heaven to plead for the sinners (vv. 60–66). The vision ends with God's assurance that the slave who serves his master will receive his freedom.

It is clear that these two texts and the Apocalypse of Sedrach, a Greek text that describes Sedrach's argument with God and the departure of his soul from his body but does not contain a visionary tour, are related to each other and to 4 Ezra. M. E. Stone outlines the relationships thus: All three texts come from a "common stock." They are all concerned with the fate of souls after death, an interest of the first three visions of 4 Ezra (3–9:25) as well. Although all three texts show points of contact with 4 Ezra, it is impossible to explain any two as derived from the third, because each has parallels to 4 Ezra that are unique to it.[59]

The argumentative personality of the hero in the Apocalypse of Ezra and to a lesser extent in the Vision of Ezra is a striking characteristic of the hero of 4 Ezra too. In the Apocalypse of Ezra the close verbal correspondence makes it clear that it is to 4 Ezra and not to Paul's pleading in the Apocalypse of Paul that Ezra's efforts at intercession should be traced. Ezra's refrain in the Vision of Ezra, "Lord, spare the sinners," is closer to the pleading of Paul and of Mary in the Greek Apocalypse of Mary; but the absence of the motif of Sabbath (or Pentecost) rest for the sinners (as also in the Apocalypse of Ezra) may mean that it is from 4 Ezra and not from the Apocalypse of Paul that it derives. On the other hand, it is worth noting that in Apoc. Ezra 7:1 God alludes to Matt. 27:34, in which Jesus is given vinegar and gall to drink; such an allusion appears in similar contexts in Apoc. Paul 44 and Gk. Apoc. Mary 29.

The Testament of Isaac

The Testament of Isaac is extant in Sahidic and Bohairic versions, as well as in Arabic and Ethiopic.[60] K. H. Kuhn considers the Sahidic the original of

---

59. M. E. Stone, "The Metamorphosis of Ezra: Jewish Apocalypse and Medieval Vision," *JTS* n.s. 33(1982):5 (4–11 on our Ezra apocalypses generally). Stone does not provide textual evidence, and it is not clear to me that there are any parallels to 4 Ezra in the Vision of Ezra that are not found also in the Apocalypse of Ezra.

For a list of parallels of the Apocalypse of Ezra to 4 Ezra, see M. R. James, Introduction to Bensly, *Fourth Ezra*, lxxxvii–lxxxviii. For a list of parallels of the Apocalypse of Sedrach to both the Apocalypse of Ezra and 4 Ezra, see M. R. James, "On the Apocalypse of Sedrach," *Apocrypha Anecdota*, 128–29. For a summary of the older views of the relationships of the various Ezra texts to one another, see Wahl, *Apocalypsis Esdrae*, 2–5.

60. Numbers given in parentheses in the body of the text refer to K. H. Kuhn, "An English Translation of the Sahidic Version of the Testament of Isaac," *JTS* n.s. 18(1967):325–36.

the two Coptic versions.[61] It seems reasonable to assume that the text passed into Arabic from Coptic and from Arabic into Ethiopic. The data allow no conclusions about a Greek original.[62]

The Testament of Isaac is closely related to the Testament of Abraham, elements of which it takes over into its story, and to the Testament of Jacob, which appears to be modeled on it. While many scholars regard the Testament of Abraham as early and Jewish, this is far from certain. Even if it were, it would not establish the date of the Testament of Isaac, which is Christian in its present form.[63] The only fixed date is that of the Sahidic manuscript, 894/5.[64] Conclusions about the age of the vision of punishments and its relation to the other visions here will be one more piece of evidence to add to the discussion of the age and provenance of the Testament of Isaac.

Isaac's vision of hell is only a small part of the Testament. Before his death, Isaac is taken to heaven by the angel of Abraham, who looks exactly like Abraham (326–27). The angel reassures Isaac about Jacob's future, and

---

61. K. H. Kuhn, "The Sahidic Version of the Testament of Isaac," *JTS* n.s. 8(1957) : 225–26. The Bohairic contains a number of Sahidicisms. This suggests that it was translated from Sahidic, the usual direction for translation activity. The two texts differ considerably, however, and the Bohairic may preserve some features of an earlier stage of the text.

62. P. Nagel ("Zur sahidischen Version des Testaments Isaaks," *Wissenschaftliche Zeitschrift der Martin-Luther-Universität Halle-Wittenberg* 12[1963] : 259–63) argues for a Greek original. Kuhn, who was agnostic about the possibility of a Greek original before Nagel's remarks ("Sahidic Version"), remains so afterward ("English Translation," 325), arguing that the features Nagel points to as indicating a Greek original, like frequent use of ⲗⲉ and vocative ⲱ, and the manner of using Greek adjectives, are so common in texts composed originally in Coptic as to be of no use in determining whether a text is a translation.

63. In a recent study of the Testament of Abraham, M. Delcor argued that the Testament of Isaac is an Essene work because of the interest in fasting, the emphasis on ritual bathing and sacrifice, and the prominence of priests (*Le Testament d'Abraham*, SVTP 2 [Leiden: Brill, 1973], 78–83). Yet all the features Delcor mentions make sense as the concerns of Egyptian monks. Delcor's claim that the river of fire shows Essene influence is easily dismissed. Rivers of fire, as it will appear below, are quite common in visions of hell, and they have predecessors in Greek and Jewish, but non-Essene, literature. James's remarks (*The Testament of Abraham*, Texts and Studies 2.2 [Cambridge: Cambridge University, 1892], 157–58) about the three forty-day fasts of the Testament of Isaac are worth noting. He writes, "The three periods of forty days are possibly the three 'τεσσαρακοσταί' (Anastasius Antiochenus, *de tribus quadragesimis*) of the Greek Church, those of Lent, of the Nativity, and of the Virgin; or something corresponding to the 'three Lents' of the Montanists, in which they practised a ξηροφαγία, very like that ascribed to Isaac."

64. Nagel ("Sahidischen Version") argues for a date between 380 and 410 on the basis of the doxology and the similarity of the Testament of Isaac to the History of Joseph the Carpenter. Kuhn ("English Translation," 325–26) argues that the date that Nagel assumes for the History of Joseph the Carpenter has been challenged and questions the dating of the doxology, which could in any case be a copyist's addition.

Isaac tells Jacob that he is about to die. He predicts the coming of Christ. Christians will offer up sacrifices to prevent the coming of the antichrist (327–30). The household and then others gather to hear Isaac's farewell. Isaac exhorts them to lead the good life (330–32). He ascends to heaven, where he sees souls undergoing torture. Only two punishments are assigned sins (332–33). Then he sees Abraham and other saints. Abraham gets God to agree to various means for men to obtain mercy. These include copying Isaac's testament, offering incense in Isaac's name, reciting the testament, or listening to others recite it (333–35). Now Isaac, lying on his couch, sees God coming forth to get him. He embraces Jacob, offers him a little more advice, and dies (335–36).

THE LIFE OF PACHOMIOS

Pachomios' vision of hell appears in a Bohairic life of the founder of cenobitic monasticism.[65] The relationship of the various lives of this Egyptian holy man in their several languages and dialects is the subject of much debate.[66] Because the vision of hell is found in only one version of the life, this debate can be sidestepped here. The universe of discourse for dating is provided by the death of Pachomios in the middle of the fourth century at one end and the Bohairic manuscript in the ninth century on the other.[67]

The vision is a separable unit, unrelated to what precedes or follows. "One day it happened that our father Pachomios was taken up at the Lord's command in order to show him the punishments and torments by which men are tortured; was it in the body that he was taken up, or was it outside the body? God knows that he was taken up."[68] This vision shares with the Apocalypse of Paul the allusion to 2 Cor. 12 : 3. It is not impossible that the author of this Life of Pachomios referred to a passage from the New Testament that seemed appropriate without knowing the Apocalypse

---

65. The life is translated into French by L. T. Lefort, *Les vies coptes de Saint Pachôme et de ses premiers successeurs*, Bibliothèque du *Muséon* 16 (Louvain: *Muséon*, 1943). The passage treated here is chap. 88 of the Bohairic life in the second series (148–51). I know of no discussions of this passage.

66. For a general discussion, J. Timbie, "Dualism and the Concept of Orthodoxy in the Thought of the Monks of Upper Egypt" (Ph.D. diss., University of Pennsylvania, 1979), 23–35. For a more detailed discussion, A. Veilleux, *La liturgie dans le cénobitisme pachômien au quatrième siècle*, Studia Anselmiana 57 (Rome: Pontifical Institute of St. Anselm, 1968), 16–114, esp. 36–48.

67. Lefort, *Saint Pachôme*, lxv.

68. I translate Lefort's French; ibid., 148.

of Paul, but the Apocalypse of Paul was available in Coptic and the text from 2 Corinthians itself provides no indication that Paul saw the tortures of hell during his visit to the heavens.

One of the most striking of the punishments of Pachomios' relatively brief tour is the torture of monks who, though completely pure in body, sowed dissension among the other monks by spreading gossip. The sins of those undergoing several of the punishments are never explained. At the end of his tour, Pachomios is directed to report what he has seen to his brethren.

INTRODUCTION TO THE HEBREW TEXTS AND THE LATIN ELIJAH FRAGMENT

Tours of hell that have many features in common with those discussed above are found in medieval Jewish literature. Like many of their Christian counterparts, these texts are extremely difficult to date and place.

Before examining the Jewish tours of hell, I wish to discuss briefly a related text of importance for the development of these tours, a passage from the Palestinian Talmud. Because of the status of the Palestinian Talmud, this text must have been widely known; it is clear that it had some influence on at least one of the tours. The vision of a pious man of Ashkelon is found in p. Ḥagigah 2.2 and p. Sanhedrin 6.6, among several stories about Simeon b. Sheṭaḥ, a Pharisaic hero of the first century B.C.E.

When both an unworthy tax collector and the man of Ashkelon's pious companion in study die on the same day, the man of Ashkelon is troubled by the contrast between the elaborate mourning for the tax collector and the lack of attention to the death of his friend until it is revealed to him in a dream that both the tax collector and his friend have received their just deserts.

His friend had sinned a single sin in his life: he had once put on the phylacteries for the head before the phylacteries for the arm. Thus he dies unmourned. The tax collector in his life had done one good deed, a charitable act of feeding the poor. Thus he receives a splendid funeral. In his dream the man of Ashkelon sees his friend strolling in the midst of "gardens and orchards and fountains," while the tax collector, his tongue stretched out over the river, tries unsuccessfully to drink from it. This incident illustrates the principle made explicit in the related midrash from *Darkhei Teshuvah* discussed below. In this world the righteous are punished for every sin they commit so that they may enjoy more completely the bliss of the world to come. The wicked, on the other hand, receive any reward due them in this world so that they may be more completely punished in the world to come.

In addition the pious man is shown a certain Miriam suffering punishment for hypocrisy. Alternate versions of her punishment are given. One consists of hanging by the breasts. This punishment and the passage as a whole will be discussed in greater detail in Chapter 3 under the story from the Palestinian Talmud.

THE MIDRASH FROM *DARKHEI TESHUVAH*

One Hebrew tour of hell appears in *Darkhei Teshuvah*, "The Ways of Repentance," an appendix to the responsa of one of the leading German rabbis of the thirteenth century, Meir of Rothenburg.[69] R. Meir does not indicate any source for the midrash, which can be understood as an expanded and rationalized retelling of the story from the Palestinian Talmud.

R. Meir uses the midrash to show that God gives the righteous the reward promised them in the next world and that those righteous people who have committed some small misdeeds are punished for them in this world so that they enter the next world with their debts paid off. The story runs as follows: In a certain city a righteous man and a wicked man die on the same day. The whole community tends to the burial of the wicked man, but no one cares for the righteous man except his son-in-law, who is brokenhearted over the neglect shown his father-in-law.

When the son-in-law falls asleep, Elijah appears to him and takes him to Gehenna, where he shows him the soul of the wicked man tormented by his inability to drink of the water so near him. The son-in-law sees four other punishments, which Elijah explains to him. They are all measure-for-measure, "to show that the Holy One, blessed be he, is a righteous judge; the limbs that commit the sin are punished in Gehenna more than the other limbs." Two of the punishments involve hanging by the sinful limb and are close to the hanging punishments of the Christian texts. Finally, Elijah takes the son-in-law to paradise, where they see angels preparing a throne for the righteous man.

Now, as in the Palestinian Talmud, Elijah explains the meaning of the incident that troubled the son-in-law. The wicked man, a tax collector, received a glorious burial because he had done one good deed during his life. The father-in-law, whose death was ignored by the community because he

---

69. The responsa of R. Meir were first published in 1608 in Prague. In that edition this midrash appears on 114c.

had committed one sin during his lifetime, will enjoy the fullness of his reward in paradise.

Elijah goes his way and the young man awakes to find the whole community gathered in his house for his father-in-law's funeral. If possible, the ending is even happier than that in the Palestinian Talmud.

THE ISAIAH FRAGMENT

The prophet Isaiah's vision of hell with God himself as guide comes down to us in four slightly different versions: as part of the Chronicles of Yeraḥme'el; as part of a short text entitled "A Description of Judgment in the Grave," published by A. Jellinek in *Bet ha-Midrasch*; and in two copies from the Cairo Geniza, published by L. Ginzberg.[70] Wherever it appears, Isaiah's tour is placed among, but never actually integrated with, several other descriptions of hell.

Ginzberg offers no comment about the age of the manuscripts from the Geniza, but he points out that the scribe's note at the end of one of the versions claims that it is excerpted from Seder Eliyyahu Rabbah.[71] The vision does not, however, appear in any of the printed editions of Seder Eliyyahu. This connection is particularly interesting because Elijah appears as the revealer or the recipient of revelation in three of the four other Jewish

---

70. The Chronicles of Yeraḥme'el is a twelfth-century compilation of midrashim and other materials that survives in a unique MS now located in the Bodleian Library. The work has been published only in translation (with some omissions) (*The Chronicles of Jerahmeel*, ed. and trans. M. Gaster, 2d ed. with prolegomenon by H. Schwarzbaum [New York: KTAV, 1971; 1st ed. 1899]). Jellinek publishes "A Description of Judgment in the Grave" in a collection that he titles "Paradise and Hell" (*Bet ha-Midrasch* [reprint; Jerusalem: Wahrmann, 1967; 1st ed. 1853–78], 5:49–51). The Geniza MSS appear in L. Ginzberg, ed., *Ginze Schechter: Genizah Studies in Memory of Dr. Solomon Schechter*, vol. 1: *Midrash and Haggadah* (Hebr.), Texts and Studies of the Jewish Theological Seminary of America 7 (New York: Jewish Theological Seminary, 1928), 196–98, 204–5.

71. Ginzberg (*Genizah*, 189–91) understood the scribal note's reference to the "great Talmud" to refer to Seder Eliyyahu and put forward a theory about the development of Seder Eliyyahu Rabbah and Zuta based on this note. (A discussion in English of Ginzberg's theory can be found in M. Kadushin, *The Theology of Seder Eliahu* [New York: Bloch, 1932], 13–16.) Ginzberg's understanding of the scribal note is disputed by J. Mann ("Genizah Studies," *American Journal of Semitic Languages and Literature* 46[1930]:267–68). Mann argues that the term "great Talmud" is not part of the subscription to the Isaiah fragment, but part of a superscription to the next work in the MS, which comes from the Babylonian Talmud, the proper referent of the term "great Talmud." B. Marmelstein (review of Ginzberg, *Genizah*, *Kiryat Sefer* 6[1929–30]:324) expresses doubts about Ginzberg's theory for similar reasons. (I owe the references to the articles by Mann and Marmelstein to a communication from Dr. P. Fenton of the Taylor-Schechter Genizah Research Unit at Cambridge University.)

tours of hell considered here. There is no consensus about the age or provenance of Seder Eliyyahu,[72] and in any case the date of a rabbinic collection does not set the date of individual elements in the collection.

Ginzberg considers the five courts of Isaiah's vision as dependent on the Babylonian Talmud's schema of seven levels of hell and thus relatively late; the five courts are a truncated form of an original seven.[73] He offers no evidence for this view, however.

Isaiah's tour describes the five courts of hell and their inhabitants in stylized terms; the description of each court is phrased in the same way. In the three middle courts, the sinners hang by the limb that sinned. The sins are close to those that give rise to such hanging punishments in the Apocalypse of Peter, the Acts of Thomas, and the midrash in *Darkhei Teshuvah*. The descriptions of the first four courts include biblical quotations in the two Geniza versions.

THE JOSHUA B. LEVI FRAGMENT

The Babylonian Talmud reports of Joshua b. Levi, a first-generation Palestinian amora, that he outwitted the angel of death and succeeded in entering paradise alive.[74] In the medieval midrashim, Joshua is the rabbi most commonly sent on tours of heaven and hell.

Many of these midrashim do not fit the pattern of the tours of hell discussed here. The tour of interest for this study appears in the Chronicles of Yeraḥme'el and in a medieval midrash called "Tractate of Gehenna."[75] It recounts Joshua b. Levi's visit to hell with Elijah as his guide. There he sees several unexplained hanging punishments and some other punishments, of

---

72. See J. Elbaum, "Tanna de'vei Eliyahu," *EJ* , for a summary of different views. For a more complete discussion of the older views, see Kadushin, *Seder Eliahu*, 3–16.

73. Ginzberg, *Genizah*, 190–91. Ginzberg made a similar claim about the five heavens of 3 Baruch in "Baruch, Apocalypse of (Greek)," *JE*. It is worth noting that there are only five compartments in the hell of the vision of the Acts of Thomas.

74. B. Ketubot 77b; cf. b. Berakhot 51a. For the image of Joshua b. Levi in rabbinic literature and Jewish folklore, see H. Schwarzbaum, "The Prophet Elijah and R. Joshua b. Levi" (Hebr.), *Yeda'-'am* 7(1960): 22–31. M. Gaster, "Hebrew Visions of Hell and Paradise," *Journal of the Royal Asiatic Society* 23(1893): 571–611, translates most of the accounts of Joshua's journeys to heaven and hell into English and provides bibliographical information (591–607). He does not mention that the Aramaic journey (605–7) is also found in Jellinek, "Paradise and Gehenna," *Bet ha-Midrasch* 5: 43–44.

75. "Tractate of Gehenna" was first published by Elijah ben Moses da Vidas in *Reshit Hokhmah*, Sha 'ar ha-yirah, chap. 13, sec. 2 (1579). It was reprinted by Jellinek in *Bet ha-Midrasch* 1: 147–49. A slightly shorter version appears in the Chronicles of Yeraḥme'el, chaps. 14–15. M. E. Stone (Stone and J. Strugnell, *The Books of Elijah, Parts 1 and 2*, Texts and Translations 18; Pseudepigrapha Series 8 [Missoula, Mont.: Scholars Press 1979], 16–18) reproduces

which one is explained in one of the two versions of this passage that survives. In what follows, both versions will be considered.[76]

Peter the Venerable, the twelfth-century abbot of Cluny, quotes part of a story about Joshua b. Levi's travels in his *Tractatus Contra Judaeos*.[77] The quotations, which have clearly been tampered with in the interests of anti-Jewish propaganda, represent a version of the story more like those passed over here, but they do contain some details that will be of interest below.

GEDULAT MOSHE

The last and lengthiest of the Hebrew visions is Moses' tour of heaven and hell.[78] According to Lieberman, this text is found only in Arab countries;[79]

---

his own transcription of the relevant text from Yeraḥme'el. Gaster's translations of the passage in *Chronicles of Jerahmeel* and the passage from *Reshit Ḥokhmah* ("Hebrew Visions," 600–601) include explanations of all the punishments that Joshua sees, and *Jerahmeel* also adds several groups of sinners not found by Stone in the MS. If Gaster had a source for these additions, he does not say what it was. Thus his additions will be ignored, and discussion will be restricted to the text of "Tractate of Gehenna" from *Reshit Ḥokhmah* and Stone's transcription of the MS of the Chronicles of Yeraḥme'el.

76. The two versions also differ in the punishments they contain. The shorter text found in the Chronicles of Yeraḥme'el lacks two groups of hanging sinners to be found in the longer version as well as the last group of sinners of that version and contains somewhat shorter descriptions of some of the common punishments. The twelfth-century Chronicles of Yeraḥme'el is earlier than the late sixteenth-century *Reshit Ḥokhmah*, the first place that the longer version appears. Yet these dates are not decisive. In both works already extant material is incorporated. One of the missing hanging punishments in Yeraḥme'el is hanging by the breasts. This punishment appears in all the other Jewish texts discussed here, and thus one might argue that the version from Yeraḥme'el is original while *Reshit Ḥokhmah* adds punishments under the influence of other texts. Yet of the other two hanging punishments found in Yeraḥme'el, one, hanging by the nose, is unknown in the other Jewish texts. The other, hanging by the hands, occurs in the Elijah fragment and *Gedulat Moshe*, but not in the midrash from *Darkhei Teshuvah* or the Isaiah fragment. Thus it is difficult to choose one version over the other. In fact, it may not be correct in a case like this to assume that a single original ever existed.

77. *Patrologia Latina* 189:631–43. The work was written c. 1140. Lieberman (*Shkiin*, 2d ed. [Jerusalem: Wahrmann, 1970], 31–35) suggests that Peter took his tale from a lost version of the Alphabet of Ben Sira once current in France.

78. This text is known not only as *Gedulat Moshe*, "The Greatness of Moses," but also as "Like an Apple Tree Among the Trees of the Forest." *Gedulat Moshe* was first published in Salonika in 1726–27 and has been printed many times since (A. J. Wertheimer, additions to S. A. Wertheimer, *Batei Midrashot*, 2d ed. [Jerusalem: Mosad ha-Rav Cook, 1954; 1st ed. 1893–97], 1:273). A Yemenite MS bearing the other title was first published by Wertheimer in *Batei Midrashot*. In the second edition of *Batei Midrashot*, differences between the two versions are noted.

79. Lieberman, "Sins," 29.

and Ginzberg reports an Arabic translation in the "library of Berlin."[80] Lieberman argues that the contents of *Gedulat Moshe* too betray Muslim influence, for example, the five purgatorial compartments and the sixth compartment that is hell itself.[81]

The text begins with Moses at Sinai receiving the Torah. It is at that moment that the ascent takes place (chap. 1). Metatron is Moses' guide. In order to be able to ascend to heaven, Moses' body is turned to fire. He then ascends through the seven heavens and sees the various angels who live there (chaps. 2–10). In the seventh heaven he sees the throne of glory. After Zagzagel, an angel in the seventh heaven, has taught him Torah (chap. 11), Moses is sent to see paradise and Gehenna (chap. 12). Gehenna is first on the agenda (chaps. 13–14). Nesargiel, the chief of Gehenna, is Moses' guide. This Gehenna contains many more sights than those of the other Jewish texts, including hanging punishments, fire, and scorpions. The text concludes with Moses' brief visit to paradise (chap. 20).

THE ELIJAH FRAGMENT

Among the Jewish texts this fragment is an anomaly. It survives as a citation in a Latin Christian work of perhaps the fifth century, and thus, while it contains nothing of an obviously Christian character, it cannot be treated as a Jewish text without discussion. The work in which the Elijah fragment appears is entitled Epistle of Titus, Disciple of Paul, on the Estate of Chastity. The epistle preaches asceticism with frequent quotations from apocryphal texts, many, like the Elijah fragment, otherwise unknown. The fragment consists of Elijah's description of a vision revealed to him by an angel in which sinners hang by the sinful limb.

This Elijah fragment is only one of many traces of an early Elijah apocalypse or apocalypses. M. R. James's view that the "original Apocalypse contained all the ingredients that the fragments show us, descriptions of hell—torments, eschatological prophecy, descriptions of Antichrist and didactic matter," is shared by Stone and Strugnell in their collection of Elijah apocrypha.[82]

Despite its preservation in Latin in a Christian work, Lieberman argues that the Elijah fragment was drawn from a Jewish text.[83] He takes the com-

---

80. L. Ginzberg, *The Legends of the Jews* (Philadelphia: Jewish Publication Society, 1909), 5:416–18, nn. 117–18.

81. Lieberman, "Sins," 29–30.

82. M. R. James, *LAOT*, 61. Stone and Strugnell, *Elijah*, 1.

83. Lieberman, "Sins," 47.

ment that introduces the fragment, "By the limb with which a man sinned, by the same limb will he be punished," as part of the fragment, an understanding that is not shared by any of the editors of the text.[84] On this basis he argues that the Elijah fragment and the midrash from which R. Meir drew the vision in *Darkhei Teshuvah* go back to a common source, for the vision in *Darkhei Teshuvah*, in which Elijah is the revealer, concludes with the sentence, "The limbs that commit the sin are punished in Gehenna more than the other limbs."

But the two sentences do not say the same thing. The sentence in the Epistle of Titus says that people are punished by the limb that sinned; the sentence in *Darkhei Teshuvah* says that the limb that sinned is punished more than other limbs. Both sentences express sentiments appropriate to the passages they accompany; there is no need to assume a common source to explain what similarity there is.

Lieberman makes a more compelling case for the Jewish provenance of the Elijah fragment in relation to its punishments. The men who hang by their genitals and the women who hang by their breasts, he claims, occur elsewhere only in the Jewish texts. It seems likely, however, that the men who hang by their loins in Eth. Apoc. Pet. 7 are suffering a more modestly described version of the punishment of hanging by the genitals. Further, the women in the Elijah fragment are not described as hanging by their breasts, although hanging is probably implied; rather, they are said to be tortured in their breasts. But despite these objections, Lieberman is correct in claiming that the combination of punishments of the Elijah fragment, and especially the two punishments that he singles out, have their closest parallels in Jewish texts. (See the section on hanging in hell in chap. 3, below, for a full discussion of these punishments. Tables 3 and 4 present the material schematically.)

But there is an obstacle in the way of considering the Elijah fragment a Jewish text that Lieberman does not seem to feel: the presence of virgins roasting on a gridiron. If the Elijah fragment is Jewish, it is the only Jewish text that shows defiled virgins being tortured. Not even the expansive *Gedulat Moshe* has defiled virgins in its hell. Several Christian texts, on the other hand, have: Eth. Apoc. Pet. 11, Apoc. Paul 39, Eth. Apoc. Mary (64), Eth. Apoc. Bar. (70–71), Vis. Ezra 43–44, and the vision in the Life of

---

84. D. de Bruyne, who first published the fragment ("Nouveaux fragments des Actes de Pierre, de Paul, de Jean, d'André et de l'Apocalypse d'Élie," *Revue bénédictine* 25[1908]: 149–60), treats the sentence as the work of the author of the epistle (153–54). Stone (*Elijah*, 14) does not include the sentence as part of the fragment; and the paragraphing of A. de Santos Otero's translation (HSW 2:157–58) suggests that he does not view the sentence as part of the apocryphon.

Pachomios. (See the section on the loss of virginity before marriage in chap. 3, below, for a full discussion of these punishments.)

The virgins are the penultimate group of sinners enumerated in the Elijah fragment; they are followed only by "other souls" who are tortured unceasingly. These last groups of sinners share two traits exceptional in the Elijah fragment: their sin is not specified, and their punishment is not a hanging punishment. A moment ago it was assumed that the virgins were to be compared to the no-longer-virgins of other tours of hell, and I believe that assumption is correct. Still, it must be noted that the nature of the virgins' sin is not here spelled out as it is in other texts and as the sins of the other inhabitants of the Elijah fragment are.

These anomalies suggest the possibility that the virgins and "other souls" are an editor's addition to the Elijah fragment. The author of the Epistle of Titus, inspired by the ideal of celibate chastity, might have felt the lack of sinful ex-virgins in the work from which he was quoting and have decided to supply them himself. If so, he was not particularly skillful in his alterations, for the punishment assigned the virgins, while drawn from the view of hell as fiery so prominent in Christian (and Jewish) literature, does not match the other tortures of the Elijah fragment. The "other souls" suit the fragment even less well. The author of the epistle may have preferred to omit an explanation for these sinners and their punishments because his additions so strained the principle of measure-for-measure operating throughout the fragment.

In any case, the virgins alone do not show the fragment to be drawn from a Christian work. Though unparalleled in Jewish texts, they are by no means impossible. Certainly the rest of the fragment finds its closest parallels in Jewish tours. Despite the problems in Lieberman's argument, then, there are good grounds for treating the Elijah fragment as Jewish.

APPENDIX: THE EPISTLE OF TITUS

The first editor of the Epistle of Titus, D. de Bruyne, believed that the epistle had been translated from Greek into Latin. Harnack thought that de Bruyne was wrong about the epistle as a whole, but regarded the Elijah fragment as a translation from Greek.[85] M. R. James early pointed out that the peculiar punishment of the men said to be burning by their eyes can be explained by assuming that the

---

85. De Bruyne, "Nouveaux fragments," 150. Harnack, "Der apokryphe Brief des Paulus-schülers Titus 'De dispositione sanctimonii'," *Sitzungsberichte der preussischen Akademie der Wissenschaften*, Phil.-hist. Klasse 17(1925): 191–93. For bibliography for the epistle, de Santos Otero, HSW 2:141–43.

Greek κρεμαμένοι, "hanging," was transformed into the Latin homonym *creman-tur*, "are burned."[86]

De Bruyne considered the epistle to be a Manichean work. Despite the liberal use of apocrypha, he preferred not to identify the work as Priscillianist on the grounds that too little was known about the Priscillianists. De Santos Otero suggests fifth-century Spain and Priscillianist influence, although he argues that the author of the epistle need not have been a Priscillianist himself.[87]

Some of the apocrypha in the epistle that can be identified with known works are clearly Christian, mainly from the apocryphal acts. Others, including several excerpts from works otherwise unknown, show no signs of Christian origin.[88]

RELATED TEXTS

Three groups of texts related to those cataloged here might have been in-cluded in this study.[89] Several early Jewish and Christian apocalypses contain descriptions of paradise and hell in the context of ascents through the heavens. While they share the formal features of the demonstrative explanation with the tours of hell (see the section on the extent of the form in chap. 2), they differ significantly in content. None contains a scene of sinners and their punishments.

Another group of texts that will not be treated here consists of medieval visions of hell from western Europe, some of which are probably contemporary with or earlier than texts included in this study. These texts, Latin, Irish, or Anglo-Saxon, contain tours of hell that have some similarities to the texts discussed here,[90] but they are less conservative in several ways. They have as their heroes not ancient worthies but medieval monks and

---

86. De Bruyne reports James's observation in "Nouveaux fragments," 154.

87. De Bruyne, "Epistula Titi, Discipuli Pauli, de Dispositione Sanctimonii," *Revue bénédictine* 37(1925):70–72. Harnack, "Brief," 205–13. De Santos Otero, HSW 2:142–43.

88. De Bruyne, "Epistula," 66–68. De Santos Otero, notes to trans., HSW 2:144–66.

89. I do not refer here to unpublished MSS omitted because of practical considerations. Unpublished MSS of Armenian apocalypses of the Virgin Mary (note 52, above) and MSS of a Christian Ethiopic Apocalypse of Baruch have been alluded to; surely there are many more such works. It is likely that most are relatively late monastic products. The more such texts examined, the clearer our picture of development and transmission.

90. The best listing of these texts is the general bibliography in Silverstein's *Visio* (223–29). The texts are interspersed among the other entries. Silverstein discusses some of them at different points in his book in relation to the Apocalypse of Paul. For a general discussion of the Anglo-Saxon texts, see E. J. Becker, *A Contribution to the Comparative Study of the Medieval Visions of Heaven and Hell with Special Reference to the Middle-English Versions* (Baltimore: J. Murphy, 1899). On the Irish texts, see St. J. Seymour, *Irish Visions of the Other World* (London: SPCK, 1930).

noblemen.[91] Many elements of these pictures of hell are drawn from eschatological traditions important in Western Christianity from the sixth or seventh century.[92] The Irish texts include details that derive from beliefs peculiar to Irish Christianity.[93]

The medieval Latin redactions of the Apocalypse of Paul require special mention because of their dependence on the Apocalypse of Paul and their points of contact with the Vision of Ezra (see chap. 5, below, on sins and punishments appearing only in the Vision of Ezra).[94] The redactions are all abridgments of the original; most contain only Paul's tour of hell. They differ from the medieval works just described in their close relationship to an earlier work which provides both their hero, one of the leading figures of Christian tradition rather than a contemporary, and many of the elements of their pictures of hell.

Yet much of the interest of the redactions lies in their additions to this inherited material, and these additions are drawn from the same stock of traditions on which the other medieval texts draw. Redaction 6 makes use of Irish materials. Most of the redactions, which are interrelated in various ways, were written between the tenth and the twelfth century.[95]

The medieval texts have been studied by Dante scholars in search of the sources on which the poet drew. A careful examination of these texts from a different point of view might yield some interesting results about the knowledge and transmission of earlier texts. This kind of study must be done extremely carefully, however, with allowance made for missing links. Some scholars who have attempted it have not been aware of later texts like the Vision of Ezra, which preserve early traditions and perhaps served to transmit them to the medieval works.[96]

Finally, tours of hell appear in Islam in the context of legends about the

---

91. Visions are attributed, e.g., to a Cistercian novice (Vincent of Beauvais, *Speculum historiale*), to a monk of Wenlock Abbey (Epistles of Boniface and Lull), to a nobleman (Vision of Tundale), to King Charles the Fat (Hariulf, *Chronicon centulense*), to a knight (Vision of the Knight Owen). Of course, several heroes of the tours of hell treated in this study, Gorgorios, Pachomios, and Joshua b. Levi, are drawn neither from the Hebrew Bible nor from the New Testament, but from more recent history or lore.

92. Silverstein, *Visio*, 77–81.

93. Seymour, *Irish Visions*, esp. 15–96.

94. Silverstein, *Visio*, is concerned primarily with these redactions.

95. Ibid., 12.

96. E.g., Becker, *Comparative Study*, 48–49, argues on the basis of certain parallels between the Apocalypse of Peter and the Vision of Alberic that the Apocalypse of Peter must have been known in Western Europe in the twelfth century. Of the three details to which he points, however, the lake of blood is not a true parallel. A second motif, women hanging by their hair for adultery, appears also in Apoc. Paul 39. Finally, the children in the enclosure in the Vision of Alberic find a parallel not only in the Apocalypse of Peter, but also in Vis. Ezra

isrā', Mohammed's nocturnal journey from Mecca to Jerusalem, or the *mi'rāj*, Mohammed's ascent to heaven. Both these cycles of legends are related to a passage in Sura 17 of the Qur'an: "Praised be He who called upon His servant to travel by night from the sacred Temple [of Mecca] to the far-off temple [of Jerusalem], whose precinct we have blessed, in order to show him our works." Since the Qur'an does not offer any more information about these events, the hadith attempt to fill in.

The most important proponent of the theory of Dante's debt to Muslim literature, M. Asín Palacios, discusses these hadith and translates some of them into Spanish.[97] According to Asín, they date from the ninth century on. Asín divides them into three cycles. The first consists of two accounts of the *isrā'*. Mohammed sees sinners suffering punishments and the blessed enjoying their reward.

The second cycle contains three accounts of the *mi'rāj*. Text 2A does not include a vision of hell, and Asín says that 2C, which is not translated in full, includes an "abortive attempt to introduce the vision of hell into the ascension."[98] The contents of 2B, however, are familiar: Mohammed sees both the sinners and the blessed.

The third cycle combines the *isrā'* and the *mi'rāj*. The one text Asín includes in this cycle contains a vision of hell, but its punishments are largely allegorical. For example, Mohammed sees a bull attempting to get back into the narrow structure that he has just left. This represents the torment of someone who cannot recall words he wishes he had not spoken.[99]

In 1949, E. Cerulli published thirteenth-century Latin and Old French

---

53. Indeed the Vision of Alberic shares with the Vision of Ezra the striking detail of the punishment of serpents sucking at the breasts of women who refused to care for orphans. (On this punishment, see chap. 3, below, under punishments for abortion and infanticide.) The Vision of Ezra is both late and Latin. Thus it is far from "evident" that the Vision of Alberic depends on a lost MS of the Apocalypse of Peter. Becker's alternative suggestion, "some now forgotten church father" as the channel of transmission, seems more reasonable, but it is probably unnecessary.

97. M. Asín Palacios, *La escatalogía musulmana en la Divina Comedia*, 2d ed. (Madrid-Granada: Escuelas de Estudios Arabes, 1943; 1st ed., 1919). These hadith are translated into Spanish in an appendix, 425–43. The English translation of the book, *Islam and the Divine Comedy* (trans. and abridg. H. Sunderland; London: John Murray, 1926), does not include the appendix. There is some discrepancy between the descriptions of the texts, found in both the Spanish volume and the English, and their actual contents as translated into Spanish, because the descriptions include variant texts that Asín does not actually translate.

I do not wish to discuss here the question of the influence of Muslim texts on Dante. For a rejoinder to Asín, see Silverstein, "Dante." Silverstein has the better of the argument, for Asín is ignorant of much of the development of the vision literature in medieval Western Christianity.

98. Asín, *Islam*, 17.

99. Asín, *Escatalogía*, 441; *Islam*, 34.

translations of an Arabic text called the *Book of the Ladder*.[100] Much of the description of hell consists of lists of the contents and names for each level, much like some of the medieval Hebrew descriptions found in "Tractate of Gehenna," for example.[101] It is chapter 79 (paras. 199–201) with its sinners and their punishments that is of interest for the Jewish and Christian texts discussed here.

These four texts, Asín's 1A, 1B, and 2B, and chapter 79 of the *Book of the Ladder,* will be treated when relevant in the discussions of the demonstrative explanations and sins and punishments of the Jewish and Christian texts.

---

100. *Il "Libro della Scala" e la questione delle fonti arabo-spagnole della Divina Commedia,* Studi e Testi 150 (Rome: Vatican, 1949). The translations were made not directly from the Arabic but from an intermediate Castilian translation (17). Neither the Arabic nor the Castilian version of the text has yet come to light.

101. Jellinek, *Bet ha-Midrasch,* 1:147–49.

Chapter 2

DEMONSTRATIVE EXPLANATIONS AND THE LITERARY CONTEXT OF THE TOURS OF HELL

DIETERICH'S *NEKYIA*

The year of the Akhmim discoveries was 1887, in 1892 the *editio princeps* of the Akhmim text of the Apocalypse of Peter was published, and in 1893 Dieterich published *Nekyia*, subtitled *Beiträge zur Erklärung der neuentdeckten Petrusapokalypse*.[1] The term νέκνια originally meant the rite used to conjure up the spirits of the dead, but it came to be applied to book 11 of the *Odyssey* and by extension to any encounter with the dead. Dieterich's is the only book-length study of this earliest Christian tour of hell, and it has enjoyed great influence. Of course, Dieterich did not know the Ethiopic version of the Apocalypse of Peter, which was not published until 1910, and those of his arguments based on the peculiarities of the Greek text are necessarily out of date.

Dieterich holds that the Apocalypse of Peter is a Christianized version of an Orphic-Pythagorean nekyia that goes back to archaic Greece. To make this case, he seeks first to demonstrate the existence of an unbroken Orphic-Pythagorean tradition from perhaps the sixth century B.C.E. to the

---

1. The second edition of *Nekyia*, published in 1913, after Dieterich's death, by R. Wünsch, contains a helpful listing of the major reviews of *Nekyia* and is annotated with comments drawn from those reviews and from the remarks of important classicists. These comments are published at the beginning of the book; their presence is noted by asterisks in the body of the text where the comment is relevant.

second century C.E. He points to motifs like the springs of forgetfulness and memory, *refrigerium* (the refreshing rest of the blessed), and Heaven and Earth as the parents of mankind, which appear in texts ranging from grave inscriptions to Plato to Plutarch.[2]

Having proved to his own satisfaction the existence of such a tradition, Dieterich attempts to demonstrate the existence of an actual text. A poem called "Descent into Hades" is ascribed to Orpheus by several ancient writers. Dieterich argues that the similarities in the picture of the afterlife in the works of Empedocles, Pindar, and Plato should be attributed to borrowing from that "Descent." The verses inscribed on the gold tablets found in graves in southern Italy and Crete are actually fragments of the text of the poem. This text soon came to be transmitted in variant versions, and Dieterich does not claim that all the aforementioned authors knew precisely the same version. Yet he argues that the context of the original nekyia can be reconstructed with some degree of certainty. It must have included "the judges of the dead, the judgment, those being punished and their punishments, rivers of torture and Tartarus, those being rewarded and the fields of the blessed, the second selection of lots in life, and in addition the first fall and the penalty decreed for it."[3]

Similar nekyiai with Pythagoras and other semi-legendary figures as their heroes soon began to circulate. Classical Athens knew these descents. Sophocles alludes to them (*Electra* 62),[4] and Aristophanes pokes fun at them, initiating a tradition of satire that goes through Menippus to Lucian. At the beginning of the common era the Orphic-Pythagorean nekyia is still making its influence felt in the works of Platonists and neo-Pythagoreans like Posidonios, Xenocrates, Plutarch, and others.[5] Thus the appearance in the second century of a Christian version of the Orphic-Pythagorean nekyiai should come as no surprise. After all, Plutarch and Lucian were probably contemporaries of the author of the Apocalypse of Peter.[6]

Next Dieterich devotes a chapter to sins and punishments. After surveying Greek and early Christian literature, Dieterich provides a set of parallels to the sins and punishments of the Apocalypse of Peter taken from texts he has already identified as drawing on the Orphic-Pythagorean nekyiai. "There is nothing analogous to the hell punishments of the Apocalypse

2. Dieterich, *Nekyia*, 84–108.

3. Ibid., 108–29; quotation, 126–27.

4. Ibid., 133. Wilamowitz' rejection of this claim is noted there in the 2d ed. of *Nekyia*.

5. Dieterich is not sure whether the influence is direct (knowledge of the nekyiai themselves) or indirect; see esp. ibid., 148, on Plutarch.

6. Ibid., 129–62.

of Peter except the subterranean punishments of the Orphic-Pythagorean nekyiai." [7]

One short chapter is devoted to Jewish apocalyptic literature. Dieterich recognizes certain parallels to the Apocalypse of Peter in 1 Enoch, but suggests that these come to it by way of the Essenes, who combined Judaism and Orphic-Pythagoreanism. "But of all the characteristic types of sins and punishments that are enumerated in the Apocalypse of Peter, no trace is found in the older Jewish apocalyptic books." [8]

Despite the central place of Orphism in his theory, Dieterich never confronts the problems involved in identifying texts as Orphic. The common use of the term provides an outstanding example of circular definition. I. M. Linforth writes,

> It is enough to mention the fact that the Gold Tablets from southern Italy and Crete are regarded by some as the very cornerstone for the reconstruction of Orphism, while others reject them as not Orphic at all. In fact, ideas and practices are arbitrarily attributed to an Orphism which is largely composed of just the ideas and practices thus attributed to it, and an Orphic religion is built up of ideas and practices which are only assumed to be Orphic. Scholars cannot always resist the temptation to fatten the spare body of Orphism by dubbing conjecturally as Orphic whatever they find in religion or art that bears any resemblance to what they conceive Orphism to be. [9]

Perhaps the vagueness of the designation accounts for the ease with which Dieterich slips in a hyphen and turns it into Orphic-Pythagoreanism.

Dieterich's mode of identifying the nekyia behind the gold tablets, Empedocles, Pindar, and Plato, is also open to criticism. He finds evidence of literary dependence on the hypothetical nekyia in the teaching of metempsychosis, the belief in world cycles, and the presence of figures like Persephone and Rhadamanthos in the underworld. [10] All are part of that diffuse collection of beliefs that he calls "Orphic-Pythagorean." Even granting the existence of such a world view, it is hard to see why the presence of these ideas and figures in diverse texts suggests literary dependence. The correspondences are of the general kind one would expect from authors with similar outlooks who live in the same culture. It would be one thing if Die-

---

7. Ibid., 163–213; quotation, 212.

8. Ibid., 214–24; quotation, 224.

9. I. M. Linforth, *The Arts of Orpheus* (Berkeley and Los Angeles: University of California, 1941), x–xi.

10. Dieterich, *Nekyia*, 108–23. Plato's belief in a 10,000-year cycle of rebirth corresponds perfectly to Empedocles' 30,000 seasons, since the early Greeks had only three seasons (119). These correspondences would be more impressive if the numbers were not so round.

terich had been willing to limit himself to suggesting the possibility of the existence of a "Descent to Hades" that served as a source for several other texts. It is another when he uses the existence of this hypothetical nekyia and its influence on other texts as a given in the further development of his argument.[11]

Finally, even if one accepts Dieterich's claim about this Ur-nekyia and the tradition it engenders, it is not clear that this tradition provides the closest parallels to the Apocalypse of Peter. Not even later works like Lucian's and Plutarch's contain anything like the number of punishments to be found in the Apocalypse of Peter, nor are most of the characteristically "Orphic-Pythagorean" features delineated by Dieterich found in the Apocalypse of Peter. The sentiment engraved on more than one of the gold tablets, "I am the child of earth and the starry sky; I too am of heavenly race," reflects a world of thought very different from that of the Apocalypse of Peter.[12]

Despite these problems, Dieterich has set the tone for subsequent discussion of the Apocalypse of Peter and thus of the later tours of hell.[13] M. R. James, who expressed some reservations about Dieterich's view that the paradise of the Apocalypse of Peter is Orphic, accepted his conclusion that the hell is derived from such sources.[14] Lieberman refers frequently to Dieterich's work in "On Sins and Their Punishments." In his introduction to the Apocalypse of Peter in the most recent edition of Hennecke-Schneemelcher, *New Testament Apocrypha*, Maurer still considers Dieterich to be right, "broadly speaking," in his belief that the hell of the Apocalypse of Peter derives from Orphic-Pythagorean sources, although he considers Jewish apocalyptic texts an important source for other parts of the work.[15]

---

11. See ibid., 212.

12. A. Olivieri, ed., *Lamellae Aureae Orphicae*, Kleine Texte für Vorlesungen und Übungen 133 (Bonn: A. Marcus & E. Weber, 1915), 12 (lines 6–7), 14 (line 3).

13. One or two of *Nekyia*'s reviewers were critical of Dieterich's claims of exclusively Greek origins. E. von Dobschütz (review of *Nekyia, Zeitschrift für Kulturgeschichte*, 1894, 340–48) criticized the lack of attention to Jewish sources, while C. Schmidt (review of *Nekyia, Theologische Literaturzeitung*, 1894, 560–65) argued also for the importance of Egyptian influence.

When a scholar of Dieterich's learning produces a work so biased in its approach, one wonders if there is not a hidden agenda. Von Dobschütz (346) remarked disapprovingly at the time the book appeared that Usener and his pupils, of whom Dieterich was one, always seek to demonstrate that the oldest forms of Christianity are gnostic, closely related to the mysteries. This remark helps to make Dieterich's fanciful reconstruction and nearly blind eye to Jewish sources a little easier to understand. It may be an expression of a certain kind of history-of-religions anti-Christian (and Jewish), pro-Greek feeling.

14. James, "Recovery," 24–25.

15. HSW 2:667.

It is to the tradition of Jewish apocalypses that I wish to turn in order to suggest an alternate ancestry for the Apocalypse of Peter and the other tours of hell.

DEMONSTRATIVE EXPLANATIONS IN THE TOURS OF HELL

The visions of hell under consideration here take the form of guided tours. Usually the guide is an angel.[16] In many of the texts, the visionary questions his guide about each sight. The interchanges between visionary and guide, or in some cases the guide's unsolicited explanations, provide the structure for the tours. The following passage from the Apocalypse of Paul is typical.

And in that place I saw another set of pits and in the middle of it a river full of men and women whom worms were devouring. I then wept, and with a sigh I asked the angel and said: Sir, who are these? And he said to me: These [17] are those who exacted usury at compound interest and trusted in their riches and did not hope in God that he would be a helper to them [chap. 37, HSW].

In all the texts except *Gedulat Moshe* the explanations appear primarily in the form of sentences beginning with demonstratives. "These are those who . . ." or simply "These . . ." are particularly common. In *Gedulat Moshe* the questions contain the demonstratives. In the Greek texts the demonstrative is usually a form of οὗτος; in the Latin texts, *hic* or *iste*; in the Hebrew texts, אלו or הם; in Coptic, ⲡⲉⲓ. For the Ethiopic, I have relied on translations.[18]

The presence of questions and explanations with demonstratives in the

---

16. Peter's guide in the Apocalypse of Peter is Jesus, Isaiah in the Isaiah fragment has his questions answered by God himself, and Joshua b. Levi is taken to hell by Elijah. The guide in the vision of the Acts of Thomas is demonic rather than angelic, but the visionary is a sinner rather than a particularly righteous person.

17. Duensing in HSW translates "*hii*" as "they." "These" is more literal, and it serves my purposes better.

18. All four Greek texts, the Greek version of the Apocalypse of Peter, the Acts of Thomas, the Greek Apocalypse of Mary, and the Apocalypse of Ezra, use forms of οὗτος.

Two of the Latin texts, the Apocalypse of Paul and the Elijah fragment, use forms of *hic*. The third Latin text, the Vision of Ezra, uses *iste*.

Of the Hebrew texts, the Isaiah fragment uses אלו, as do the questions of *Gedulat Moshe*, which does not have demonstratives in its answers. The one demonstrative in *Reshit Ḥokhmah*'s version of the Joshua b. Levi fragment is אלו. The midrash in *Darkhei Teshuvah* uses הם. (On הם as a demonstrative, see Gesenius' *Hebrew Grammar* [ed. Kautzsch and Cowley], no. 136a, b.)

Table 1. THE NUMBER OF DEMONSTRATIVE EXPLANATIONS AND QUESTIONS IN
TOURS OF HELL

	Explanations	*Questions*
Apoc. Pet. (Eth.)	18	—
Apoc. Pet. (Gk.)	11	—
Acts Th.	9	—
Apoc. Zeph.	8	8
Apoc. Paul	24	20
Eth. Apoc. Mary[a]	22	15
Eth. Apoc. Bar.	7	16
Apoc. Gorg.	13	12
Gk. Apoc. Mary	20	20
Apoc. Ezra	6	5
Vis. Ezra[b]	15	13
T. Isaac	2	1
L. Pach.	2	1
Dar. Tesh.	5	—
Isa. frag.	5	5
Josh. frag.[c]	1	—
Ged. Mosh.	—	6
Elij. frag.	4	—

[a] The Ethiopic Apocalypse of Mary also includes eight questions and answers of the form
"What is his name?" "——— is his name."

[b] I follow the texts printed by Wahl, which contain several punishments absent in Mercati's
version.

[c] In the text transcribed by Stone from the Bodleian MS of Chronicles of Yeraḥme'el, none
of the explanations is demonstrative. In the form in *Reshit Ḥokhmah*, there is one demonstrative explanation.

tours of hell of the texts considered here can be represented as shown in
Table 1. In general, demonstrative questions and explanations appear
throughout the texts considered here, in tours of paradise and encounters
with angels as well as in tours of hell; for the purposes of Table 1, I have
included only those that appear in the tours of hell proper.

The determination of what constitutes a demonstrative explanation is to
some extent arbitrary. I have insisted on the presence of a demonstrative
adjective or pronoun. In the Elijah fragment, for example, I did not count

---

Of the Coptic texts, the Apocalypse of Zephaniah, in the Akhmimic dialect, uses ⲛⲉⲓ (pl.),
while the vision in the Bohairic Life of Pachomios uses ⲛⲁⲓ (pl.), and the Sahidic Testament
of Isaac, ⲡⲉⲓ (sing.) and ⲛⲁⲓ (pl.).

The demonstrative pronouns in Ethiopic are cognate with those of other Semitic languages and seem to function in the same way syntactically. (See M. Chaîne, *Grammaire éthiopienne*, rev. ed. [Beirut: Imprimerie Catholique, 1938], no. 194.)

a number of clauses of the form "*qui* . . . , *sunt* . . . ," because no demonstrative like *hii* or *isti* appears. The clauses in which those demonstratives do appear are otherwise of exactly the same form. There is also an element of subjectivity involved in counting questions and explanations. I have chosen to count several clauses, each beginning with a demonstrative, separately, even when all are in response to a single question.

But the point that Table 1 is intended to demonstrate is a simple one. Central to all the texts considered here, with perhaps the exception of the visions in the Testament of Isaac, the Life of Pachomios, and the Joshua b. Levi fragment, are explanations and often questions in which demonstratives appear.

This characteristic is not limited to the Jewish and Christian texts considered here. Questions and answers with demonstratives also appear in the Muslim tours of hell published by Asín. According to Asín's translation, they correspond exactly to a form common in the Jewish and Christian texts: "Who are these?" "These are they who . . ." or "These who . . . are. . . ." Chapter 79 of the *Book of the Ladder* also contains demonstrative explanations.

The Arda Viraf, the single Zoroastrian tour of heaven and hell to reach us, contains almost one hundred questions and answers of the form "What sin was committed . . . ?" "This is the soul of the wicked man who. . . ." The demotic tale of Setme contains one explanation beginning "These men. . . ."[19] One explanation, of course, is not a pattern.

Implicit in my discussion of the Jewish and Christian texts is the claim that the presence of these demonstratives is not accidental, that it places the texts in a tradition, literary or otherwise. Yet it must be admitted that the presence of demonstrative questions and explanations is not particularly surprising. After all, "What (or who) is this?" is the most natural of questions in a strange setting, and real-life tours are full of explanations that begin with demonstrative pronouns reinforced by pointing fingers. Indeed, the presence of the pattern of demonstratives in other texts, Muslim and Zoroastrian, might suggest that the form is so commonplace as to lack any special significance.

Both the Muslim texts and the Arda Viraf, however, may have been influenced by texts that form part of the Jewish and Christian tradition delineated here. The question of the relationship between Muslim and Chris-

---

19. *The Book of Arda Viraf*, ed. and trans. M. Haug, assisted by E. W. West, text prepared by Destur Hoshangji Jampaspji Asa (Bombay: Government Central Book Depot; London: Trubner & Co., 1872). The Setme tale appears as "The Tale of Khamuas and His Son Si-Osiri," in F. L. Griffith, ed. and trans., *Stories of the High Priests of Memphis* (Oxford: Oxford University, 1900). Demonstrative explanation, 49.

tian texts in Europe in the late Middle Ages has been a controversial one in Dante studies, but Silverstein has argued convincingly that those scholars like Asín who view the Christian texts as dependent on the Muslim are simply unaware of the existence of an ongoing Christian tradition of tours of hell.[20] It is clear that the traditions are not unrelated, but given the presence of demonstratives in Christian texts that pre-date the rise of Islam, on this point at least the Muslim texts are more likely to show the influence of the Christian texts.

The Arda Viraf in its present form comes from the ninth or tenth century C.E. M. Boyce argues that it contains an ancient "kernel" and that through its influence on Muslim texts it contributes to the *Divine Comedy*.[21] This position is based on the works of students of Islam like G. Levi della Vida, who follow Asín on the relationship between Muslim and Christian texts.

Casey suggests that the Arda Viraf may be dependent on the Nestorian Syriac version of the Apocalypse of Paul.[22] Even if this claim is too strong, it is more reasonable to suggest that the Christian tradition of tours of hell, attested much earlier and in some quantity, influenced the single late example of a Zoroastrian tour than vice versa. The plausibility of the suggestion of Persian origins for the tour form diminishes drastically when the actual dates of texts are considered.

The Greco-Roman works that Dieterich views as the predecessors of the Apocalypse of Peter lend support to the position that the demonstratives of the Jewish and Christian tours of hell are significant, for almost all of them lack such features completely. Dieterich himself ignored demonstrative explanations altogether, despite their striking presence in the Apocalypse of Peter. Perhaps his exclusively Hellenic frame of reference blinded him to them, or perhaps, consciously or unconsciously, he preferred not to take note of them because they place the Apocalypse of Peter so clearly in the context of Jewish apocalyptic literature.

The earliest of the Greco-Roman texts lack not only the demonstratives but even their prerequisite, a guide. In most of book 11 of the *Odyssey*, the dead appear to Odysseus on earth. Even when Odysseus finds himself in Hades (11:565–627), he has no guide. Plato's Er (*Republic* 613e–end) travels without a guide. The gold tablets do not mention a guide.

---

20. Asín, *Escatología*; Silverstein, "Dante." Neither author considers demonstrative explanations in his discussion.

21. M. Boyce, "Middle Persian Literature," in *Iranistik* 4.2.1, Handbuch der Orientalistik I (Leiden: Brill, 1968), 48, esp. n. 3. Boyce argues for an ancient kernel based on the hero's name, which appears in the Avesta.

22. R. Casey, "Apocalypse of Paul," 32.

In the view of I. Lévy, Pythagoras is the first figure with whom a guided descent to Hades is associated.[23] A fragment of a work of Heraclides of Pontus (c. 390–310 B.C.E.) mentions a δαίμων νεανίας γενόμενος who showed the visitor a tree (probably the tree from which Homer was hanging for his blasphemy, according to the account of Pythagoras' descent by Hieronymos of Rhodes as quoted by Diogenes Laertius) and instructed him to believe that the gods exist and care for human affairs.[24] Lévy believes that Pythagoras is not the visitor, but the δαίμων.[25] In either case this fragment contains a guide who converses with his charge.

The guide becomes a standard feature of Greek tours of hell in the Roman period.[26] The guides in Plutarch's descents, *Divine Vengeance* and the *Sign of Socrates*, converse with the visitor to hell, but the conversations are not at all stylized, and demonstratives play no special role. Guides are of less importance in Lucian's work. The guides of *Lover of Lies* and *Menippus* are silent, while *True Story* lacks a guide altogether. (*Downward Journey* and *Dialogues of the Dead* are set in Hades, but they are not tours.) The Bologna Orphic fragment, which is clearly recognizable as a description of punishment in hell for various kinds of sins despite its extremely fragmentary condition, lacks any trace of a guide or of a dialogue or explanation.[27]

It is the *Aeneid*, a Latin poem deeply indebted to the Hellenic tradition, that provides the closest parallels to the interchanges of the Jewish and Christian texts. During his descent (book 6) Aeneas enters into conversation with the dead themselves, questioning them about their fate (e.g., Palinurus, 6.337–83), and much of the description is given in narrative form. At one point, however, Aeneas asks his guide, the Sibyl, "What forms of crime are these? Say, O maiden! With what penalties are they scourged? What cry so loud uprises?" (6.559–61).[28] The Sibyl's answer (6.561–627) contains three sentences that begin with the adverb *hic*, "here": "Here the

---

23. I. Lévy, *La légende de Pythagore de Grèce en Palestine*, Bibliothèque de l'École des Hautes Études, Sciences Historiques et Philologiques 250 (Paris: Champion, 1927), 84–85.

24. Heraclides of Pontus, quoted in the grammatical treatise Περὶ Συντάξεως, in I. Bekker, ed., *Anecdota Graeca* (Berlin: G. C. Nauck, 1814), 1:145. Diogenes Laertius, *Lives of Eminent Philosophers* 8.21.

25. Lévy, *Pythagore*, 83–84.

26. According to Lévy (*Pythagore*) all these late tours and some of the Jewish tours of hell (as well as Lithuanian folk tales!) are indebted to the lost descent of Pythagoras; this explains their similarity. Pan-Pythagoreanism is not very different in its consequences from pan-Orphism!

27. R. Turcan, "La catabase orphique du papyrus de Bologne," *Revue de l'histoire des religions* 150(1956):136–72. The grounds for considering the text Orphic seem shaky at best.

28. I quote the translation of H. Rushton Fairclough (*Virgil I*, LCL [Cambridge: Harvard University; London, William Heinemann, 1967]).

ancient sons of Earth . . . writhe in the lowest abyss" (580–81); "Here . . .
I saw the twin sons of Aloeus" (582); and "Here were they who in lifetime
hated their brethren" (608). Two sentences begin with the demonstrative
pronoun *hic*:[29] "This one sold his country for gold" (621) and "This one[30]
forced his daughter's bed" (623).

The Greco-Roman nekyiai, then, show that it is possible to describe a
tour of hell without questions and answers or even demonstrative explanations. Aeneas' trip to the underworld shows that demonstrative explanations can take other forms. The Sibyl's answers to Aeneas begin more
often with "here," a word that never appears as the demonstrative in the
explanations of the Jewish and Christian texts, than with "this one." The
distinguishing feature of the questions and answers of the Jewish and
Christian tours of hell is the relentless use of "this" and "these." In the later
texts, the demonstratives can be explained as part of an established tradition. But what gave rise to this tradition?

DEMONSTRATIVE EXPLANATIONS IN THE BOOK OF THE WATCHERS

With the publication of the Aramaic fragments from Qumran, the first
book of the anthology traditionally referred to as 1 Enoch has been shown
on the basis of paleography to be not later than the early part of the second
century B.C.E. The presence of literary seams suggests that parts of it are
even older.[31] For convenience, this text, chapters 1–36 of 1 Enoch, may be
referred to as the "Book of the Watchers."[32]

Chapters 17–36 of the Book of the Watchers describe Enoch's tour of the
cosmos. As R. H. Charles had already noted, Enoch takes not one but two
separate tours.[33] Charles saw chapters 17–19 as "certainly foreign to the rest
of this section. They are full of Greek elements. . . . Notwithstanding

---

29. While *hic*, the adverb "here," and *hic*, the masculine singular demonstrative pronoun
for objects near at hand, are visually identical (in fact, the adverb is a form of the pronoun),
the difference in grammatical function and in meaning is clear from the context.

30. "One" is my addition to the translation, to show that at both points the Latin is the
same.

31. Milik, *Books of Enoch*, 25. See also M. E. Stone, "The Book of Enoch and Judaism in the
Third Century B.C.E.," *Catholic Biblical Quarterly* 40(1978):484, who points out that since
there is no reason to believe that the earliest fragments represent the autograph copy, the text
in this form may well come from the third century.

32. Milik (*Books of Enoch*, 22) suggests this title. Syncellus refers to the excerpt in his chroni-
cle as taken from "the first book of Enoch about the Watchers."

33. See Charles's titles to chaps. 17–19 and chaps. 21–36 of *The Book of Enoch* (Oxford:
Oxford University, 1912).

these chapters belong to the Enoch tradition."[34] This cryptic last sentence is not explained. The rest of the tour, Charles's notes suggest, is indebted primarily to the biblical tradition.

More recently, Milik has argued for a different understanding of the relationship between the two tours based on his analysis of the book as a whole. For Milik, chapters 17–19 are part of a larger literary unit, chapters 6–19. This very ancient text was inserted by the compiler of the Book of the Watchers between two sections of his own composition, the introductory material of chapters 1–5 and the second tour of chapters 20–36. Chapters 21–25 are the compiler's rewriting of chapters 17–19; the rest of the tour is his own contribution.[35] The cosmology of both sections of the tour is Babylonian.[36]

Both accounts of Enoch's tour differ significantly from later cosmic tours, for they are imagined as tours of the earth. In the first tour, chapters 17–19, Enoch travels toward the west or northwest.[37] It is true that Enoch sees heavenly sights ("the places of the luminaries" [17:3], "the treasuries of the winds" [18:1]), but it appears that he sees them from the earth. Many of the sights he sees are earthbound: "the mouths of all the rivers of the earth and the mouth of the deep" (17:8), for example. He is said explicitly to come to the ends of the earth (18:10, 14); elsewhere he arrives at "a mountain the point of whose summit reached to heaven" (17:2; see also 18:8). The tour is concerned primarily with cosmological phenomena. It ends with the punishment of the Watchers.

The second tour is both more elaborate and more explicit about direc-

---

34. Ibid., notes to chaps. 17–19 (38).

35. Milik, *Books of Enoch*, 25. Milik believes that he can identify this compiler with some precision. He was a third-century (28) Judaean, perhaps a Jerusalemite; this accounts for the "excellent knowledge" of Jerusalem and its surroundings displayed in the part of the tour for which he was responsible (25–26). By profession he was "a modest official, in the perfume and spice trade." Later Milik calls him a merchant (28); perhaps this is what was originally intended by "modest official." This conclusion is suggested by the information about spice trees "obviously gained from hearsay" and by the description of the Nabatean city that Milik detects in chap. 28 (26).

This analysis of the tour assumes that no more than two hands are involved. The evidence of the questions and answers seems to suggest that the situation is more complicated. (See below.)

36. Ibid., 29–31. Like Charles, however, Milik (38) considers the fiery river of chap. 17 to be the Greek Pyriphlegethon. He does not make any suggestions about how this Greek element made its way into an essentially Babylonian cosmology; in fact, he in no way indicates surprise at the presence of Pyriphlegethon in a work of Babylonian inspiration.

37. The direction is implied by the description of the sights that Enoch sees, the fire of the west (17:4) or the seven mountains, three toward the east, three toward the south (18:6), which suggests the northwest. See ibid., 33, 38.

tions. Enoch goes "to the west of the ends of the earth" (23:1), to "the middle of the earth" (26:1), to "the midst of the desert" (28:1),[38] "to the east" (30:1), "to the east of the ends of the earth" (31:2),[39] "to the north-east" (32:1),[40] to the "ends of the earth," and east of them, to "the ends of the earth whereon the heaven rests" (33:1–2), "north to the ends of the earth" (34:1), "west to the ends of the earth" (35:1), "south to the ends of the earth" (36:1), "east to the ends of the heaven" (36:2). The contents of this tour are the punishment of the Watchers (chap. 21), the chambers of the souls (chap. 22), a fiery place in the west (chap. 23), the seven mountains, one of which is the throne of God, and the tree of life (chaps. 24–25), Jerusalem and Gehenna (chaps. 26–27), the desert and its spice trees (28–32:2), the garden of righteousness with the tree of knowledge (32:3–6), and finally the portals of heaven with the stars, winds, and rains (chaps. 33–36).[41]

If the contents of the first tour have any similarity to the contents of the tours of hell, it is in the description of the punishment of the Watchers. The second tour is much more concerned with reward and punishment: following the descriptions of the punishment of the Watchers, Enoch sees the chambers in which souls are stored to await the day of judgment. In these chambers the souls are separated according to righteousness and wickedness. The description of God's mountain throne and the tree of life says that the righteous will enjoy the tree's fruit at the end of time while the wicked suffer in the valley of Gehenna. The similarity of the contents of this tour to the tours of hell is of a very general nature; 1 Enoch knows nothing like the detailed descriptions of particular punishments for particular sins that dominate the tours of hell.

In the first tour Enoch is accompanied by an angel identified in the speech in chapter 19 as Uriel. The list of seven archangels in chapter 20 seems to suggest that all seven accompany Enoch on this second tour. Charles notes, however, that only four of them are actually mentioned in the course of the tour as it has come down to us.[42]

The two tours together contain ten conversations between Enoch and his guide. Each of these conversations contains a demonstrative explana-

---

38. Ethiopic has "towards the east, into the midst of the mountain range of the desert."

39. Missing in Ethiopic.

40. Ethiopic has "towards the north."

41. Milik (*Books of Enoch*, 38) understands this last part of Enoch's tour (33:2–36:3) as a tour of the heavens. "After his linear journey towards the East Enoch makes a circular flight along the boundaries of the sky and earth. . . ." If "boundaries," why "flight"? As in the first tour, Enoch seems to be viewing heavenly phenomena from an earthly vantage point.

42. Charles, *Book of Enoch*, notes to chap. 20 (43).

tion by the angelic guide; two contain two such explanations.[43] Five of the explanations are in response to questions. These will be discussed later.

The ten conversations are not distributed evenly through chapters 17–36. Only one (18:13–19:2) appears in the first tour. In the second tour, they cluster in chapters 21–27. From chapter 28, where the description of the wilderness begins, through the end of the tour, only one explanation appears. This is in chapter 32, where Enoch is taken to the garden of righteousness. An analysis of the literary sources that make up the tour of the kind attempted by Milik should take account of this extremely uneven distribution, which may suggest more than one source for the second tour.

The ten interchanges are as follows: (1) 18:13–19:2, (2) 21:4–6, and (3) 21:8–10, about the prison of the stars or angels; (4) 22:2–4, (5) 22:6–7, and (6) 22:8–13, about the hollows where the souls are stored; (7) 23:3–4, about the fire of the heavenly luminaries; (8) 24:5–25:6, about the tree of life, with two demonstrative explanations; (9) 27:1–4, about the accursed valley; (10) 32:5–6, about the tree of knowledge.

The finds at Qumran have resolved once and for all the debate about the original language of 1 Enoch, with the exception of chapters 37–71, the Parables, which do not appear at Qumran at all. Unfortunately, the fragmentary nature of the Qumran Aramaic makes it impossible to rely on it for a discussion of the demonstrative explanations; relevant readings from the fragments will be discussed below.

The cosmic tour up to chapter 32 has been preserved in the Greek of the Gizeh manuscript. Since the Greek is certainly a translation of the Aramaic while the Ethiopic is usually considered a translation of Greek, the Greek will be used here in preference to the Ethiopic.[44]

The explanations from Enoch's cosmic tour exhibit the same characteristics as the explanations found in the tours of hell. All begin with a form of the demonstrative οὗτος, except 27:2, where the Greek text is corrupt.[45] At that point I follow the Ethiopic, according to Charles's translation.

---

43. I have not included 22:4 in this count. It repeats the demonstrative of 22:3.

44. For a recent discussion of this point, see M. A. Knibb in consultation with E. Ullendorf, *The Ethiopic Book of Enoch: A New Edition in the Light of the Aramaic Dead Sea Fragments* (Oxford: Oxford University, 1978), 2:37–46. Knibb follows Ullendorf in arguing that the Ethiopic translators had access to an Aramaic version of Enoch, but he believes that on the whole the Ethiopic is based on the Greek version. Thus the Ethiopic may at times be independent of and superior to the Greek, but generally the Greek is closer to the original Aramaic.

45. The Greek text as it stands does not make sense. Enoch's question about the valley runs into the answer without an indication of a change in speakers. The answer begins abruptly, γῆ κατάρατος. The Ethiopic suggests that the Greek once read αὕτη ἡ γῆ. Charles takes γῆ as a transliteration of Hebrew גיא (notes to 27:2 [56]).

The opening phrases of the explanations are as follows:

18:14 οὗτός ἐστίν
18:15 οὗτοί εἰσιν
21:6 οὗτοί εἰσιν
21:10 οὗτος ὁ τόπος
22:3 οὗτοι οἱ τόποι
22:7 τοῦτο τὸ πνεῦμα
22:9 οὗτοι οἱ τρεῖς
23:4 οὗτος ὁ δρόμος
25:3 τοῦτο τὸ ὄρος
25:4 τοῦτο τὸ δένδρον
27:2 this accursed valley
32:6 τοῦτο τὸ δένδρον

Only one of these phrases has been preserved in Aramaic. For 23:4, οὗτος ὁ δρόμος τοῦ πυρός, 4QEn^{d}1 xi preserves the reading ונורא הוא, "and this fire." The Greek, "this path of fire," is not an exact translation of this Aramaic. The Ethiopic, according to Charles, omits "of fire."[46] The demonstrative, however, is constant in all three versions. One possible Aramaic *Vorlage* for οὗτος as adjective, then, is הוא, the third-person masculine singular personal pronoun, which can also serve as a demonstrative.[47]

4QEn^{e}1 xxii begins at the end of 22:3, too late to provide an Aramaic version of οὗτοι οἱ τόποι. This fragment does, however, offer an Aramaic version of 22:4, which begins in the Greek, καὶ οὗτοι οἱ τόποι. This verse refers back to the places pointed to in 22:3. It is useful here because it provides the Aramaic behind one Greek phrase beginning with οὗτοι. Again, however, the Greek and the Ethiopic, which here agree with each other, do not correspond exactly to the Aramaic, והא אלן אנון פחתיא, "And behold, these are the pits. . . ." Despite this discrepancy, it appears that the plural οὗτοι can stand for אלין, as it is spelled in biblical Aramaic and sometimes in the Aramaic fragments of Enoch.[48] אלין is cognate with the Hebrew אלה, which figures in some of the Hebrew tours of hell.

The third-person masculine plural personal pronoun אנון is one of several in biblical Aramaic; like הוא, it can serve also as a demonstrative or as a copula, as it does here.[49] Thus a possible Greek translation of אנון as used

---

46. See Milik, *Books of Enoch*, 220, notes to 4QEn^{d}1 xi, for a discussion of the relation of the Greek and Ethiopic to the Aramaic.

47. F. Rosenthal, *A Grammar of Biblical Aramaic* (Wiesbaden: Otto Harrassowitz, 1961), 20–21 (no. 32).

48. Ibid., 20 (no. 32) for biblical form. For אלין in Enoch, e.g., 4QEn^{a}1 iii, 5, 13.

49. Ibid., 19 (no. 30).

here would be εἰσιν; alternately, the verb might be omitted altogether in Greek, as it is in 21:10 or 22:3, for example. The reading of 4QEnᵃ1 iii 13 for the opening phrase of 6:8, אלין אנון, is rendered in the Greek as οὗτοί εἰσιν.

Οὗτος and οὗτοι, then, can correspond to הוא and אלין in the Book of the Watchers. But there is no guarantee that these equivalents are used consistently. Elsewhere in the Book of the Watchers forms of οὗτος translate דן, a singular demonstrative (6:4), and אנון, the plural pronoun discussed above (7:1). These two examples were gleaned from Milik's glossary; there are surely others. Thus it is quite likely that the Greek with its consistent use of a single word produces a more powerful impression of pattern than did the Aramaic. Nevertheless, the limited evidence provides no reason to doubt that the pattern of demonstrative explanation was present in the Aramaic of the Book of the Watchers.

Five of the explanations, 21:4, 22:6, 22:8, 23:3, 27:1, correspond to actual questions. The form of the question varies.[50] One explanation is introduced by an allusion to a question, "When I asked concerning them. . ." (18:13). The remaining explanations are prompted by exclamations of terror or delight.[51]

All the explanations of the Book of the Watchers, then, are offered as

---

50. The interrogatives are as follows:

  21:4 διὰ ποίαν αἰτίαν/ διὰ τί
  22:6 τίνος ἐστίν
  22:8 διὰ τί
  23:3 τί ἐστιν
  27:1 διὰ τί

51. It is interesting that most of the responses, whether to questions or not, are introduced by ἀποκρίνειν, often with a form of λέγειν:

  18:14 εἶπεν
  21:5 εἶπεν (question)
  21:9 ἀπεκρίθη καὶ εἶπεν
  22:3 ἀπεκρίθη καὶ εἶπεν
  22:7 ἀπεκρίθη λέγων (question)
  22:9 ἀπεκρίθη λέγων (question)
  23:4 ἀπεκρίθη (question)
  25:3 ἀπεκρίθη λέγων
  27:2 (Ethiopic) answered (question)
  32:6 ἀπεκρίθη

The verb ἀποκρίνομαι is the usual rendering of Hebrew ענה in Jewish and Christian translation literature of the period, and it is used in much the same way as ענה is used in the Hebrew Bible. Just as ענה is often joined to the verb אמר, ἀποκρίνομαι is often joined to λέγω. Further, ענה ואמר does not necessarily indicate that the speaker is answering a ques-

part of conversations, but only about half are prompted by actual questions. This is especially interesting in light of the fact that two of the earliest tours of hell, the Apocalypse of Peter and the Acts of Thomas, lack questions altogether. On the other hand, the Apocalypse of Zephaniah, also relatively early, contains questions for all the relevant explanations, and the Apocalypse of Paul, later than these others but still relatively early, has questions for almost every explanation. In later Christian texts, perhaps because of the influence of the Apocalypse of Paul, questions are the rule.

EZEKIEL'S TOUR AND THE PESHER FORM

The Book of the Watchers is not the earliest tour in Jewish literature. Even more ancient is Ezekiel's tour of the new temple in chapters 40–48 of the biblical book.[52] The prophet Ezekiel was active during the first half of the sixth century. Even those who hold that part or all of chapters 40–48 is not the work of the prophet place these chapters within the sixth century, although perhaps later than Ezekiel's time.[53]

In chapters 40–42 Ezekiel is led around by an angelic guide who measures each feature of the new temple while Ezekiel notes the measurements for the reader. In chapter 43 the glory of God returns to the temple, and God issues instructions about the temple. These instructions continue through chapter 46. In chapter 47 the angel leads Ezekiel along the bank of the river that flows east from the temple. The angel offers a relatively long

---

tion. It may simply indicate that the speaker's words are related to what went before. The same combination appears in biblical Aramaic, ענה ואמר, e.g. Dan. 2:8. Thus, neither in Greek nor in the Aramaic *Vorlage* do these verbs necessarily suggest questions (Bauer-Arndt-Gingrich, *Greek-English Lexicon of the New Testament*, s.v. ἀποκρίνομαι; P. Joüon, "Respondit et dixit," *Biblica* 13[1932]: 309–14).

52. The Book of the Heavenly Luminaries (1 Enoch 72–82) is cast in the form of a tour, although this feature is not emphasized; it too is older than the Book of the Watchers. On the basis of paleography, Milik (*Books of Enoch*, 7) places the earliest fragments from Qumran in the late third or early second century B.C.E., but he believes the text to be considerably earlier than that. As preserved in Ethiopic the tour contains no dialogue, but there are a number of speeches in chaps. 80–81.

53. See O. Eissfeldt, *The Old Testament: An Introduction*, trans. from the 3d German ed. of 1964 by P. R. Ackroyd (New York: Harper & Row, 1976), 372–80. M. Greenberg ("Ezekiel," *EJ*) considers the whole book Ezekiel's work. See S. Talmon and M. Fishbane, "The Structuring of Biblical Books: Studies in the Book of Ezekiel," *Annual of the Swedish Theological Institute* 10(1975–76): 138–53, for a detailed discussion of the relationship of Ezek. 40–43:12 to chaps. 40–48 and to the book as a whole. They regard Ezekiel as the author of chaps. 40–48.

description of the course of the river, which has special powers to freshen water, and of the trees on the river's bank. The rest of chapter 47 and all of chapter 48 consist of instructions for dividing the land among the tribes.

Ezekiel does not speak at all in the course of the tour, but the angel does comment on what Ezekiel is shown. In the first part of the tour, chapters 40–43:12, the angel speaks only four times (40:4, 40:45, 41:22, 42:13), and twice his comments begin with the demonstratives of the tour guide (40:45, 41:22). When the glory of God returns to the temple, God himself says, "This is the place of my throne . . ." (43:7).

The unit 40–43:12 concludes with a demonstrative used in a different way. Again God himself is speaking: "This is the law (תורה; probably better translated, "instructions") of the temple. . . ." Here, as in 43:18, the demonstrative is part of a formula for concluding a set of rules.[54]

In the remainder of the tour, a number of sentences beginning with demonstratives appear. Some appear in the course of instructions about land distribution and laws of sacrifice (chaps. 45 and 48 especially) without the function of the tour guide's demonstrative. There are, however, a number of appearances of זה and אלה that point to particular sights, although some also serve to convey instructions: 43:13(2); 44:2; 46:20, 24; 47:8, 13, 15.[55] Thus, while the demonstratives are used sparingly and the demonstrative sentences are less explanations than signals, the oldest extant tour in Israelite literature contains at least the seed of a feature that becomes so prominent in the hell tours.

The connection between Ezekiel 40–48 and the cosmic tour of the Book of the Watchers consists of more than the tour form itself and the presence of demonstratives. Enoch's tour shares the interest of Ezek. 47:1–12 in Jerusalem and the trees of the surrounding area. Like Ezekiel's Jerusalem, Enoch's has a stream flowing out of it, although this one flows southward (26:2). J. D. Levenson has shown that Ezekiel's prophecies about Zion merge Zion traditions, which draw on Canaanite beliefs about the sacred mountain of the north, with traditions about the Garden of

---

54. On 43:12 see Talmon and Fishbane, "Ezekiel," esp. 140–42. On the formula "This is the law of . . ." more generally, see Fishbane, "Accusations of Adultery: A Study of Law and Scribal Practice in Numbers 5:11–31," *HUCA* 45(1974):31–35.

55. It is not clear whether the measurements in 43:13 describe an altar that Ezekiel actually sees. If they are purely directions, they should not be included in this list.

The same problem arises in 47:13, 15. Is Ezekiel actually looking out on the land, or is he receiving theoretical instructions?

Ezek. 47:31 reads גה (meaningless) rather than זה in the MT. Biblia Hebraica suggests reading זה with Greek, the targumim, and the Vulgate.

Eden, primarily Mesopotamian in provenance.[56] The mountain throne of God and the Garden of Eden are also associated with each other in Enoch's tour. On the tallest of seven mountains, identified by Michael as God's throne, is a fragrant tree, apparently the eschatological tree of life (chaps. 24–25). Seven mountains are mentioned again immediately before the description of the garden of righteousness (chap. 32).[57]

A book with the prestige of Ezekiel might well have served as a model for the author(s) of the Book of the Watchers. Yet there are many elements in the tour of the Book of the Watchers that cannot be explained by reference to Ezekiel 40–48. In the case of the demonstrative explanations, Ezekiel's tour may contain the seed, but the development in the Book of the Watchers has gone far beyond it.

Perhaps the ancient tradition of interpretation of dreams and visions that appears in a number of places in biblical literature, in the Qumran pesharim, and in several Jewish and Christian apocalypses influenced this development. This form of exegesis breaks up the dream or text to be decoded into component sections. The interpretation is usually linked to the lemma by means of a connective.[58] For example, Joseph interprets Pharaoh's dream as follows: "The seven good cows, they are seven years, and the seven good ears, they are seven years . . ." (Gen. 41:26). Here the linking term is הנה, "they (are)." In the Hebrew Bible such dreams and visions appear also in Amos, Jeremiah, and Ezekiel.[59]

Zechariah 1–8, usually dated to the late sixth century, not much later than Ezekiel, contains a new departure of particular importance for apocalyptic literature.[60] It offers elaborate symbolic visions and for the first time an angelic interpreter. Many of the angel's interpretations are prompted by Zechariah's questions, "What is this?" "What are these?," the best biblical parallels to the question-and-answer form of the Book of the Watchers and many later tour apocalypses.[61]

---

56. J. D. Levenson, *Theology of the Program of Restoration of Ezekiel 40–48*, Harvard Semitic Monographs 10 (Missoula, Mont.: Scholars Press, 1976), 25–36.

57. The seven mountains appear in the first tour (18:6–8), and the middle one is described as reaching "to heaven like the throne of God." There is no link to Eden here, however.

58. See M. Fishbane, "The Qumran Pesher and Traits of Ancient Hermeneutics," *Proceedings of the Sixth World Congress of Jewish Studies* (Jerusalem, 1977), 1:106–10 for discussion of examples.

59. Amos 7:7–9; 8:1–3; Jer. 1:11–19; 24; Ezek. 17 (not a vision); 37:1–14.

60. For the date, Eissfeldt, *Old Testament*, 429. On the importance of Zechariah for apocalyptic literature, see, e.g., D. S. Russell, *The Method and Message of Jewish Apocalyptic* (Philadelphia: Westminster, 1964), 88–91.

61. Zech. 1:9; 2:2; 4:4; 5:6; 6:4. Sometimes in Zechariah (4:2; 5:2, 6) and in other texts (e.g., Jer. 1:11), the prophet is asked by the divine interpreter, "What do you see?"

In Daniel (chaps. 2, 4, 5, 7, 8) symbolic visions appear for the first time with obviously eschatological content.[62] The combination of symbolic vision and eschatology reappears in later apocalypses like 4 Ezra (9:26–10, 11–12, 13) and 2 Baruch (chaps. 36–40, 53–74). Indeed, it is often considered a characteristic element of apocalyptic literature generally since most of the attention given apocalyptic literature has been directed at the historical apocalypses.[63]

In his article on the ancient Near Eastern background of the Qumran pesharim, M. Fishbane terms the method of treating the text, dream, or vision employed by the works mentioned above "citation and atomization."[64] The biblical texts and the pesharim (Fishbane does not discuss the noncanonical apocalypses) should be viewed as part of an extremely old tradition of interpretation of oracles, dreams, and finally scripture with roots in Egypt and Mesopotamia.[65] Most of these texts share other exegetical techniques involving various kinds of wordplay.

The interpretations of the dreams in Genesis, the visions of Zechariah, and the dream visions of Daniel are based not primarily on wordplay but on symbolic equivalence, as are the interpretations in the noncanonical apocalypses.[66] While such equivalences are not absent from the other texts Fishbane discusses, there they are of less importance than wordplay.

Demonstrative pronouns are prominent as linking terms in the texts that rely on symbolism. 4 Ezra 10:44–48, for example, reads as follows:

See Fishbane, "Qumran Pesher," 106–8, for a detailed discussion of the formal features of the angelic interpretation in Zech. 1–8 and its transitional place between earlier biblical dream and vision interpretation and the interpretation in Daniel.

62. See J. J. Collins, *The Apocalyptic Vision of the Book of Daniel*, Harvard Semitic Monographs 16 (Missoula, Mont.: Scholars Press, 1977), 78–87, on the relation between the tales and the visions.

63. E.g., Russell, *Jewish Apocalyptic*, 122–27.

64. Fishbane, "Qumran Pesher," 98–99, 101–2, 105–10.

65. Here Fishbane draws on the work of, among others, A. L. Oppenheim, "The Interpretation of Dreams in the Ancient Near East," *Transactions of the American Philosophical Society* 46(1956):179–255; S. Lieberman, "Rabbinic Interpretation of Scripture," in *Hellenism in Jewish Palestine* (New York: Jewish Theological Seminary, 1962), 68–82; L. Silberman, "Unriddling the Riddle," *Revue de Qumran* 3(1961):323–35 on petirah midrashim. See also Collins, *Daniel*, 78–87, on Daniel, the Qumran pesharim, and biblical visions.

Some of the materials from the Hellenistic Near East considered by Fishbane are discussed from the point of view not of form but of content by Collins, "Jewish Apocalyptic Against Its Hellenistic Near Eastern Environment," *Bulletin of the American School of Oriental Research* 220(1975):31–33, and J. Z. Smith, "Wisdom and Apocalyptic," in *Religious Syncretism in Antiquity: Essays in Conversation with Geo Widengren*, ed. B. A. Pearson (Missoula, Mont.: Scholars Press, 1975).

66. The interpretation of the writing on the wall, Dan. 5, does use wordplay. The dreams of the court stories, in chaps. 2 and 4, however, do not.

This woman whom you saw, this (*haec*) is Zion, whom you now see as a city that is built. And as for her telling you that she was barren for thirty years, (this is) because there were three thousand years in which there was not an offering offered in her. And it came to pass after three thousand years that Solomon built the city and offered offerings. Then it happened that the barren woman bore a son. And as for her saying to you that she raised him with great care, this (*haec*) was the time of dwelling in Jerusalem. And as for her saying to you, "When he entered the marriage chamber, my son died" and that misfortune had come upon her, this (*haec*) was that Jerusalem had been laid waste.[67]

The same demonstratives that introduce the explanations of the tour apocalypses serve as the link between symbol and interpretation in the exegesis of the visions of the historical apocalypses. The scenes of the tour apocalypses are not complex symbolic constructions, but simply sights that need to be identified. Yet the tours are so structured that they conform to the pattern of vision followed by angelic interpretation found in Zechariah 1–8 and some of the historical apocalypses. Of course the tours considered here are not ordinary tours; like the symbolic visions, they are God's means of revealing his secrets to his chosen ones.

The angelic tour guide's explanation of sights in the tour apocalypses and the angelic interpreter's decipherment of symbolic visions in the historical apocalypses are indebted, then, to the same tradition of exegesis. In the historical apocalypses both function and style of this tradition of exegesis are preserved. In the tour apocalypses the style remains relatively unchanged, but the function is altered significantly: decipherment becomes description. In the light of our new knowledge of the early date of the Book of the Watchers, it now appears that this pesher style of exegesis was adapted by the tour apocalypses before the historical apocalypses made use of it in a more conservative way.

The new interest in tour apocalypses generated by the Qumran Enoch fragments has raised the question of the relationship between tour apocalypses and historical apocalypses: are we justified in speaking of a single genre on literary or historical grounds? Our investigation of the demonstrative explanations suggests that for this feature at least the tour apocalypses and the historical have different histories. While the two varieties of apocalypse draw on the same sources, there is no single line of development to be traced through the tour apocalypses to the historical apocalypses.[68]

67. My translation from B. Violet's text, *Die Esra-Apokalypse*, Griechische christliche Schriftsteller 18 (Leipzig: J. C. Hinrichs, 1910), 308–10.

68. J. J. Collins treats the question of the relationship of the tour apocalypses to the historical apocalypses in Collins, ed., *Apocalypse: The Morphology of a Genre* (*Semeia* 14[1979]:

THE EXTENT OF THE FORM

Demonstrative explanations are not restricted to the tour apocalypses studied here. They appear also in 3 Baruch, the ascent of the Testament of Abraham, the Parables of Enoch, 2 Enoch, and the Ascension of Isaiah. But there are also tours in early Jewish and Christian apocalyptic literature in which they do not appear: the Book of the Heavenly Luminaries (1 Enoch 72–82) and the ascents of the Testament of Levi and the Apocalypse of Abraham.[69]

I think it can be shown that the distribution of demonstrative explanations in these tours is significant. This is not the place for a full investigation of the subject; I shall offer only a few observations about the relationship between the contents of the heavens in each text and the presence of demonstrative explanations. Briefly, I think that demonstrative explanations appear in those texts with ties of some kind to the Book of the Watchers or the tours of hell.

The two texts that come closest to sharing the concerns of the tours of hell are 3 Baruch and the Testament of Abraham. The structure of 3 Baruch, as much as that of any of the tours of hell, is determined by conversation between the visionary and his angelic guide as they travel through five heavens.[70] Most of the conversations consist of questions

---

16–17). He argues for the existence of a single genre on the basis of various features distributed throughout apocalyptic literature. But Collins points to a direction of development that seems to me problematic: from the "clear distinction" between "'historical' apocalypse" and "otherworldly journey" found in early apocalypses like Daniel and 1 Enoch 1–36 to the blurring of these categories in the Parables of Enoch and Revelation. (The examples here are Collins'.) Might this not suggest that two once-separate genres came together in perhaps the first century C.E.?

The evidence I have presented above relates to only one feature of the texts, and any discussion of this question must consider as many features as possible. Still, I think that the thrust of Collins' own discussion shows that further consideration is required.

69. In the Apocalypse of Abraham a pesher form of exegesis is used to decipher Abraham's vision of world history. Demonstrative explanations do not appear in the description of the contents of the heavens, however.

70. On 3 Baruch, see G. W. E. Nickelsburg, *Jewish Literature Between the Bible and the Mishnah* (Philadelphia: Fortress, 1981), 299–303. For a brief discussion and recent bibliography, see J. H. Charlesworth, *The Pseudepigrapha and Modern Study with a Supplement*, SCS 7S (Chico, Calif.: Scholars Press, 1981), 86–87, 275.

The work certainly postdates the destruction of the Second Temple in 70, and Nickelsburg suggests Egypt as the place of origin. The work as it has reached us contains indisputably Christian passages, and M. R. James (*Apocrypha Anecdota* II, Texts and Studies 5.1 [Cambridge: Cambridge University, 1897], lxxi) considers the work as a whole Christian. If there

and answers; many of the answers are demonstrative explanations.[71]

In the third heaven Baruch learns about the comings and goings of the sun and moon in a description that shares certain features with the description of these heavenly phenomena in 2 Enoch. But the main concern of 3 Baruch is the fate of souls. The first and second heavens are inhabited by the builders and planners of the Tower of Babel in demonic guise. In the third heaven is found the monster whose belly is hell. The fourth heaven contains the souls of the righteous. In the fifth the archangel Michael receives the prayers of the righteous.

The contents of the first two heavens are not easy to interpret;[72] they seem to reflect interest in reward and punishment as the higher heavens certainly do. M. R. James saw in the description of the angels who gather the prayers of the righteous in 3 Baruch 12 a point of contact with Apoc. Paul 7–10.[73] It is not clear that the similarities are so strong as to require a common source. The demonstrative explanations of 3 Baruch may be explained as the result of contact with a particular text or tradition (a common source of 3 Baruch and the Apocalypse of Paul, for example) or simply as an attempt to conform to the pattern of tours concerned with reward and punishment like the Book of the Watchers and any of the tours of hell that its date would have permitted the author of 3 Baruch to know, perhaps the Apocalypse of Zephaniah (chap. 5 under the Apocalypse of Zephaniah and the Book of the Watchers) and a Jewish tour or tours no longer extant (see chap. 5, below, under the Apocalypse of Peter and the Jewish texts).

Abraham's ascent in the Testament of Abraham is concerned with the judgment of sinners. It includes dialogue between Abraham and his guide, the archangel Michael, some in the form of questions and answers with demonstratives.[74]

---

can be said to exist a scholarly consensus on this little-studied text, it is that 3 Baruch is a Jewish work. The Slavonic lacks many of the Christian elements of the Greek (U. Fischer, *Eschatologie und Jenseitserwartung im Hellenistischen Diasporajudentum* [Berlin: de Gruyter, 1978], 72–76).

71. There are twenty-nine exchanges of question and answer in the course of the seventeen chapters of the text. Some consist of several questions at once and a lengthy answer. Ten of the answers are of the form οὗτός ἐστι . . . or οὗτος ὁ. . . .

72. Nickelsburg sees the inhabitants of the first and second heavens as the destroyers of Jerusalem (*Jewish Literature*, 302–3). J.-C. Picard ("Observations sur l'Apocalypse grecque de Baruch," *Semitica* 20[1970]:77–103) thinks that the inhabitants of the second heaven are Greek sophists (79, n. 6; to the best of my knowledge, the continuation of the article, in which Picard promised to argue for this view, has never appeared).

73. M. R. James, *Apocrypha Anecdota* II, lxix–lxxi.

74. On the Testament of Abraham, Nickelsburg, *Jewish Literature*, 248–53, and Charlesworth, *Pseudepigrapha*, 70–72, 270–71. This work, with its two quite different recensions, is

The description of the judgment of the soul after death in the Testament of Abraham shows points of contact with the descriptions in the Apocalypse of Zephaniah and the Apocalypse of Paul.[75] All these descriptions contain demonstrative explanations. The relationship of the three texts probably indicates a shared tradition rather than borrowing from one text by another. Even if we accept the dominant view of the Testament of Abraham as a first-century Jewish work,[76] its author could have known the same works that the author of 3 Baruch knew, and the use of demonstrative explanations in the Testament of Abraham beyond the judgment scene may reflect, as in 3 Baruch, the author's feeling that tours concerned with reward and punishment require them.

The Parables of Enoch, chapters 37–71 of 1 Enoch, contains several instances of questions and demonstrative explanations.[77] The tour discernible in this work is combined with poetic pronouncements about the end of days and the fate it will bring for the wicked and the righteous. Unlike the Testament of Abraham and 3 Baruch, the Parables of Enoch is interested in reward and punishment of individual souls only as part of a wider range of concerns, including traditions about the fallen angels related to those in the Book of the Watchers. As a later stage in the development of Enoch literature, the Parables of Enoch is unmistakably indebted to the Book of the Watchers, and the demonstrative explanations should be seen as a sign of that debt.

Like the Parables of Enoch, 2 Enoch is in part a reworking of the Book

---

extremely difficult to date or to place geographically. There are advocates of both Jewish and Christian origins. Of course the date of the Testament of Abraham is crucial for determining what other works its author might have known.

The questions and answers with demonstratives appear as follows. Recension A: chap. 10 (1 question and answer), chap. 11 (1), chap. 12 (1), chap. 13 (4); Recension B: chap. 8 (1 question, 2 answers), chap. 9 (1), chap. 11 (1 question, 2 answers).

75. On the judgment scene, see Nickelsburg, "Eschatology in the Testament of Abraham," in Nickelsburg, ed., *Studies on the Testament of Abraham*, SCS 6 (Missoula, Mont.: Scholars Press, 1976), 23–64.

76. See the discussions in the works listed in n. 74 above.

77. On the Parables of Enoch, see Nickelsburg, *Jewish Literature*, 214–23, and Charlesworth, *Pseudepigrapha*, 98–103, 278–83. If there can be said to be a consensus on date and provenance, it is that the Parables of Enoch is a Palestinian Jewish work of the first century c.e. For Milik's controversial views on the parables, see his *Books of Enoch*, 89–98. For a critique of these views, see J. C. Greenfield and M. E. Stone, "The Enochic Pentateuch and the Date of the Similitudes," *Harvard Theological Review* 70(1977): 51–66. There are nine demonstrative explanations, seven with questions (40:8–9, 43:3–4, 46:2–3, 52:3–4, 53:4–5, 54:4–5, 60:24–no question, 61:2–3, 64:2–no question). I have counted only those sentences that refer to sights actually extant at the time of Enoch's tour. There are many such sentences about the future in the Parables of Enoch.

of the Watchers or its traditions.[78] Second Enoch modernizes the earth-bound tour of the Book of the Watchers in light of new ideas about the structure of the heavens. Only in three of the seven heavens does Enoch ask about or comment on the sights. These heavens, the second, third, and fifth, are the ones in which reward and punishment are at issue. The first and fourth heavens contain cosmological phenomena; the sixth and seventh contain angels. In the seventh heaven angels encourage Enoch as he goes to meet God, and Enoch expresses his fear, but without demonstratives.

The third heaven contains the paradise of the righteous and the place of torment for the wicked (chap. 5). In reponse to Enoch's exclamations, the guides describe the final abodes with sentences that begin "This place . . . "; retroverted to Greek, this would be the phrase οὗτος ὁ τόπος, so familiar from the Book of the Watchers.

The second and fifth heavens are occupied by angels identified as the Watchers known from 1 Enoch. (This identification is made explicitly only in the fifth heaven [chap. 7]). Those in the second heaven are being pun-ished, and like the Watchers of 1 Enoch, they ask Enoch to intercede for them (chap. 4). Those in the fifth heaven are sad and sullen not because of their own sin, but because of the fate of their brothers who descended to earth and sinned. The guide's explanations of the sights of the second and fifth heavens, one explanation per heaven, begin "These are . . . ," in Greek most likely οὗτοί εἰσιν. Both explanations are prompted by questions.

The contents of the three heavens in which demonstrative explanations appear, then, are closely related to the Book of the Watchers. The contents of the other heavens are far less so. The demonstrative explanations seem likely to be a formal feature borrowed together with content.

Up to this point the texts under discussion have combined demonstra-tive explanations with content concerned with reward and punishment or otherwise indebted to the Book of the Watchers. Now we turn to an apoc-alypse with demonstrative explanations, but very different interests.

In the seven heavens of the Ascension of Isaiah, there appear neither cosmological phenomena nor scenes of reward and punishment, but only angels and finally God himself.[79] Isaiah and his guide converse during the

---

78. On 2 Enoch, see Nickelsburg, *Jewish Literature*, 185–88, and Charlesworth, *Pseudepi-grapha*, 103–6, 283. Egypt is usually suggested as the place of origin. The date is uncertain, and the issue of Jewish or Christian authorship is still discussed.

I follow the chapter divisions in the text of A. Vaillant, *Le livre des secrets d'Hénoch* (Paris: Institut d'Études slaves, 1952).

79. On the Ascension of Isaiah, see Charlesworth, *Pseudepigrapha*, 125–30, 289–90. In its present form it is a composite Christian work of perhaps the late second century. But one of

ascent, but there are only about six demonstrative explanations in the ascent, most preceded by questions. All but two appear in the description of the seventh heaven.[80]

In its angelological interests the Ascension of Isaiah is close to two tour apocalypses from which demonstrative explanations are absent altogether, the ascents of the Testament of Levi[81] and the Apocalypse of Abraham.[82] These three ascents, together with 2 Enoch, share some of the following motifs with merkavah literature: an ascent through seven heavens, angels as the contents of the heavens, angelic crowns, angelic hymns, the visionary's mistaking an angel for God, danger to the visionary during the ascent, the vision of the throne of God.[83] The Apocalypse of Zephaniah stands in a special relationship to these works. While it contains many of

---

the documents that makes up the work, the Martyrdom of Isaiah, is clearly Jewish, and I shall argue below (in chap. 5, under ascent apocalypses and merkavah mysticism) that the ascent itself contains elements that connect it to hekhalot literature.

80. The complete Ascension of Isaiah is preserved in Ethiopic, and it is from the Ethiopic that both R. H. Charles (*The Ascension of Isaiah* [London: A. & C. Black, 1900]) and J. Fleming and H. Duensing (HSW 2:642–63) translate. For chaps. 6–11 there are Latin and Slavonic versions preserved. Charles prints the Latin and Bentwetsch's Latin translation of the Slavonic as an appendix to his translation. According to the translations of the Ethiopic text, there are demonstrative explanations at 7:11–12; 9:4, 25–26, 32, 36; and 10:6. There is no demonstrative at 9:4 according to the Latin and Slavonic; and at 9:23 the Latin and Slavonic contain an extra question and answer with demonstratives lacking in the Ethiopic.

81. On the Testament of Levi, see Nickelsburg, *Jewish Literature*, 235–37, and Charlesworth, *Pseudepigrapha*, 211–20, 305–7. The history of the Testament of Levi is quite complicated. In its Greek form as part of the Testaments of the Twelve Patriarchs, it is a Christian reworking of Jewish traditions attested by several Aramaic MSS from the Cairo Geniza and Qumran. The material from Qumran is fragmentary. A fragment that preserves a small portion of an Aramaic form of the ascent is published by Milik, "Le Testament de Lévi en araméen: Fragment de la grotte 4 de Qumrân," *Revue biblique* 62(1955):398–406. On the layers of tradition in the chapters that include Levi's ascent, see M. de Jonge, "Notes on the Testament of Levi II–VII," in de Jonge, ed., *Studies on the Testaments of the Twelve Patriarchs*, SVTP 3 (Leiden: Brill, 1975), 247–60.

Nickelsburg argues for a close relationship between the ascent in the Testament of Levi and the earlier ascent of 1 Enoch 12–16 ("Enoch, Levi, and Peter: Recipients of Revelation in Upper Galilee," *Journal of Biblical Literature* 100[1981]:575–600).

82. On the Apocalypse of Abraham, see Nickelsburg, *Jewish Literature*, 294–99, and Charlesworth, *Pseudepigrapha*, 68–69, 269–70. Although it is preserved only in Slavonic and contains Christian elements as it now stands, the Apocalypse of Abraham is usually treated as a first- or second-century C.E. Jewish work.

83. I. Gruenwald, *Apocalyptic and Merkavah Mysticism* (Leiden: Brill, 1980), devotes a chapter to merkavah motifs in apocalyptic literature ("The Mystical Elements in Apocalyptic," 29–72). In this context he considers or mentions not only the five texts that I treat as related to hekhalot literature (with the exception of the Apocalypse of Zephaniah, which he does not seem to know), but also texts like the Apocalypse of Paul and the Revelation. I do not dispute

the motifs listed above, it is not structured as an ascent. Many of these motifs appear in chapter 14 of the Book of the Watchers, an early example of the tradition of visions of the throne of God that extends from Ezekiel to the hekhalot texts. The hekhalot texts do not make use of demonstrative explanations.

These apocalypses, then, represent a different variety of tour apocalypse, related not so much to chapters 17–36 of the Book of the Watchers as to chapter 14. Demonstrative explanations are not standard features of these tours, as they are of the tours of hell; such explanations are absent from chapter 14 of the Book of the Watchers.

This distinction is not hard. Second Enoch, for example, contains demonstrative explanations in those heavens concerned with reward and punishment, but not in those concerned with cosmology and angelology. The Ascension of Isaiah, despite its Christian content, is in some ways particularly close to the hekhalot texts, but it contains several demonstrative questions and answers, although they do not function as a structuring device since most appear in a single heaven. In the Apocalypse of Zephaniah demonstrative questions and answers appear throughout. Indeed, the Apocalypse of Zephaniah spans these categories, sharing interests with the tours of hell and with the ascents. If I am right about the early date of the work, it represents an intermediate stage between the Book of the Watchers with its broad interests and the full-blown tours of hell.

Finally, the content of the Book of the Heavenly Luminaries places it neither among texts concerned with reward and punishment nor among those related to hekhalot texts.[84] Its interests are almost exclusively astronomical and calendrical. The absence of demonstrative explanations hardly requires explanation. Since it predates the Book of the Watchers, no such feature had yet been developed.

Conclusions

All the tours of hell and many other tour apocalypses contain the feature I have been calling "demonstrative explanations." While the presence of

---

Gruenwald's identification of individual merkavah motifs in the works he discusses, but a distinction needs to be made between texts that contain individual merkavah elements and texts that share the structure of ascent through seven heavens as well as particular motifs with the hekhalot literature.

84. On the Book of the Heavenly Luminaries, see Nickelsburg, *Jewish Literature*, 47–48, and Charlesworth, *Pseudepigrapha*, 98–103, 278–83. This work, apparently the earliest preserved apocalypse, can be dated on the basis of paleography to the third century B.C.E.

these explanations in any one text is not particularly noteworthy, their presence in text after text requires explanation.

Demonstrative explanations make their appearance as a structuring feature of apocalyptic tours as early as the Book of the Watchers. The Book of the Watchers had available the model of Ezekiel 40–48, a tour in which the angelic guide uses demonstratives, although not exactly in the manner of the later tours. The development of the demonstrative explanations into a central feature of the tours of hell reflects the influence of the tradition of pesher-style exegesis, which finds its most important expression for both tour and historical apocalypses in Zechariah 1–8. These explanations distinguish the texts in which they appear from other texts with similar interests like the Greco-Roman nekyiai.

It is one thing to speak about a "tradition." It is another thing to uncover the dynamics of transmission of the elements that define the tradition. Without attempting to account for all the texts discussed above, let me offer a few remarks about the possible modes of transmission. At one extreme stand literary models and direct dependence. The similarities between the Apocalypse of Paul and the Ethiopic Apocalypse of Mary can probably be accounted for in this way (see chap. 1 above, under the Ethiopic Apocalypse of Mary). At the other extreme is the consciousness derived from familiarity with a number of texts, with no particular text or texts serving as a model, that a genre requires certain features. This may be the best way to understand the presence of demonstrative explanations in texts like the Testament of Isaac and the Life of Pachomios (see chap. 5, below).

On the basis of structure, then, Dieterich's view of the Apocalypse of Peter as a Greek work with only the lightest Christian retouching must be challenged. Demonstrative explanations are important not only in the Apocalypse of Peter and the other tours of hell. Rather they are characteristic of a range of Jewish and Christian tour apocalypses going back to the Book of the Watchers. This is by no means to deny that there are Greek elements in the Apocalypse of Peter. Similarly Charles is probably correct in viewing the tours of the Book of the Watchers as containing motifs drawn from Greek beliefs. It should come as no surprise that a Jew in third or even fourth century B.C.E. Palestine or a Christian in second century C.E. Egypt should be influenced by Greek conceptions. What Dieterich fails to see is that the various motifs in the Apocalypse of Peter, whatever their origin, have been shaped in consciousness of a Jewish and Christian literary tradition.

Chapter 3

SINS AND PUNISHMENTS I
Sins and Measure-for-Measure Punishments

"There is nothing analogous to the hell punishments of the Apocalypse of Peter except the subterranean punishments of the Orphic-Pythagorean nekyiai."[1] By finding Greek precedents for the sins and punishments of the Apocalypse of Peter, Dieterich sought to strengthen his claim that the Apocalypse of Peter was a lightly Christianized Orphic-Pythagorean katabasis.

In the preceding chapter Dieterich's view that an ancient Greek descent to Hades stands behind the structural features of the Apocalypse of Peter was criticized, and it was shown that predecessors to and relatives of the tours of hell could be found in Jewish apocalyptic literature. In this chapter Dieterich's view of the exclusively Greek provenance of the sins and punishments of the Apocalypse of Peter will be scrutinized, although the discussion here will not be restricted to the Apocalypse of Peter, but will include all the tours of hell. No attempt to determine either/or—either a Jewish provenance, or a Greek—will be made, however. The direction of recent scholarship has been toward rendering that particular distinction increasingly hazy.

Even without the problems related to the Jewish/Greek distinction, Dieterich's quest for origins is problematic. It was suggested in the preceding chapter that the demonstrative explanations characteristic of the tours of hell are influenced by a very ancient form of exegesis that appears in Mesopotamian literature. No one would suggest, however, that the authors of the Jewish apocalypses of the Hellenistic period read cuneiform. Rather, the form was known to them because it appeared in a variety of

---

1. Dieterich, *Nekyia*, 212.

texts with which they were well acquainted. Nor has the question of the ultimate origin of the tour form in Jewish literature been resolved by pointing to 1 Enoch and Ezekiel. Should the tours be understood as going back to Babylonia? Or are they native Jewish developments?

Perhaps a more appropriate object for the historian, certainly one more easily achieved, is the determination of proximate sources. One goal of the following investigation will be to form a picture of the kinds of sources on which the authors of the earliest tours of hell might have drawn.

The other goal is to point out certain distinctive sins and punishments that appear in several texts and to use them to illumine the relations of the various texts to one another. Observations about the development of particular groupings of sins and punishments will be offered in this chapter and the next; the attempt to provide a more comprehensive picture of the development of the texts will be reserved for Chapter 5.

SINS

In the following pages most of the attention will be directed at punishments rather than at sins, since the punishments prove to be more useful for determining relationships among texts. Thus a few general words about the sins treated in the tours of hell are in order.

The sins in the tours of hell range from murder to idle chatter in church or synagogue, but the two most common kinds of sins are sexual sins and sins of speech. As Table 2 indicates, sexual sins appear in all the texts except the Apocalypse of Zephaniah. No attempt has been made to indicate on the table the occurrence of a sin more than once in a text. Adultery and fornication are treated together because they are so difficult to distinguish. The Ethiopic version of the Apocalypse of Peter, for example, calls the sin of the women hanging by their hair fornication (chap. 7), while the women described in the same way in the Greek version (chap. 24) are guilty of adultery. It is difficult to say whether the women of the fourth court in the Isaiah fragment are guilty of adultery or fornication when they "lead men astray." Abortion and infanticide also prove extremely difficult to separate. Does killing infants mean infants already born or not? Thus these categories too are treated together here.

The emphasis on proper sexual behavior in early Jewish literature is so overwhelming that comment is hardly necessary.[2] Sexual purity is one of

---

2. For references, see F. Hauck, "μοιχεύω," *TDNT* 4(1967):729–35; F. Hauck and S. Schulz, "πόρνη," *TDNT* 6(1968):579–95; J. Jensen, "Does *Porneia* Mean Fornication? A Cri-

Table 2. SEXUAL SINS IN THE TOURS OF HELL

Text	Adultery/Fornication	Immodesty	Loss of Virginity Before Marriage	Abortion/Infanticide	Homo-sexuality	Incest
Apoc. Pet.	X		X	X	X	
Acts. Th.	X	X		X		
Apoc. Zeph.						
Apoc. Paul	X		X	X	X	
Eth. Apoc. Mary	X		X	X	X	X
Eth. Apoc. Bar.	X		X	X	X	X
Apoc. Gorg.	X					
Gk. Apoc. Mary	X			X		
Apoc. Ezra				X		X
Vis. Ezra	X		X	X		X
T. Isaac					X	
L. Pach.			X			
Dar. Tesh.	X	X				
Isa. frag.	X					
Josh. frag.[a]						
Ged. Mosh.	X				X	X
Elij. frag.	X		X		X	

[a] For most of the punishments in this text, no sin is mentioned. There are several hanging punishments that in other Hebrew texts are applied to sexual sins, primarily adultery/fornication.

the important ways in which the Hebrew Bible directs Israelites to differentiate themselves from their neighbors who practice the "abominations" that eventually cause the land to vomit them out. Adultery is forbidden in the Ten Commandments, and death is the punishment for all kinds of sexual misbehavior. This attitude continues to make itself felt in the apocrypha and pseudepigrapha, in Philo's works, at Qumran, and in rabbinic literature.

The emphasis in early Christian literature is similar and equally overwhelming. Perhaps the major difference is that Christian literature tends to encourage celibacy, while this is a relatively uncommon attitude in Jewish circles before the year 70 and almost unheard of after.[3]

Sexual sins also play a part in texts of the Hellenistic and Roman period that are neither Jewish nor Christian, although they do not seem to have rated among the major sins of archaic and classical Greece.[4] The earliest appearance of adulterers in Hades seems to occur in the fragment of Hieronymos of Rhodes's (third century B.C.E.) Life of Pythagoras preserved by Diogenes Laertius (*Lives* 8.21), where Pythagoras is said to have seen men hanging in Hades "who did not wish to have intercourse with their own wives." I. Lévy is certain that this enigmatic phrase refers to adultery.[5] (Dieterich, who reads the passage the same way, points out that Pythagoras [or Hieronymos] has chosen "a most remarkable mode of description."[6]) Later authors describe punishments in hell for sexual wrongs: incest (Virgil, *Aeneid* 6.623) and adultery (Lucian, *Menippus* 11, *True Story* 2.26). Sexual wrongdoing and even the tendency to such wrongdoing, a lustful disposition, are found in pagan lists of vices.[7]

Adultery/fornication is the most widely diffused category of sexual sin, as Table 2 shows. It appears almost everywhere. Loss of virginity before marriage and abortion/infanticide, on the other hand, appear almost exclusively in Christian texts;[8] the ex-virgins of the Elijah fragment make it

tique of Bruce Malina," *Novum Testamentum* 20(1978) : 161–84. All these articles are intent on showing that early Christian sexual ethics were superior to contemporary Jewish sexual ethics; Jensen is somewhat more subtle than the two *TDNT* articles. Despite this bias, the texts assembled offer an impression of the insistence of the Jewish and Christian literature on the importance of chastity.

3. For a brief discussion of the practice of celibacy at Qumran and among the Therapeutae and of favorable attitudes toward celibacy in rabbinic literature, see G. Vermes, *Jesus the Jew* (Philadelphia: Fortress, 1981; first published 1973), 99–102.

4. Dieterich, *Nekyia*, 163–70, esp. 168–69.

5. Lévy, *Pythagore*, 82.

6. "*Eine sehr bemerkenswerte Art der Bezeichnung*," Dieterich, *Nekyia*, 169.

7. E.g., Plutarch, *Education of Children* 5b, 12b; Claudius Ptolemy, *Tetrabiblos* 3.13.

8. I include the Ethiopic Apocalypse of Baruch among the Christian texts since Leslau believes that it is a copy of a Christian text. (See chap. 1, above.)

the single exception (see chap. 1, above). In fact, it is worth noting that the two sins are closely linked; five of the seven texts that mention the loss of virginity before marriage also contain a punishment for abortion/infanticide.[9] The two exceptions are not unexpected. One is the Elijah fragment, which is probably not a Christian work. The other is the very brief vision of hell in the Life of Pachomios, where the sin that I have classified as loss of virginity before marriage is described in veiled language as soiling one's body without the parents' knowledge. No clear pattern emerges in the distribution of homosexuality and incest.

Sins of speech include blasphemy, false witness, slander, and gossip, categories that overlap in so many cases that it seemed best to group all these sins of the tongue together. A sinner may be said, for example, to have blasphemed his neighbor. Here "to blaspheme" has nothing to do with God, but seems to mean either to slander or to bear false witness. Further, it is difficult to know how to compare the range of meanings of terms in different languages. Sins of speech appear in all the texts except the Apocalypse of Zephaniah, the Apocalypse of Ezra, and the Testament of Isaac.

Sins of speech are condemned in the Hebrew Bible, in early Jewish literature, in rabbinic literature, and in early Christian literature.[10] In pagan Greco-Roman literature the concern is not entirely absent. Blasphemy in its strict sense and the breaking of oaths are important crimes in classical Greek thought.[11] Less clear-cut sins of speech are not neglected altogether. Plutarch condemns flatterers, an important social type in his milieu.[12] Ptolemy includes among the undesirable personality traits created by certain configurations of the stars the tendency to slandering, swearing falsely, blaming, speaking evil, speaking abusively, and speaking frivolously.[13] References to such failings are not common, however.

The prominence of sexual and verbal sins in the tours of hell, then, seems to owe more to biblical tradition than to Greek. Surprisingly, it goes hand in hand with a relative lack of attention to other central sins of the biblical tradition. Murder appears in only three tours of hell (the Apocalypse of Peter, the Apocalypse of Gorgorios, and *Gedulat Moshe*) while stealing appears in four (the Acts of Thomas, the Apocalypse of Gorgo-

---

9. Three of those five texts, the Apocalypse of Peter, the Apocalypse of Paul, and the Ethiopic Apocalypse of Mary, dress the ex-virgins in dark raiment. A trace of this punishment appears in a different context in the Ethiopic Apocalypse of Baruch, also among these five texts, where dark raiment is the punishment of avaricious virgins.

10. E.g., Ps. 34:12–13; Prov. 6:17; 1 Enoch 96:7; 1QS 4; b. Soṭah 42a; Rom. 1:29–30; Col. 3:8–9; 2 Tim. 3:3; Didache 2:3–5.

11. Dieterich, *Nekyia*, 163–70.

12. *Education of Children* 5b.

13. *Tetrabiblos* 3.13.

rios, the Joshua b. Levi fragment, and *Gedulat Moshe*). Yet murder and stealing are forbidden in the Decalogue just as clearly as are adultery, blasphemy, and bearing false witness.[14]

It may be that the strong interest in sexual sins and sins of speech in the tours of hell is a result of the invisibility of these sins.[15] Gossip and slander are daily occurrences, impervious to legislation. The smaller the social group, the more intense such sins are likely to be. There is great psychological realism in Pachomios' vision of monks punished in hell for having gossiped about other monks. Sexual sins, too, are almost by definition private, precisely the sins that never come before a court. Murder is difficult to conceal, and the murderer is likely to be brought to justice by an earthly court. But to see slanderers and adulterers reap the just reward for their hidden crimes, one must await the punishment of heaven.

The sins and punishments of the tours of hell at first glance appear to be a promising source for social history. Unfortunately, the condemnation of a practice does not necessarily indicate that it was a living issue for the author of the text and his community, for these texts are part of a tradition. They draw consciously on earlier tours of hell, and consciously and unconsciously show the influence of the canonical texts of Judaism and Christianity. Thus the appearance of certain sins in the later texts may indicate no more than this dependence; the social problems that lay behind the original mention may have vanished long since. In the absence of even a rough date or location for many of the texts or extensive knowledge of the social world of those texts that can be dated and located with some accuracy, restraint must be exercised in trying to reconstruct the social setting of the texts on the basis of the sins proscribed.

Variations in the descriptions of sins and punishments might also appear to hold out promise as clues to the social world of the texts. For example, it is tempting to suggest on the basis of the fact that women hang by their

---

14. It is interesting to compare the catalogs of vices in the New Testament, which draw on the same background, Jewish and Greek, as the early tours of hell. There fornication is more common than murder and theft, but murder and theft are among the most common sins (B. S. Easton, "New Testament Ethical Lists," *Journal of Biblical Literature* 51[1932]:5). For more recent discussion of these catalogs, see S. Wibbing, *Die Tugend- und Lasterkataloge im Neuen Testament und ihre Traditionsgeschichte unter besonderer Berücksichtigung der Qumran-Texte* (Berlin: A. Töpelmann, 1959).

15. I wish to thank G. D. Cohen for pointing out to me that the curses in Deut. 27:15–26 have been understood by many commentators to be unified by their reference to invisible sins. (See, e.g., A. Phillips, *Deuteronomy*, Cambridge Bible Commentary [Cambridge: Cambridge University, 1973], 181; G. von Rad, *Deuteronomy: A Commentary*, Old Testament Library [London: SCM, 1966], 168–69.) Several of these sins are sexual, but none is a sin of speech.

breasts for adultery/fornication in Jewish texts, but by their hair in Christian texts, that women's hair was associated with their sexuality by Christians but not by Jews. Yet Lieberman has assembled evidence to show that not only the Romans and their Byzantine successors, but also the Jews of the geonic period, punished sexual immodesty by shaving the head.[16]

On the other hand, when enough information about the background of the texts is available, it may be possible to make sense of the presence of particular sins in some texts but not in others. The lopsided presence of loss of virginity before marriage and abortion/infanticide in Christian texts is a good example.

Unlike Judaism, Christianity holds celibacy as an ideal and institutionalizes it in monasticism. The ex-virgins of the Apocalypse of Paul are said to have been "appointed as virgins." Some of the aborters and infant killers are specifically identified as nuns (Ethiopic Apocalypse of Mary) or as priests and widows (Ethiopic Apocalypse of Baruch). This supports the reasonable a priori assumption that loss of virginity before—or without—marriage and abortion and infanticide are especially likely to be problems in a society that has institutionalized celibacy. For nuns, marriage is not a solution to pregnancy.

In Jewish society premarital pregnancy could be legitimized by marriage. While sex before marriage was certainly not acceptable, its consequences were less visible, and it is thus likely to have been less a subject of discussion.[17]

Yet Christian monasticism alone does not explain the configuration of the texts. Abortion/infanticide is prominently punished in the Apocalypse of Peter, which comes from the period before the institutionalization of monasticism, although the favorable view of celibacy certainly goes back to the earliest Christian literature.

Tacitus' famous remark on the Jewish failure to practice infanticide (*Histories* 5.5) is a good indication of how widespread that practice was in the ancient world. Not only in Tacitus' Rome, but also in the Hellenistic world and classical Greece, abortion was a perfectly acceptable form of contraception.[18] The earliest Roman law against abortion comes under Septimius Severus and is directed against divorced women who procured

---

16. Lieberman, "Shaving of the Hair and Uncovering of the Face Among Jewish Women" (appendix to "On Sins and Their Punishments," 52–54).

17. L. Epstein, *Sex Laws and Customs in Judaism* (New York: Bloch, 1948), 126–31, assembles evidence for the relatively common practice of intimacy of engaged couples from the tannaitic period to the late Middle Ages. Naturally the rabbis were not pleased.

18. S. Pomeroy, *Goddesses, Whores, Wives, and Slaves: Women in Classical Antiquity* (New York: Schocken, 1975), 69, 164–69.

abortions to deprive their ex-husbands of the child. Under Caracalla there was legislation against drugs and magic.[19] Only when the empire became Christian did infanticide become illegal.[20] The law on abortion did not change even after the empire had become Christian.[21]

Thus it may be that the causes for the practice of abortion and infanticide punished in the hells of these tours changed from the earlier period to the later. In the early period, when many Christians were converts to the religion, abortion and infanticide may simply have been a continuation of the accustomed Greco-Roman practices. Later, when Christians were likely to be descended from many generations of Christians, celibacy had become institutionalized in monasticism. Thus some pregnancies could not be legitimized by the simple expedient of marriage. The fact that a number of the later texts specifically designate the sinners as nuns, widows, or priests suggests that in this case these later texts are not simply copying automatically the sins listed in earlier texts.

MEASURE-FOR-MEASURE PUNISHMENTS IN ANCIENT GREECE, ROME, AND ISRAEL

One large and important group of punishments in the tours of hell consists of those based on the principle of measure-for-measure. The principle appears in many ancient legal systems. The biblical formulation, "an eye for an eye, a tooth for a tooth" (Exod. 21:24, Lev. 24:20), is part of a wider ancient Near Eastern pattern.[22] Although it is important in other

---

19. Ibid., 168.

20. J. T. Noonan, Jr., *Contraception: A History of Its Treatment by the Catholic Theologians and Canonists* (Cambridge, Mass.: Harvard University, Belknap, 1965), 85–86. In 318 it became a crime, parricide, for a father to kill his child (*Codex Theodosianus* 9.15.1). Only in 374 did killing an infant become homicide (*Codex Theodosianus* 9.14.1).

21. Noonan, *Contraception*, 86. There were, to be sure, dissenting voices in the Greco-Roman world. The Hippocratic oath forbade the administration of abortifacients; and Aristotle distinguishes between the period before the fetus has sensation, when abortion is perfectly acceptable, and after, when it is not (Pomeroy, *Goddesses*, 69). Galen claims that Solon and Lycurgos had legislated against abortion, and Musonios claims other antiabortion legislation (S. Reinach, "Morale orphique et morale chrétienne," in *Cultes, mythes et religions* [Paris: E. Leroux, 1908–23], 3:280). One of the inhabitants of hell in the apparently pagan Bologna papyrus is a woman who has had an abortion (Turcan, "Catabase orphique," 149–55).

22. Elsewhere in the Bible in a legal context: Gen. 9:6; Deut. 19:19. For ancient Near East, Code of Hammurabi, Laws 192–231 (*ANET*, 175–76); J. Greenberg, "Crimes and Punishments," *Interpreter's Dictionary of the Bible* (New York and Nashville, Tenn.: Abingdon, 1962); H. H. Cohn, "Talion," *EJ*.

areas of Greek thought, talion does not seem to have played a part in the Greek legal system.[23] At Rome, on the other hand, the *lex talionis* goes back to the Twelve Tables.[24]

Talion, as the principle of measure-for-measure is called after the Roman legal term, did not long exist in its pure form. In many of the texts that have come down to us the principle has already undergone interpretation. Just retribution for bodily injury may be a fine rather than infliction of a matching injury. In many codes, the two types of punishment exist side-by-side.[25]

Talion is also found as a principle of justice outside the legal codes. There are several instances in the Bible. For example, Adoni-bezeq, a Canaanite king, understands his disgrace at the hands of the Israelites as an instance of talion, retribution for what he had done to other kings (Judg. 1:7), and the men who insisted that Daniel be thrown into the lion's den are punished by being thrown in themselves (Dan. 6:24).[26]

Among the Greeks the belief in talion is associated particularly with shadowy groups like the Pythagoreans or those learned in the mysteries. Aristotle refers disapprovingly to the Pythagoreans' belief that "it is just for one to suffer that which he did" (*Magna Moralia* 1194a = 1.33.13). The chorus in Aeschylus' *Libation-Bearers* expresses a point of view similar to the one attributed to the Pythagoreans (306–14).[27]

Such retribution is often placed in the afterlife. Plato (*Laws* 870 d–e = 9.10) refers to a popular belief taught by the initiates of the mysteries that murderers will suffer punishment in Hades and then return to this world to be murdered by others.[28] Aristotle, again disapproving, says that the Pythagoreans attribute to Rhadamanthos, the judge of the dead, the maxim "If one suffers what he himself did, it is true justice" (*Nichomachean Ethics* 1132b = 5.5.3).[29]

---

23. The concept is not mentioned by A. R. W. Harrison, *The Law of Athens: Procedure* (Oxford: Oxford University, 1971), nor does Herdlitczka, "Talio," PW, refer to its presence in Greek law.

24. For a discussion of the development of the concept from the Twelve Tables to the *Corpus Iuris Civilis*, see Herdlitczka, "Talio."

25. E.g., Code of Hammurabi; Exod. 21:19, 22, 24. In the Twelve Tables, provision is made for payment rather than dismemberment in certain cases (Herdlitczka, "Talio," 2070–71).

26. Cohn, "Talion," offers these and many other biblical examples, some of which are not quite measure-for-measure.

27. Aeschylus is often considered to have been influenced by the mysteries. E.g., G. Thomson, *Aeschylus and Athens*, 2d ed. (1946; reprint ed., New York: Haskell House, 1972), feels able to identify Aeschylus as "an early Pythagorean" (291).

28. An odd combination—punishment in Hades and on return!

29. See Dieterich, *Nekyia*, 205–10, for references to other classical texts.

Jubilees is probably the first extrabiblical Jewish text to make use of the principle. According to Jubilees, Cain, who killed his brother with a stone, died when his stone house fell on him. "With the instrument with which a man kills his neighbor with the same shall he be killed; after the manner that he wounded him, in like manner shall they deal with him" (Jub. 4:32, *APOT*).

The formulation in Jubilees is very close to various rabbinic rules. The rabbis delight in multiplying examples of God's just punishments and rewards according to the principle "By the measure a man measures out, so it is measured out to him" or "All the measures of the Holy One, blessed be he, are measure for measure."[30] The principle can be applied to good behavior or to evil.

Mishnah Soṭah 1:8–9 (Danby) provides an excellent example of the rabbinic use of talion:

[8] Samson went after [the desire of] his eyes—therefore the Philistines put out his eyes, as it is written, *And the Philistines laid hold on him and put out his eyes* (Judg. 16:21); Absalom gloried in his hair—therefore he was hanged by his hair; and inasmuch as he came in upon the ten concubines of his father, therefore they thrust ten spear-heads into his body, as it is written, *And ten young men that bare Joab's armour compassed about and smote Absalom and slew him* (2 Sam. 18:15); and inasmuch as he stole away three hearts, the heart of his father, the heart of the court, and the heart of Israel (as it is written, *So Absalom stole the hearts of the men of Israel* [2 Sam. 15:6]), therefore three darts were thrust into him, as it is written, *And he took three darts in his hand and thrust them through the heart of Absalom* (2 Sam. 18:14).

[9] So, too, in a goodly matter: Miriam awaited Moses one hour, as it is written, *And his sister stood afar off* (Exod. 2:4), therefore Israel delayed for her seven days, as it is written, *And the people journeyed not till Miriam was brought in again* (Num. 12:15). . . .

It is interesting that there are very few instances in rabbinic literature of the application of this principle to the world to come. This is at least in part the result of the exegetical nature of so much of rabbinic literature. Talion is almost always applied to a biblical text, and biblical texts are almost always concerned with this world.[31]

---

30. See Lieberman, "Sins," 48, n. 106, for references.

31. In "Some Aspects of After Life in Early Rabbinic Literature," in *Harry Austryn Wolfson Jubilee Volume* (Jerusalem: American Academy for Jewish Research, 1965), English section, Lieberman writes: "These earlier rabbinic sources . . . do not portray the topography of Gehenna in its details. . . . They do not mention the refined tortures of Gehenna, their minutiae, and the ramified penal code which governs Hades. The rabbis certainly lacked neither the imagination nor the legal mind required for such descriptions" (496). This is a tantalizing remark. Lieberman never tells us how he would explain this situation.

Instances of the application of talion to the world to come are not entirely lacking in rabbinic literature, however.[32] B. Giṭṭin 56b–57a reports
that when Onqelos, a nephew of the Emperor Titus, decided to convert to
Judaism, he conjured up the ghosts of the notorious villains Titus and Balaam and of Israelite sinners[33] to see how they were faring in the next
world. Titus has been punished by having his ashes scattered every day
over the seven seas; he had planned to avoid God's wrath by having his
ashes scattered. (This punishment must be seen in relation to the horror
the ancients felt at lack of proper burial.)

Balaam is punished by having boiling semen poured over him. Although the motivation for this punishment is not provided in this passage,
elsewhere the rabbis charged Balaam with the responsibility for the seduction of the Israelite men by the daughters of Moab (Num. 25 : 1–9).[34] Thus
Rashi (to b. Giṭṭin 57a) comments that Balaam's punishment is "measure
for measure."

The crime of the Israelite sinners was that they had mocked the words of
the sages. Boiling excrement is poured over them. The appropriateness of
this punishment is not obvious, but perhaps the thought is that these sinners had treated what is precious as refuse.

The Story from the Palestinian Talmud

In "On Sins and Their Punishments," Lieberman argues that the dream of
the pious man of Ashkelon from the Palestinian Talmud (discussed under
the introduction to the Hebrew texts and the Latin Elijah fragment in
chap. 1, above) is another rabbinic passage that applies the principle of
measure-for-measure to the world to come. The passage is of great importance for this study. In it the tax collector is given the difficult epithet דמעין

---

32. Lieberman, "Sins," 48, n. 106, provides references. I pass over b. Soṭah 10b, an expan-
sion of the Mishnah, where Absalom hangs over Sheol. It does not provide a picture of what
goes on in Sheol itself. Similarly b. Sanhedrin 90a: "He denied the resurrection of the dead;
therefore he will have no share in the resurrection of the dead, for all the measures of the
Holy One, blessed be he, are measure for measure" is not relevant here. It rationalizes the
exceptions given by Mishnah Sanhedrin 10:1 to the rule that all Israel has a portion in the
world to come. A *b'raita* in b. Ketubot 5b says, "A man should not let his ears hear idle chatter
for they will be burnt first of his limbs." Lieberman must take this to be burning in Gehenna.

33. For "Israelite sinners" the Munich MS and the Venice first edition read "Jesus." Fas-
cinating though this is, it is not important for our purposes.

34. In Num. 31 : 16 Moses implies that Balaam was responsible. The rabbis make this point
in Sifre Numbers 131 and 157, b. Sanhedrin 106a, and elsewhere. See Ginzberg, *Legends of the
Jews*, 6 : 134–35, n. 785, for a more inclusive list of references.

בריה, which Lieberman suggests means "paunchy." If so, the tax collector, a glutton, is made to suffer a fitting punishment, thirst, while the poor man is rewarded with plenty.[35] This punishment is obviously related to the punishment of Tantalus in Greek myth; the appearance of related punishments in the Apocalypse of Paul family will be discussed in Chapter 4, below.

The passage from the Palestinian Talmud goes on to describe the fate of Miriam of "the onion bulbs," as Lieberman translates another difficult phrase. Those reporting the story disagree; either Miriam was hanging by her nipples, or the hinge of the gate of hell rested in her ear. The exact nature of her sin is also disputed. Either she bragged of her fasting, or she pretended to fast more than she actually did. In either case she was a hypocrite. This, Lieberman argues, is the meaning of her epithet.[36] This second punishment is not a measure-for-measure punishment.

In *Vom Reichen Mann und Armen Lazarus*, his study of the Lazarus story in Luke and its sources, H. Gressmann argues that the story of Lazarus shares a source with the story in the Palestinian Talmud and related Jewish texts, including *Darkhei Teshuvah*, and the Egyptian tale of Setme and his son Si-Osiri. This story survives in a late first-century C.E. demotic text.[37]

The moral of this tale, revealed by the wonder-child Si-Osiri to his father by means of a tour of the seven halls of Amente, is that social status and moral status are not necessarily equivalent. In the fourth hall of Amente men who had been poor but wicked during life undergo a kind of tantalization, reaching for the food and water that hang above them while pits are dug beneath them to prevent them from ever attaining their object. In the fifth hall a rich man is discovered with the bolt of the door of that hall fixed in his eye. In the seventh hall with Osiris and his attendants stands a

---

R. A. Kraft suggests to me that Balaam's punishment may be related to the LXX's translation of the chamber, קבה (Num. 25:8), in which Phineas finds and kills the Israelite man and Moabite woman. According to the LXX, the chamber is a furnace, κάμινος. It should be noted, however, that the punishment of those who mocked the words of the sages is *boiling* excrement. The measure-for-measure nature of semen in relation to Balaam's crime is clear; boiling may be no more than an added touch.

35. "Sins," 34–35.

36. Ibid., 35–36, on the relation of onions to hypocrisy.

37. H. Gressmann, *Vom Reichen Mann und Armen Lazarus*, Abhandlungen der königlich preussischen Akademie der Wissenschaften, Phil.-hist. Klasse 1918. The back of the papyrus in Greek is dated 46–47 C.E. It is thus assumed that the copy of the Setme tale must be later, but not too much later. The style and spelling point to the last century of Ptolemaic rule or the first century of Roman rule; this is quite compatible with the date on the verso (Griffith, *Stories*, 41, 67–70). Quotations in the body of the text are taken from Griffith's translation.

poor man dressed in the funeral garment of the rich man. It was the contrast between the rich man's splendid funeral and the poor man's unceremonious burial that led to the tour of Amente; when Setme wishes aloud to share the fate of the rich man, his son takes him to Amente to show him his error.

The setting for the story of the Palestinian Talmud is similar: the observation of the pious man of Ashkelon of the difference between the funeral of the rich tax collector and his pious friend. Like Setme the pious man exclaims about the contrast. Unlike Setme the pious man sees the difference as unjust. The punishment of the tax collector is equivalent to that of the poor men of the fourth hall in Setme's vision, while the punishment of the rich man in Setme's vision is one of the punishments given to Miriam in the Palestinian Talmud.

The moral of the story in the Palestinian Talmud is different from that of the Setme tale. The story in the Palestinian Talmud attempts to explain why the wicked flourish and the righteous suffer. The answer is, first, that this injustice matters very little because the righteous will be rewarded in the world to come while the wicked are punished, but further that even the suffering of the righteous in this world is not arbitrary, for the righteous do occasionally sin, and it is because of those sins that they suffer here. On the other hand, even the wicked occasionally do good, and thus they are allowed their reward here so that they may find only punishment awaiting them in the world to come.

The explanation given the pious man eliminates the apparent injustice in the fates of his friend and the wicked tax collector not only by describing the glorious life after death of the one and the sad condition of the other, but also by justifying their conditions in this world.[38] The rabbinic passion for perfect justice exemplified in the passage from Mishnah Soṭah quoted above may explain why the rich man of the Palestinian Talmud receives the punishment of Tantalus rather than a pivot in the eye like the rich man of the Setme tale, for, as Lieberman argues, in the Palestinian Talmud the rich man's punishment is measure-for-measure.[39] Although Miriam's punishments do not appear to be explicable on the measure-for-measure prin-

---

38. Gressmann, *Armen Mann*, 43–46, makes many of the same observations about the relation between the two stories. He wants to understand their differences as a result of the difference in form of the two stories. For him Setme's tale belongs to the category of *Märchen*, while the story from the Palestinian Talmud belongs to the category of *Legende*. Thus for Gressmann the Setme story is typologically prior.

39. Lieberman, "Sins," 35. Even if we remain agnostic about Lieberman's interpretation of the tax collector's epithet, tantalization is a fitting punishment for a rich man.

ciple, both of them are later doled out on a measure-for-measure basis.[40]

Gressmann sees the story in the Palestinian Talmud as literarily dependent on the Setme tale.[41] Of the motifs common to both stories, reversal, tantalization, and the pivot, only the presence of the pivot seems to require explanation. Reversal is a natural human solution to inequity. Tantalization originates in classical Greece[42] and thus was available to writers of the Hellenistic period.

While the pivot appears a number of times in later rabbinic literature and once in a Christian tour of hell, the only earlier example of this motif is a sculpture of a man in whose chest the pivot of a door rests. This sculpture comes from the fourth millennium B.C.E.; it was found at Hieraconopolis in Egypt.[43] Gressmann views the use of the chest as the resting place for the pivot as a concession to architectural necessity and argues that this sculpture is an exact parallel to the torture described in the Setme tale and the story from the Palestinian Talmud.[44] But this parallel is extremely early and, despite Gressmann's explanation, not as close as one might wish. Without evidence of an ongoing Egyptian tradition of pivots in the body, it is reasonable to ask whether this motif too might have been the common property of the Hellenistic Mediterranean. While the Setme tale and the story from the Palestinian Talmud are undeniably similar, the hypothesis of a common nonliterary source seems more defensible than the claim of literary influence in one direction or the other.

But the precise nature of the relationship between the story in the Palestinian Talmud and the Setme tale is not of great importance for present

---

40. Hanging by the breasts appears as a measure-for-measure punishment in the Isaiah fragment, *Darkhei Teshuvah*, *Gedulat Moshe*, and the Elijah fragment. The pivot in the ear becomes a measure-for-measure punishment in *Darkhei Teshuvah* and the Apocalypse of Ezra.

41. Gressmann argues that the story in the Palestinian Talmud is a combination of two independent stories, one of the tax collector and the pious man, the other of Simeon b. Sheṭaḥ and the witches. According to him, Miriam comes from the Simeon b. Sheṭaḥ story. By rights, the pivot should be in the ear of the tax collector. This is indeed the case in Rashi's version of the story in his comments to b. Sanhedrin 44b (*Armen Mann*, 17). Miriam properly hangs by her breasts (23). (Gressmann thinks that she is Mary, the mother of Jesus.)

42. Gressmann points out that the description of the poor men as men whose wives robbed them while they were alive is reminiscent of Oknos in Pausanias' description of the painting of Polygnotos at Delphi (ibid., 33–34).

43. Griffith (*Stories*, 46, note to line 3) refers to a sculpture, discovered by Quibell at Hieraconopolis, of a man whose chest is used as the rest for the door pivot. Gressmann (*Armen Mann*, 38–39) suggests a date of 3800 B.C.E. for the sculpture. Its grotesque form, he argues, was intended to scare demons away from the building, the same function many ascribe to the Aramaic incantation bowls.

44. Gressmann, *Armen Mann*, 38–39.

purposes. What is important is that the idea of measure-for-measure punishment in the next world is not restricted to (culturally) Greek sources.
Indeed, the idea is so natural that it probably appears in some form in most
cultures without any influence of one on another.

In Jewish literature we have seen a well-developed tradition of measure-
for-measure punishments from the Bible through Jubilees into tannaitic
and later rabbinic texts. Twice in rabbinic literature the principle is applied,
although not explicitly, to the next world. One of these instances, the story
from the Palestinian Talmud, is likely to be quite early.

MEASURE-FOR-MEASURE PUNISHMENTS IN THE TOURS OF HELL

Measure-for-measure punishments are a significant component of the punishments in most of the tours of hell, as Table 3 makes clear. Since most of
these punishments are not explicitly described as measure-for-measure, the
determination that a punishment is measure-for-measure contains an un-
avoidable element of subjectivity. This explains the occasional vacillation
about numbers in the table.

Several forms that measure-for-measure punishments take will be discussed below. Only forms that appear a number of times will be treated.
Unlike the environmental punishments to be discussed in the next chapter,
each measure-for-measure punishment has its own history; thus no general
conclusions will be offered at the end of the chapter.

HANGING IN THE ANCIENT WORLD IN LITERATURE AND IN PRACTICE

Hanging by the sinful limb is a form of measure-for-measure punishment
of particular importance in the Jewish texts, the Apocalypse of Peter, and
the Acts of Thomas. It plays a more minor role in the other texts with a
significant number of measure-for-measure punishments.

In the ancient world hanging was used less for execution than for public
disgrace. A modern historian of capital punishment commenting on Tacitus' description of hanging among the Germans writes, "It is clear that
hanging was originally chosen not as a good way of killing the offender—
sometimes indeed he was killed first—but as an excellent device for en-
hancing the deterrent effect of the death penalty by exposing his body to
the public gaze in the most ignominious and abject of postures."[45]

---

45. E. Gowers, *A Life for a Life?* (London: Chatto & Windus, 1956), 9.

Table 3. MEASURE-FOR-MEASURE PUNISHMENTS IN THE TOURS OF HELL

	No. Punishments	No. Measure-for-Measure	Percent Measure-for-Measure
Apoc. Pet. (Eth.)	20	8	40
Apoc. Pet. (Gk.)	15–16	5–6	33–40
Acts Th.	6–7	4	57–67
Apoc. Zeph.	3	1	33
Apoc. Paul	24	9–10	38–42
Eth. Apoc. Mary	26	7–8	27–31
Eth. Apoc. Bar.	23	7–8	30–35
Apoc. Gorg.	11	3	27
Gk. Apoc. Mary	20	5	25
Apoc. Ezra	7–9	4	44–57
Vis. Ezra	15	5	33
T. Isaac	5	—	—
L. Pach.	6	—	—
Dar. Tesh.	5	5	100
Isa. frag.	5	5	100
Josh. frag. [a]	7/11	1	—
Ged. Mosh.	13	6	46
Elij. frag.	8	5	63

[a] The figures for Josh. frag. take account of both versions. The shorter contains four punishments of hanging by a limb, the longer, six. Since sins cannot be specified for any of these punishments, it is impossible to determine whether they are measure-for-measure punishments. Certainly many of them function as measure-for-measure punishments in other texts.

Deuteronomy assumes the practice of hanging the criminal's corpse in its legislation against allowing the humiliation to last more than one day: "And if a man has committed a crime punishable by death and he is put to death, and you hang him on a tree, his body shall not remain all night upon the tree, but you shall bury him the same day, for a hanged man is accursed by God" (Deut. 21:22–23, RSV).

Several biblical passages illustrate the use of hanging implied by this law. The baker who is Joseph's companion in prison is first decapitated and then hung on a tree (Gen. 40:19). Joshua first kills and then hangs five Canaanite kings (Josh. 10:26). The Philistines hang the bones of Saul and Jonathan in a public square (2 Sam. 21:12). David hangs the hands and feet of the murderers of Ish-Bosheth in public (2 Sam. 4:12). On the other hand, Haman and his sons seem to have been put to death by the process of hanging (Esth. 8:7, 9:13).

In the Hebrew Bible the verb "hang" is תלה or תלא. It is almost always translated into Greek by κρεμάννυμι or a derivative. In Esther, it is translated by σταυρόω, crucify. Perhaps this is a reflection of the Mesopotamian practice of impaling.[46] Paul (Gal. 3:13) uses Deut 21:22–23 as a proof text in relation to Jesus' crucifixion.

Whatever the precise nature of Israelite practice, hanging and impaling are closely linked. In what appears to be the most ancient text in any literature containing a reference to hanging, the Sumerian "Inanna's Descent to the Netherworld," the goddess, temporarily dead, is hung from a stake.[47] For the rabbis, hanging after death was restricted to blasphemers and idolaters. Mishnah Sanhedrin 6.4 provides a fairly detailed picture of the rabbis' image of what the practice had been like, if not of the practice itself: "How did they hang someone? They sank a beam into the ground and a piece of wood extended from it. They placed the two hands together and hanged him."[48]

Hanging as a form of punishment and disgrace appears also in Greek and Roman sources. In the *Gorgias* (525c) Plato speaks of the worst sinners hanging (ἀναρτάω) in the prison of Hades as examples. He does not include any further details in his description. Diogenes Laertius (*Lives* 8.21) preserves the report of Hieronymos of Rhodes that during his descent to Hades Pythagoras saw the soul of Hesiod bound (δέω) to a bronze pillar while the soul of Homer hung (κρεμάννυμι) from a tree as punishment for their sacrilegious stories about the gods.

It is not clear whether Hesiod is to be visualized as hanging from his pillar. The verb δέω sometimes seems to imply hanging. In Lucian's *True Story* 2.26, Rhadamanthos sentences Cinyras and Helen to be bound (δέω) by their genitals, whipped with mallow, and sent away from the Isles of the Blest for their adulterous elopement. A little later (2.31) Lucian sees Cinyras *hanging* (ἀπαρτάω) by his genitals during his tour of the Isles of the Wicked.

In the tours of hell men frequently hang by their genitals for fornication. Only in a Muslim text, the *Book of the Ladder* (chap. 79), do *women* hang by their genitals. This is not surprising given the realities of human anatomy. In the Jewish tours of hell adulterous women hang by their breasts, in the Christian tours, by their hair, the parts of the body the women used for seductive display.

Hanging by the hair appears for other reasons in the *Elegies* of Propertius (4.7.45). Propertius' dead lover Cynthia appears to him in a dream

---

46. G. Bertram, "κρεμάννυμι," *TDNT* 3(1964):918.

47. *ANET*, 55.

48. See also S. Mendelsohn, "Capital Punishment," *JE*; Sifre Deuteronomy 221 and b. Sanhedrin 46b.

and describes her loyal slave Lalage "hanging by her twisted hair and scourged" by a rival. Lalage's only crime is loyalty to her mistress.

Hanging was actually used as a punishment by the Romans. Plautus (*Asinaria* 301) and Terence (*Phormio* 220, *Eunuch* 1021) describe the whipping of slaves who are hanging (*pendere*) by their heels. The Acts of the Martyrs and rabbinic accounts also provide evidence for the practice. Sifre Deuteronomy 221 says that the Bible does not prescribe hanging a *live* criminal "the way the empire does." Lieberman shows that the rabbis' account of an instrument they call גרדון (= *gradus*) corresponds to the *catasta* known from Christian accounts.[49] The *catasta* was a raised platform used for the questioning and torture of slaves. The person under torture was said to be lifted or suspended (Hebrew, תלה; Latin, *levare, suspendi, extendi*). The descriptions I have read do not make it clear whether the victim was actually hanging, but the verbs used suggest that he was. The use of this form of questioning and torture was extended from its original application to slaves and applied to Christians and, during certain periods, Jews.

HANGING IN HELL

Hanging in the ancient world, then, is not primarily a method of execution. As a form of punishment that has humiliation as a major goal, it is particularly appropriate for the never-ending torment of hell, when execution is meaningless.

Hanging has one other important virtue in a world where the law of talion has such great appeal. It is a punishment that can be applied—at least in the imagination, where the laws of gravity need not operate—to any crime. The author of the Epistle of Titus quotes the Elijah fragment, devoted almost entirely to hanging punishments, to prove the point: "By the limb with which each man sinned, by the same limb will he be punished."

The midrash in *Darkhei Teshuvah* makes the same point. People are punished by the sinful limb "to show that the Holy One, blessed be he, is a righteous judge. The limbs that committed the sin are punished in Gehenna more than the other limbs." A similar though less general formulation is found as early as the Mishnah (Soṭah 1.7): "With the measure a man

49. S. Lieberman, "Roman Legal Institutions in Early Rabbinics and in the Acta Martyrum," in *Texts and Studies* (first published in *Jewish Quarterly Review* 35[1944]:1–55) 69–71. See also H. Leclerq, "Catasta," *Dictionnaire d'archéologie chrétienne et de liturgie* (Paris: Letouzey & Ané, 1907–53).

metes out, it is meted out to him. . . . [The adulterous woman] began to sin with the thigh, and afterwards the belly—therefore the thigh suffers first, and then the belly. . . ." (This mishnah is followed by the account of punishments by the sinful limb quoted above.) A more general formulation offered in the exegesis of the same biblical text (Num. 5:21–29) is found in Sifre Numbers 18: "The limb which began the transgression, from it will begin the punishment."

Almost all the tours of hell contain some hanging punishments, but many of these punishments consist not of hanging by the sinful limb but simply of hanging or hanging upside down. Most often such hanging is combined with other tortures. In both Ezra apocalypses, for example, beasts suck at the breasts of hanging women in punishment for abortion or infanticide. Thus, while the hanging forms part of a measure-for-measure punishment, it is not itself measure-for-measure.

An examination of punishments of hanging by the sinful limb uncovers a striking emphasis on two kinds of sins, sexual and verbal (Tables 4 and 5). Of course, it has already been noted that these two types of sins are special concerns of the tours of hell, but their dominance is overwhelming. In fact, when the results of Table 4, where all the punishments of hanging by the sinful limb are listed, are reclassified in Table 5 into the categories of sins of speech and female and male sexual sins, only two punishments from the Acts of Thomas, one from the Greek Apocalypse of Mary, and three from *Gedulat Moshe*, less than a fourth of all hanging punishments, are eliminated.[50]

The verbal sins are uniformly punished by hanging by the tongue. The sins mentioned include slander, gossip, blasphemy, and false witness, sometimes several in a single text.

The results of sexual sins are different for men and women, and for women there is some variation between Jewish and Christian texts. In the Isaiah fragment, *Darkhei Teshuvah*, the Joshua b. Levi fragment (*Reshit Ḥokhmah*), and *Gedulat Moshe*, women hang by their breasts. In the Latin Elijah fragment, women are said to be tortured in their breasts, but hanging is not specifically mentioned. Still, hanging is the dominant form of

---

50. The Joshua b. Levi fragment is not counted here because in neither version are its hanging punishments assigned sins. *Gedulat Moshe* contains two hanging punishments for women, hanging by the hair and hanging by the feet, to which no sins are assigned. Without the seven hanging punishments that can be culled from the two versions of the Joshua b. Levi fragment and the two unexplained punishments of *Gedulat Moshe*, a total of twenty-eight punishments of hanging by the sinful limb emerges. Of these, six are not assigned sins that are verbal or sexual.

Table 4. MEASURE-FOR-MEASURE HANGING PUNISHMENTS

Text	Limb	Sin
Apoc. Pet.	tongue	blasphemy
	hair (women)	Eth.: fornication
		Gk.: adultery
	Eth.: thighs ⎱ (men)	Eth.: fornication
	Gk.: feet ⎰	Gk.: adultery
Acts Th.	tongue	slander, lying
	hair (women)	immodesty
	hands	stealing
	feet	running to do evil
Apoc. Paul[a]	eyebrows (men)	adultery
	hair (women)	adultery
Apoc. Ezra	eyelids (men)	incest
Gk. Apoc. Mary	ear	eavesdropping, gossip
	tongue	slander, false witness
Dar. Tesh.	genitals (men)	fornication
	breasts (women)	immodesty
Isa. frag.	tongue	slander
	genitals (men)	fornication with gentile women
	breasts (women)	leading men astray
Josh. frag.[b]	hands	
	tongue	
	eyes	
	ears	
	nose	
	feet	
	breasts	
Ged. Mosh.	eyes	looking at married women, neighbor's money
	ears	listening to vain words, not words of Torah
	tongue	gossip, idle chatter
	feet	walking in slander, not to good deeds
	hands	stealing, murder
	breasts (women)	leading men to unchaste thoughts
	hair (women)	
	feet (women)	

Elij. frag.	genitals (men)	adultery, pederasty
	tongue	blasphemy, false witness
	eyes	stumbling through glances
	breasts (women)ᶜ	fornication
	hands (men)	fornication

ᵃThe passage in Apoc. Paul 39 reads, "I saw men and women hanging by their eyebrows and hair." Thus it is not clear whether people of both sexes hang by each part of the body or whether men hang by their eyebrows, while women hang by their hair. In light of the parallels from other texts, the latter interpretation seems more likely.

ᵇI have listed the contents of both versions combined. The longer version omits ears; the shorter omits noses, feet, and breasts.

ᶜThe women of Elij. frag. are said to be "tortured" in their breasts; hanging is not specifically mentioned. The punishment appears in the midst of the hanging punishments, however, and the women's partners hang.

punishment in the Elijah fragment. The Isaiah fragment, *Darkhei Teshuvah*, and *Gedulat Moshe* explain that in order to lead men astray these women nursed their babies in public. Thus hanging by the breasts is a perfect application of measure-for-measure.

In the Apocalypse of Peter and the Acts of Thomas, on the other hand, the women hang by their hair (Eth. Apoc. Pet., neck and hair). The Apocalypse of Peter specifically says of these women that they "plaited their hair not to create beauty, but to turn to fornication" (Eth. Apoc. Pet. 7, HSW). The wording suggests that the crime is one of seduction, as in the Jewish texts. (Similarly, Vis. Ezra 17 describes the punishment [not measure-for-measure] of married women "who adorned themselves not for their own husbands but to please other men.") In Acts Th. 56 those being punished are immodest women who "went about in the world bare-headed" (HSW). Again the fittingness of the punishment is emphasized. The Isaiah fragment notes that the women who brazenly nursed in public also uncovered their hair before men with the same goal.[51]

Apoc. Paul 39 makes no attempt to explain the punishment of its adulterous women hanging by their hair. This may suggest that the relation of hair to sexuality was obvious to the intended audience. In addition to the women hanging by their breasts, *Ged. Mosh.* 13 has women hanging by their hair, but their sin is never explained.

Men hang by their genitals, hands, feet, and eyes for their sexual sins.

51. See Lieberman, "Shaving of the Hair and Uncovering of the Face Among Jewish Women."

Table 5. HANGING PUNISHMENTS FOR VERBAL AND SEXUAL SINS

Text	Sins of Speech	Sexual Sins: Women	Sexual Sins: Men
Apoc. Pet.	tongue	hair	Eth.: thighs Gk.: feet
Acts Th.	tongue	hair	—
Apoc. Paul	—	hair	eyebrows
Apoc. Ezra	—	—	eyelids
Gk. Apoc. Mary	tongue	—	—
Dar. Tesh.	—	breasts	genitals
Isa. frag.	tongue	breasts	genitals
[Josh. frag. [a]	tongue	breasts	hands, feet, eyes]
Ged. Mosh.	tongue	breasts	eyes
Elij. frag.	tongue	breasts [b]	genitals, hands, eyes

[a] No sins are mentioned for the hanging punishments. I list the likely limbs.
[b] See Table 3, footnote c.

Usually the sin is fornication / adultery, but the Elijah fragment adds homosexuality. The Isaiah fragment specifies that the fornication of the men in its hell was with gentile women.

Part of Lieberman's argument for the Jewish origin of the Elijah fragment is that it contains men hanging by their genitals and women hanging by their breasts. These two categories, he argues, do not appear in Christian sources.[52] In fact, of the other Jewish texts, only the Isaiah fragment and *Darkhei Teshuvah* offer men hanging by their genitals, and Lieberman is not entirely correct in saying that no Christian text contains such a punishment. In Eth. Apoc. Pet. 7, men hang by their thighs (HSW; *ApNT*, "loins") for having joined the women who are hanging by their hair. "Thighs" seems to be a more modest version of what is found in the Hebrew sources. The "feet" of Gk. Apoc. Pet. 24 may be an even more modest circumlocution. Otherwise hanging by the feet is without parallel as a punishment for sexual sins.

In the Elijah fragment adulterers and pederasts hang by their genitals, but the partners of the women who are hanging by their breasts form a separate category; they hang by their hands. The Manual of Discipline from Qumran (1QS 7:13–15) contains the following rule: "Anyone who takes his hand from under his garment when he is poorly dressed so that his nakedness is seen shall be punished for thirty days." There is no unanimity among commentators about the interpretation of י, "hand," in this

---

52. Lieberman, "Sins," 47.

passage.[53] Some see Isa. 57:8 as parallel. While the new Jewish Publication Society translation takes the difficult יד there as "lust" in light of the Ugaritic *ydd*, "to love," many earlier readers have understood it as a euphemism. The conjunction of these two examples seems to suggest that "hand" could be a euphemism for penis. It is not clear, however, why the author of the Elijah fragment should choose a euphemism at one point in the text but not at another.[54]

Still another limb is singled out for a hanging punishment for sexual sin in the Elijah fragment. People (or men) who are said to have been tempted by looking, gazing with lust at guilty deeds,[55] are punished by hanging by their eyes.

If the sexual content of the sin in the Elijah fragment is not perfectly clear from the wording, there is no ambiguity in *Ged. Mosh.* 13. There adulterers (or, more precisely, "those who looked at married women," together with those who coveted the money of others) hang by their eyes. (In the last compartment of this hell other fornicators are found, tortured alternately by snow and fire.)

As Lieberman notes, there are other punishments related to hanging by the eyes in tours of hell.[56] In Apoc. Paul 39, men hang by their eyebrows

---

53. I wish to thank W. L. Lipscomb for pointing out this parallel to me. P. Wernberg-Møller (*The Manual of Discipline* [Leiden: Brill, 1957], 118, n. 30) traces the modern understanding of יד as penis to R. Marcus ("Textual Notes on the Dead Sea Manual of Discipline," *Journal of Near Eastern Studies* 11[1952]:205–11), who points to the use of יד in Isa. 57:8. Wernberg-Møller himself does not accept this suggestion. He reports, however, that his teacher Driver agrees with Marcus. H. E. del Medico (*Deux manuscrits hébreux de la Mer Morte* [Paris: P. Geuthner, 1951], 82) makes the same point as Marcus. G. Vermes (*The Dead Sea Scrolls: Qumran in Perspective* [Cleveland: William Collins & World, 1978], 94) also views "hand" as a euphemism.

54. R. A. Kraft suggests to me that this may indicate the use of more than one source in the Elijah fragment. I have already argued for editorial activity in the fragment (see chap. 1, above), but this euphemistic measure-for-measure punishment does not share the characteristics of the punishments I see as the editor's work.

55. ". . . *in videndo scandalizati sunt, respicientes in concupiscencia reatu gesta. . . .*" *Videndo* is de Bruyne's emendation of the meaningless *adtendo*. Stone (*Books of Elijah*, 15) emends to *adtendendo*, which seems better graphically. The meaning of the passage is not changed. I am unhappy with de Santos Otero's translation (HSW 2:158), ". . . who have stumbled through their glances and who have looked at foul things with craving for them. . . ." This suggests two separate sins, and the nature of the sin implied by "foul" and "craving" is not at all clear. M. R. James's translation (*LAOT*, 55), ". . . they that have [been] offended in regard of sight, because they looked upon things done guiltily in concupiscence. . . ." seems preferable.

56. Lieberman, "Sins," 47, n. 105.

for adultery, while in Apoc. Ezra 4:22–24 a man hangs by his eyelids for incest. The eyebrow and eyelid of the Apocalypse of Paul and the Apocalypse of Ezra may be adaptations of hanging by the eye intended to make the punishment more reasonable anatomically. The measure-for-measure nature of the punishment is not made explicit in these texts, since the sin is not described by reference to "looking." The Apocalypse of Ezra's description of the man's sin as "fulfilling a small desire" may be intended to suggest a link to the eyes, the instrument of desire. Perhaps this line of reasoning proved too obscure for the editor of the Vision of Ezra, who describes the sin of those who committed incest as "desiring an evil desire," but has them punished by hanging without reference to a particular limb or organ (vv. 19–21). Lieberman suggests that the eyebrow is chosen in the Apocalypse of Paul because Juno, the guarantor of the sanctity of marriage, is associated with the eyebrow. If he is right, the use of the eyebrow would not mean that the eye is perceived as the sinful limb.

To summarize, the prominence of punishments of hanging by the sinful limb in certain tours of hell seems to be a result of the suitability of hanging for the ongoing punishment necessary for the eternity of existence in hell and of the ease with which hanging can be used to apply the principle of measure-for-measure. Yet despite the potential for adaptation to a wide variety of sins, hanging is applied primarily to verbal and sexual sins. Parallels to the hanging punishments appear not only in Greek but also in Jewish literature. The most elaborate formulations of the principle of punishment by the sinful limb come from Jewish literature, although these formulations are not applied to the world to come. Roman practice, too, seems to have been an important influence; it probably accounts for the many instances of hanging upside down that figure as part of punishments that are not measure-for-measure.

The presence of some of the same sins and hanging punishments in the Apocalypse of Peter on the one hand, and the Apocalypse of Paul, the Apocalypse of Ezra, and the Greek Apocalypse of Mary on the other is not surprising. These Christian texts share other sin-and-punishment combinations (see, e.g., the discussion of punishments for abortion and infanticide, below), and the hanging punishments are not particularly close.

But the persistence of particular combinations of sin and punishment from the Apocalypse of Peter and the Acts of Thomas through the relatively late Hebrew texts certainly requires explanation. Here the correspondences are much closer. Did these later Jewish texts know the Apocalypse of Peter or a lost relative? Or did all these texts inherit the hanging punishments for verbal and sexual sins from a lost Jewish text (or texts) that predates the Apocalypse of Peter? These questions will be discussed in Chapter 5, below.

TANTALIZATION AND THE PIVOT PUNISHMENT

Another form of measure-for-measure punishment that appears in a number of tours of hell is tantalization. There are several versions of the punishment of Tantalus in Greek mythology,[57] but it is from the description in the nekyia of the *Odyssey* (11:582–92) that the English word "tantalize" is derived. There Tantalus stands up to his chin in water that recedes as he attempts to drink it, while the tempting fruit on trees above him evades his grasp.

In Apoc. Paul 39 a version of this punishment is given to people who broke their fasts early. They hang over a body of water but are unable to reach the water to drink from it, and they cannot reach the fruit that is placed in their sight. Variants on this sin-and-punishment combination appear in Eth. Apoc. Mary (65–66) and Eth. Apoc. Bar. (74). Tantalization here is a measure-for-measure punishment: inability to control the desire to eat in this world leads to the inability to partake of food in the next world. This is the principle operating in the very similar tantalization of the tax collector in the Palestinian Talmud, discussed above.

The midrash in *Darkhei Teshuvah*, which integrates the story of the Palestinian Talmud into the schema of hell with five chambers, places tantalization in the first chamber, although the trees of the Palestinian Talmud are gone and only water is mentioned.

In the Setme tale tantalization is the punishment for wicked poor men who in life struggled to find enough to eat while their wives robbed them. In death they are condemned to continue the struggle. "Food, water, and bread" hang above them, but as they reach for the food, pits are dug beneath them (45, 49).

In addition, both Eth. Apoc. Mary (55–56) and Eth. Apoc. Bar. (68–69) include a similar scene in their descriptions of heaven. Just outside the heavenly city, as in Apoc. Paul 24, stand men who were perfect in ritual but proud and (in the Apocalypse of Paul and the Ethiopic Apocalypse of Mary) lacking in good deeds. In the Apocalypse of Paul and the Ethiopic Apocalypse of Mary it is stated that these men will eventually be allowed to enter heaven. In the Apocalypse of Paul nearby trees do penance for these men by bowing over and over. This scene has been transformed into an-

---

57. Schwenn, "Tantalos," PW.

other instance of tantalization in the Ethiopic Apocalypse of Mary and the Ethiopic Apocalypse of Baruch. The trees bear delicious fruit, but as the men reach for it the trees stretch up, out of their grasp. The Ethiopic Apocalypse of Baruch adds a retreating brook.

Since a description of tantalization close to those in the tours of hell discussed above appears in the *Odyssey*, there is no need to claim that the Apocalypse of Paul and its two descendants are influenced by the Palestinian Talmud or the Setme tale. But there is one detail of the description found in the Apocalypse of Paul, although not in its descendants, that is close to the Palestinian Talmud and that does not appear in Homer or in any of the other classical sources I know.[58] The tongues of those who prematurely broke their fasts in the Apocalypse of Paul are described as "very dry." In the version of the Palestinian Talmud's story found in Hagigah, the tax collector's tongue is hanging out.[59] It is interesting that Miriam's sin in the Palestinian Talmud involves irregularity in her fasting.

Another possible link between the Palestinian Talmud and the Christian tours of hell is the pivot that appears in Miriam's ear in the Palestinian Talmud. Under the influence of the Palestinian Talmud, a pivot figures also in *Darkhei Teshuvah*, where it has become a measure-for-measure punishment: the woman's sin is now described as gossip as well as hypocritical fasting.

As noted above, the rich man of the Setme tale is punished with a pivot in his eye.[60] In Peter the Venerable's account of the visit of Joshua b. Levi to hell in *Contra Judaeos*, Pharaoh lies with his head under the threshold of hell and the pivot of the door of hell in his eye.[61]

The pivot also appears in rabbinic texts unrelated to tours of hell.[62] Both 'Avot d'Rabbi Natan (ed. Schechter, Appendix B, p. 156) and Yalqut Shim'oni (*Vayyelekh*, 940), report Moses' attempt to convince God to revoke his death sentence. In 'Avot d'Rabbi Natan, Moses offers to put his eye under the door three times a day if God will save him from death. In Yalqut Shim'oni, Moses offers to do so three times a year. The thought seems

---

58. Ibid.; J. E. Hylén, *De Tantalo* (Uppsala: Almquist & Wiksell, 1896), 63–83; W. Scheuer, "Tantalos," *Ausführliches Lexicon der griechischen und römischen Mythologie* (Leipzig: Teubner, 1916–24) 5:75–86. It is interesting that Tantalus' crime is sometimes related to speech (see Hylén, *De Tantalo*, 31–35).

59. Gressmann, *Armen Mann*, 72, apparatus, believes that the version in p. Sanhedrin, where no mention is made of the tongue, is more original because it is in Aramaic. Lieberman, "Sins," 33, apparently disagrees.

60. Griffith, *Stories*, 46, translates "bolt" but in his note says that the translation is uncertain and that "pivot" is just as likely.

61. *Patrologia Latina* 189, 632.

62. These rabbinic parallels are noted by Lieberman, *Shkiin*, 39, n. 4.

to be that this punishment is painful enough to be a fair exchange for death.

Midrash Tehillim 104 : 26 also relates the punishment to death: even putting the tongue under the pivot of the door will not save one from death or Sheol. Lieberman prefers a marginal reading in which one rabbi speaks of the tongue under the pivot, another of putting *oneself* under the pivot.[63]

Thus all the instances of this punishment in Jewish literature are related to life after death. Either they take place in the afterlife, or they are intended to save from death or hell.

In Apoc. Ezra 4 : 16–18, the only Christian tour of hell to contain a pivot as punishment, Ezra sees old men with fiery pivots in their ears. Their sin was eavesdropping.[64] As in *Darkhei Teshuvah*, the punishment has become measure-for-measure.

While *Darkhei Teshuvah* and perhaps Peter the Venerable's *Contra Judaeos* show the influence of the Palestinian Talmud, there is no reason to argue that the other texts do, especially because the torture is applied to a variety of limbs. It is interesting that the two rabbinic texts involving Moses resemble the Setme tale in making the eyes the pivot's resting place.

If a pivot appeared in the Apocalypse of Paul along with its peculiar form of tantalization, a strong case could be made for some kind of link between the story in the Palestinian Talmud and the apocalypse. The presence of the pivot in the Apocalypse of Ezra is intriguing but difficult to interpret. In light of the rabbinic evidence, it may be that the pivot was a widely known motif, not restricted to tours of hell; its presence in texts from different periods and milieux may require no more explanation than the presence of tantalization.

WATER-CARRIERS IN THE ISAIAH FRAGMENT

The Isaiah fragment contains a punishment that in English might be called tantalization but that does not derive from the punishment of Tantalus. The four versions of the Isaiah fragment show some important differences in the wording of the punishment and in the nature of the sin thus punished. All versions agree that the inhabitants of the first compartment of hell carry water to a pit that never fills up. The two Geniza fragments add

---

63. Ibid., 40, n. 4.

64. See Lieberman, "Sins," 41, n. 70. The translation "eavesdropper" is an improvement on A. Walker's translation, "they who would not listen" or "who heard wrong" ("Revelation of Esdras," *Ante-Nicene Fathers* 8 : 572).

another clause. The carriers are not "עזובין" according to the first fragment, but are "נעזובין" according to the second. Both words are passive participial forms of the verb "leave" or "allow."

Further, the first Geniza fragment says that those punished ate and drank and possessed(?) the best fields and vineyards [65] in this world and transgressed the commandment that forbids coveting. The second Geniza fragment and the version in *Bet ha-Midrasch*, although they show substantial differences in wording, mention only the sin of covetousness and not the material conditions of the lives of the sinners.

Lieberman interprets the passage as follows: The first Geniza fragment is correct in seeing two sins, for both Geniza fragments indicate two punishments, carrying water, and not being עזובין or being נעזובין. Since the other punishments in this text are measure-for-measure, these must also be measure-for-measure. The first sin, living luxuriously in this world, preserved only in the first Geniza fragment, is punished with the never-ending labor of bringing water to a well that never fills up. This is measure-for-measure for idleness. The idleness, unfortunately, is not explicit; Lieberman finds it implied in the description of living well.

The correct reading for the second half of the punishment, according to Lieberman, is the first Geniza fragment's negative. The phrase means "not permitted." The water-carriers are not permitted to drink their water in punishment for their covetousness. Lieberman compares this punishment to that of the tax collector in the Palestinian Talmud. He argues further that אינן עזובין is the exact equivalent of *non permittebantur* in the tantalization scene in the Apocalypse of Paul. [66]

Lieberman's application of the law of talion can be improved on if the futile task of trying to fill the well is given to those who coveted in life. The attempt to make this task the punishment for idleness is the weakest element of Lieberman's argument, for nowhere are the high-living sinners said to have been idle. But the never-ceasing effort to fill a bottomless well is surely appropriate for people who were never satisfied with what they had, but always wanted more.

Similarly the punishment of not being permitted to drink is more appropriate for the first part of the sin as reported in the first Geniza fragment. There it is said explicitly that the people ate and drank in this world.

---

65. The sentence in this version of the Isaiah fragment (Ginzberg, *Genizah Studies*, 197) is corrupt. Literally it reads, "These are men who, in this world, used to eat and drink and delightful fields and pleasant vineyards. . . ." Lieberman ("Sins," 37) understands the sentence to mean that the sinners owned fields and vineyards.

66. Ibid., 37–38, 41. *Non permittebantur* is the reading of the Paris MS. The St. Gall MS reads *non sinebat eos*, while, as Lieberman notes, Redaction 7 reads *non sinebantur*.

An advantage of this approach is that the first sin of the first Geniza fragment now corresponds to the first punishment, while the second sin corresponds to the second punishment.

The Isaiah fragment's version of tantalization seems unrelated to the version found in the other tours of hell,[67] but a source is not hard to find. Lieberman notes that the water-carriers of Hades are a common classical motif, according to F. Cumont one of the most common designs on sarcophagi in late antiquity.[68]

Punishment for Abortion and Infanticide

Another variety of measure-for-measure punishment is meted out to parents who have committed abortion and infanticide in the Apocalypse of Peter, the Apocalypse of Paul, the Ethiopic Apocalypse of Mary, the Ethiopic Apocalypse of Baruch, the Greek Apocalypse of Mary, the Apocalypse of Ezra, the Vision of Ezra, and perhaps the Acts of Thomas. All the punishments are related.

The "perhaps" of the Acts of Thomas applies to the description of the punishment of the sinners who "perverted the intercourse of man and woman" (chap. 55; HSW). This phrase in the context of the tours of hell usually suggests adultery or fornication. But nearby, heaps of infants identified as the children of the sinners are piled up as testimony against their parents. A common feature of the punishment for abortion / infanticide is that the children are present to accuse their parents.

It is likely, then, that the perversion of the intercourse of men and women implies abortion or infanticide, the outcome of its more obvious sense, adultery or fornication. On the other hand, it is possible that the infants are complaining about the parents' adultery, which has tainted them.[69] This would not explain why the children are infants, however. Thus the crime of perverting intercourse of man and woman is probably best understood as including abortion and infanticide.

---

67. Lieberman makes a case for the parallels between the Isaiah fragment and the Palestinian Talmud, but is cautious: "This reminds us to some extent of the passage in the Palestinian Talmud mentioned above" ("Sins," 38). His sense of a relationship grows out of his family tree for the Jewish texts, with which I take issue below (see the Apocalypse of Peter and the Jewish texts in chap. 5).

68. F. Cumont, *Lux Perpetua* (Paris: P. Geuthner, 1949), 214.

69. Methodius, *Symposium* 2.6, cites the Apocalypse of Peter about God's tender care for "children who are born before their time, even if they be the offspring of adultery" (HSW 2:675). This suggests a taint attached to adulterous conception.

Apocalypse of Peter, Ezra Apocalypses, Greek Apocalypse of Mary

The Apocalypse of Peter is the earliest of the texts that contain a form of this punishment. Chapter 8 of the Ethiopic version describes two punishments, one following the other, similar in some details. In the first, women stand up to their necks in a pit of refuse. Their children sit opposite them, and lightning comes forth from their eyes and pierces the mothers' eyes. In the second punishment men and women stand naked, as their children, who are "in a place of delight," accuse them before God. Milk comes forth from the mothers' breasts and turns into devouring beasts. These beasts then torture the parents forever, "because they forsook the command of God and killed their children."

In both punishments the parents are confronted by their children. Are the punishments doublets of a single original? The women in the first punishment are explicitly said to have undergone abortions. The second punishment includes both men and women. The logic of talion would suggest that the sin of the mothers in the second punishment involved rejection of nursing. Thus this punishment may be seen as appropriate for infanticide. If so, the Apocalypse of Peter contains separate punishments for two related sins.

The Greek version of the Apocalypse of Peter contains only the first punishment and specifies abortion as the sin. Since the preserved Greek is relatively late, it is possible to explain the absence of the second punishment as the result of the discomfort of a scribe (or redactor) with the presence of two such similar punishments.

Clement of Alexandria's citations of the Apocalypse of Peter in his *Eclogues* are the earliest witnesses to its text. In *Eclogue* 41, Clement mentions the care-taking angel ($\tau\eta\mu\epsilon\lambda\hat{o}\hat{v}\chi os$; the adjective becomes the proper name Temlakos in the Ethiopic), who appears in the Ethiopic text in the second punishment. The verb Clement uses to describe the parents' sin is $\dot{\epsilon}\kappa\tau\dot{i}\theta\eta\mu\iota$, "to expose" (children).[70] Clement goes on to describe the lightning coming forth from the children and striking the mothers' eyes.[71] In the Ethiopic version of the Apocalypse of Peter this is the punishment of the mothers who have had abortions.

In *Eclogues* 48–49, Clement again cites a passage about the care-taking

---

70. Lampe, *Patristic Lexicon*, cites Clement in *Stromateis* 2.18 as an example of this usage.

71. The translation in HSW, "a flash of fire," is misleading. Ἀστραπή means "lightning." It is true that Clement writes ἀστραπὴ πυρός, but it is unfortunate to lose the literal sense of ἀστραπή. The Greek of the Apocalypse of Peter is corrupt, but it seems to have read ἀκτῖνες πυρός.

angel, but this time in relation to children who are victims of abortion. The verb here is 'εξαμβλόω, to cause to miscarry. Clement then quotes the passage about the mothers' milk turning to beasts.

The evidence of the *Eclogues* strongly supports the originality of two punishments, as in the Ethiopic text. Clement clearly knows both punishments, although it appears that he attributes to the aborters the punishment that the Ethiopic text gives to the infanticides, and vice versa. The Ethiopic's assignment of punishments seems preferable to Clement's, since the punishment by means of mothers' milk should belong, according to the principle of measure-for-measure, to the infanticides rather than the aborters.

The motif of the children's accusation of their parents does not appear in either of the passages in the *Eclogues*. This does not necessarily mean that it was not found in the text before Clement. It was certainly known by the late third century, for it appears in Methodius' citation of the Apocalypse of Peter (*Symposium* 2.6). Although the wording is somewhat different, the content is unmistakable.

Like the Apocalypse of Peter, and perhaps dependent on it, the Vision of Ezra contains two distinct punishments. Women who bore children in adultery and then killed them are sent into a burning furnace while the children accuse their mothers before God (vv. 51–53). Other women hang in fire while serpents suck at their breasts. These women too killed their children. In addition, they "did not give their breasts to other orphans" (vv. 53a–54).[72]

This last clause seems to be an attempt to make manifest the measure-for-measure nature of the punishment, but it misses the point. The sin of these women was not that they withheld milk from other children but that they withheld milk (and all care) from their own children.

The Vision of Ezra, then, follows the Apocalypse of Peter in the presence of two punishments and in some details of the punishments, but it does not distinguish two sins. It is not clear whether "killing" children implies abortion, infanticide, or both. As opposed to the Apocalypse of Peter, only women are punished; while the beasts that emerge from the

---

72. The women with the serpents at their breasts are found only in the long form of the Vision of Ezra, although the short form (MS V) suggests an omission, for, as it stands, the angel's explanation, "These are they who killed their children and did not give their breasts to other orphans" (v. 54), appears to apply to the accusing children (v. 53). Thus Dinzelbacher's claim ("Die Vision Alberichs," 437–38) that v. 53a, which describes the women with serpents, is an interpolation is difficult to accept. Even if he is correct that the other passages peculiar to the long version are interpolations, this passage, for which the Apocalypse of Ezra supports the long version, cannot possibly be correct as it stands in the short version.

mothers' milk in the Apocalypse of Peter devour both mothers and fathers, the serpents of the Vision of Ezra ignore fathers and suck at the mothers' breasts.

The Apocalypse of Ezra contains only one punishment for abortion/infanticide (5:2–3). Four beasts suck at the breasts of a woman who is hanging for the sin of begrudging her milk and throwing her babies into rivers. This is very close to the second punishment of the Vision of Ezra, but the creatures are beasts, as in the Apocalypse of Peter, rather than serpents.

The aborters and infanticides of the Greek Apocalypse of Mary appear in chapters 5–7, where they are immersed in a river of fire up to their breasts and necks. The depths of immersion are not accidental. The crime of those immersed to their breasts, both men and women, is described as throwing off their children and committing fornication. If throwing off children were described as denying milk to them as it is elsewhere, the punishment would be measure-for-measure. The measure-for-measure nature of immersion to the neck is made explicit by describing the sin of the men and women so punished as "eating human flesh," that is, abortion.

A punishment more closely related to those in the Ezra apocalypses appears in chapter 20, where a deaconess is seen hanging while a ten-headed beast chews at her breasts. (It is typical of the Greek Apocalypse of Mary to be concerned with the sins of church officials.) Her sin is that she defiled her body in fornication. The principle of talion has been submerged here, but perhaps it can be recovered. The sins and punishments of the two Ezra apocalypses suggest the following line of reasoning. The end result of fornication is abortion or infanticide, figuratively or literally "denying milk." The breast is thus the sinful limb in relation to the results of fornication, and a beast chewing at the breasts is a measure-for-measure punishment for fornication.

A second passage in the Greek Apocalypse of Mary makes use of a similar punishment. In chapter 19, female presbyters hang by their nails while fire comes forth from their mouths and burns them. Then beasts emerge from the fire and gnaw at the women. The sin of these women is that they remarried after the death of their presbyter husbands. The beasts are not explicitly related to the breasts here, but the associations of this punishment suggest that the author of the text considered the women guilty of fornication.

Beasts sucking at the breasts of women appear also outside the tours of hell. In its description of the woes to come on Egypt in the last days, the Coptic Apocalypse of Elijah predicts a great horror: "At that time the king will command that every nursing woman be seized and brought to him in fetters and that they suckle dragons and that their blood be sucked from their breasts. . . ."[73]

In his edition of the Apocalypse of Elijah, J.-M. Rosenstiehl notes that the apocalypse in an Arabic Life of Shenouti includes a similar evil. Jesus reveals to Shenouti the catastrophes to come on Egypt: "Woe to women who are pregnant and nursing in those days! They will pierce the bellies of pregnant women, they will make serpents go in who will penetrate and suck the breasts. . . ." Rosenstiehl believes that the author of the Life of Shenouti drew on the Apocalypse of Elijah. The date of the Arabic translation of the Life is not known; Amélineau thinks that the Coptic Life from which it was translated can be dated quite precisely to 685–90 on the basis of historical allusions.[74]

The presence of this motif in texts unlikely to have been influenced directly by the Apocalypse of Peter because their concerns are so different is relevant to the question of the nature of the relationship between the Apocalypse of Peter and the two Ezra apocalypses. The Ezra apocalypses do not seem to show the influence of the Apocalypse of Peter in any other specifics, and the woes of the Apocalypse of Elijah and the Life of Shenouti contain an element present in the Ezra apocalypses, but not in the Apocalypse of Peter, beasts sucking at the breasts. Further, both the Apocalypse of Elijah and the Apocalypse of Ezra contain descriptions of the antichrist that belong to the same genre, although they do not share many details. On the other hand, the Vision of Ezra contains two separate punishments for abortion/infanticide without providing any rationale like the two separate sins of the Apocalypse of Peter. One way to make sense of the two punishments in the Vision of Ezra is to attribute them ultimately, if not directly, to the influence of the Apocalypse of Peter.

Apocalypse of Paul, Ethiopic Apocalypse of Mary, Ethiopic Apocalypse of Baruch

A somewhat different form of punishment for the same sins appears in Apoc. Paul 40, Eth. Apoc. Mary (65), and Eth. Apoc. Bar. (71–72). In the Apocalypse of Paul men and women are tortured on a fiery spit (*ApNT*),

73. A. Pietersma and S. T. Comstock, with H. A. Attridge, *The Apocalypse of Elijah*, Texts and Translations 9, Pseudepigrapha Series 19 (Chico, Calif.: Scholars Press, 1981) 37.

74. J.-M. Rosenstiehl, *L'Apocalypse d'Élie*, Textes et études pour servir à l'histoire du Judaisme intertestementaire 1 (Paris: P. Guethner, 1972), 40–41. E. Amélineau, trans., "Vie arabe de Schnoudi," *Mémoires de la mission archéologique française au Caire* 4(1888): *Monuments pour servir à l'histoire de l'Égypte chrétienne aux IVe et Ve siècles*, 342–43. I translate from the French.

while beasts tear them to pieces. The description of their sin does not allow a decision between abortion and infanticide. According to the Coptic version, the dead children watch the punishment. In the Ethiopic Apocalypse of Mary nuns hang in the midst of fire, while fiery snakes, dogs, lions, and panthers attack them. Both abortion and infanticide are explicitly mentioned here. In the Ethiopic Apocalypse of Baruch priests and widows who had abortions hang from fiery trees while fiery snakes and dogs devour them.

In these texts the devouring beasts are not associated with the mothers' breasts. The punishments offer a different kind of measure-for-measure. In all three texts an accusation similar to that in the Apocalypse of Peter is reported: the children, who are not actually present except in the Coptic version of the Apocalypse of Paul, are said to have complained that their parents threw them to the beasts (Apoc. Paul: dogs, pigs, river; Eth. Apoc. Mary: dogs, pigs; Eth. Apoc. Bar.: dogs, beasts). In turn their parents are tortured by beasts, although not precisely the ones to whom they threw their offspring.

Duensing takes this punishment as evidence of the Apocalypse of Paul's dependence on the Apocalypse of Peter.[75] But placed among the punishments assembled here, the punishment in the Apocalypse of Paul does not appear to be very close to that of the Apocalypse of Peter. The only elements of the punishment in the Apocalypse of Paul that might suggest dependence on the Apocalypse of Peter are the accusation of the children, which differs considerably in its content in each of the apocalypses and which is to be found in all the texts examined here except the Apocalypse of Ezra, and the presence of angels to whom the murdered children are entrusted. (See under the Apocalypse of Peter and the Apocalypse of Paul in chap. 5, below.)

The Angel Temelouchos

Both the Ethiopic Apocalypse of Mary and the Ethiopic Apocalypse of Baruch call the angel in charge of the souls of the dead infants Temelouchos (or a variant). This name appears also in the Ethiopic version of the Apocalypse of Peter; it is a transformation of the Greek adjective τημελοῦχος, care-taking, which describes that angel in excerpts from the Apocalypse of Peter in Clement (*Eclogue* 48) and Methodius (*Symposium* 2.6).

---

75. HSW 2:757.

The Latin version of the Apocalypse of Paul refers to the angels involved in this episode as "angels of Tartarus"; it lacks the term or name "Teme-louchos" altogether. The Greek version of the Apocalypse of Paul, which contains an unnamed angel in the episode of the infanticides, gives the name Temelouchos to the angel to whom the evil soul is entrusted after it leaves the body (chap. 16) and to the angel who participates in the torture of a gluttonous elder (chap. 34). The angel in chapter 16 in the long Latin is named "Tartaruchus"; in chapter 16 in the St. Gall manuscript and in both manuscripts in chapter 34 the angels are called "angels of Tartarus." The Coptic twice refers to an angel named "Aftemelouchos." He appears in the passage parallel to chapter 34 in the Greek and Latin versions (Coptic 12a) and also in the episode of the infanticides as the angel who presides over their punishment and to whom the souls of their victims are entrusted (14b–15a).

In his edition of the Coptic Apocalypse of Paul, E. A. W. Budge suggests that the name "Aftemelouchos" means "four angels." In Coptic ⲁϥⲧⲉ means "four," and Budge takes ⲙⲉⲗⲟⲩⲭⲟⲥ to mean "angel" on the basis of Arabic parallels.[76] It is true that four angels torture the bishop (12a) and defiled virgins (13b) in the Coptic Apocalypse of Paul. (Four angels torture the bishop [chap. 35] and the virgins [chap. 39] in the Latin version as well.) But both times the Coptic calls the four angels ⲁⲣⲅⲉⲗⲟⲥ. The word ⲙⲉⲗⲟⲩⲭⲟⲥ is not Coptic. If the Coptic text originally referred to Temelouchos where the Latin has the more easily understood "angels of Tartarus," "Aftemelouchos" may represent an attempt to naturalize the peculiar name by making at least one element meaningful in Coptic, perhaps under the influence of the four angels who appear earlier in the text.

Both the Ethiopic Apocalypse of Mary and the Ethiopic Apocalypse of Baruch put the name of the angel at the end of the episode of the infanticides, as in the Apocalypse of Peter. Contact with the Apocalypse of Peter is not out of the question for Ethiopic texts, but because there are no other signs of the Apocalypse of Peter's direct influence, either in this episode or elsewhere, it seems preferable to assume that the version of the Apocalypse of Paul on which the Ethiopic texts drew contained the name Temelouchos, probably in the position in which it is found in the Ethiopic Apocalypse of Mary and the Ethiopic Apocalypse of Baruch. This version might have been an Ethiopic translation of the Apocalypse of Paul, although it is also possible that the Ethiopic descendant texts drew on an Arabic version

76. E. A. W. Budge, *Coptic Texts*, vol. 5 (reprint of *Miscellaneous Coptic Texts in the Dialect of Upper Egypt* [1915]; New York: AMS, 1977), 1060, n. 1.

no longer extant or not yet recovered. It may well be that other copies of the Apocalypse of Paul in Coptic contained the name Temelouchos (or Aftemelouchos) at the end of the episode of the infanticides. Since none of the other versions of the Apocalypse of Paul shows any trace of the care-taking angel, the reading of the Coptic may indicate renewed contact between the Apocalypse of Paul and the Apocalypse of Peter in Egypt.

PUNISHMENT FOR LOSS OF VIRGINITY BEFORE MARRIAGE

In the discussion of sexual sins above, it was noted that there is a close correlation between the appearance of a punishment for abortion/infanti-cide in a text and the appearance of a punishment for the loss of virginity before marriage. Eight instances of a punishment for abortion/infanticide appear in the seventeen tours of hell, and seven of a punishment for loss of virginity; five texts contain both. Thus, although the punishments for loss of virginity are not measure-for-measure, this is a convenient place to discuss them.

All the punishments for abortion/infanticide, it appeared above, contain common elements. The same is true for the punishments of the ex-virgins, except the two that appear in texts that do not contain punishments for abortion/infanticide, the Life of Pachomios and the Elijah fragment. In the Elijah fragment, the ex-virgins are roasted on a gridiron; in the Life of Pachomios, souls, not identified as female, are burned inside a huge stone structure.

The earliest version of the punishment in the remaining texts is that of Eth. Apoc. Pet. 11. There the virgins are "clad in darkness for raiment" (HSW); their flesh is to be torn apart. In Apoc. Paul 39 the young women are dressed in black, and tormenting angels lead them "toward darkness" by means of blazing chains set on their necks. Eth. Apoc. Mary (64) copies the punishment as described in the Apocalypse of Paul quite closely: the women are again dressed in black, fiery chains encircle their necks, and they are led toward a fiery river.

The situation in the two remaining texts is a little more complicated. In Eth. Apoc. Bar. (70–71) "people" punished in an abyss of fire are said to have lost their virginity in deserted places without having been given in marriage by their parents. This is exactly how the sin of the ex-virgins, all female, is described in the Ethiopic Apocalypse of Mary. At the very beginning of the tour of hell, Baruch sees "virgins clothed in darkness" (70). "These are mad virgins who were avaricious." The sin-and-punishment combination of the Apocalypse of Peter, the Apocalypse of Paul, and especially the Ethiopic Apocalypse of Mary has been broken up. The punishment of dark raiment is still identified with virgins, but their sin is not loss of virginity before marriage. Loss of virginity is provided with a punishment unrelated to the others.

The description of the punishment of the ex-virgins in Vis. Ezra 43—44 contains a crucial word, apparently corrupt, that defies interpretation. Ezra sees virgins coming toward the west with a cry and with five-hundred-pound *pogines* (MS L) or *bogiis* (MSS VH).[77] Unfortunately neither *pogines* nor *bogiis* is readily understood as Latin or muddled Greek. The variants in the two textual traditions suggest that the copyists were unsure of the meaning. The phrase "toward the west" may echo the Apocalypse of Paul's "toward darkness"; as the Latin *occiduum* reminds us, the west is where the sun sets. Perhaps the five-hundred-pound burdens the women bear are chains or something similar.[78]

The dark raiment of the Apocalypse of Peter, then, is transmitted through the Apocalypse of Paul to the two Ethiopic texts. The additions of the Apocalypse of Paul to the punishment as it appears in the Apocalypse of Peter also recur in the later texts. The Apocalypse of Peter and the Apocalypse of Paul are much closer here than in the punishments for abortion/infanticide. It is interesting that the Vision of Ezra, which for abortion/infanticide showed parallels to the Apocalypse of Peter found nowhere else, is here linked to the other texts, if at all, through parallels to the Apocalypse of Paul.

BLINDNESS

Blindness appears as a measure-for-measure punishment in the Apocalypse of Peter, the Apocalypse of Paul, and the Apocalypse of Zephaniah. The importance of this cluster of texts justifies discussion of this punishment despite the relatively small number of occurrences.

One of the three groups of sinners that Zephaniah sees submerged in a sea consists of catechumens who have heard but not fulfilled the word of God (15—16). They are blind.

The blind catechumens are paralleled in Eth. Apoc. Pet. 12 by blind and

---

77. The selection of readings published by Wahl from the new MSS of the Vision ("Vier neue Textzeugen") includes nothing of use here.

78. J. R. Mueller and G. E. Robbins, "Vision of Ezra," in *The Old Testament Pseudepigrapha*, ed. J. H. Charlesworth (Garden City, N.Y.: Doubleday, in press), translate the problematic word as "neck irons." They were kind enough to inform me that their translation is based on the parallels in the other tours of hell.

dumb men and women dressed in white, who are tortured with coals of fire. Their sin is described as follows: "These are they who give alms and say, 'We are righteous before God,' while they have not striven for righteousness" (HSW). In Apoc. Paul 40 these sinners are "the heathen who gave alms and did not know the Lord God." They are blind and are dressed in bright clothing. (The St. Gall manuscript adds that they are found in a pit of fire.)

It is interesting that in the Apocalypse of Paul the clothing of the sinners and alms are mentioned, as in the Apocalypse of Peter, and that, as in the Apocalypse of Zephaniah, the sinners are not (originally) believers. The wording in the Apocalypse of Peter does not suggest that the sinners are heathen or catechumens. Thus the Apocalypse of Paul contains details found in both the other texts, while the Apocalypse of Zephaniah and the Apocalypse of Peter do not share any distinctive details. This is exactly what one would expect given the other evidence for the relationship of the Apocalypse of Paul to the two earlier texts.

The sin of the Apocalypse of Zephaniah, hearing but not fulfilling, is not exactly the same as the sin of the Apocalypse of Peter, claiming to be righteous but not striving for righteousness. Blindness is an appropriate punishment for both, however. It is the physical actualization of the lack of self-awareness or self-criticism that allows the sins to come into being.

Blindness appears as a punishment in both Greek and Jewish literature.[79] In the case of Oedipus, blindness, although self-inflicted, has much the same significance as in the case of the sinners of the tours of hell: blameworthy ignorance is crystallized into physical blindness. The blindness inflicted on Samson by the Philistines is understood as a measure-for-measure punishment by Mishnah Soṭah 1:8 (Danby): "Samson went after [the desire of] his eyes—therefore the Philistines put out his eyes. . . ."[80]

---

79. See M. E. Monbeck, *The Meaning of Blindness: Attitudes Toward Blindness and Blind People* (Bloomington, Ind., and London: Indiana University, 1973), 48–53.

80. I would like to thank G. W. E. Nickelsburg for pointing out that pseudo-Philo's treatment of this incident (43.5) makes the same point.

Chapter 4

SINS AND PUNISHMENTS II

Environmental Punishments and the Sins and Punishments of the Apocalypse of Paul Family

Environmental Punishments

Measure-for-measure punishments form one major group of punishments in the tours of hell. A second group consists of punishments inflicted by the geography of hell. This geography was a subject of interest to many ancient cultures; the Egyptians even provided the dead with maps of their new home.[1]

Both Greek and Jewish sources contribute to the picture of the geography of hell in the texts discussed here. Ancient Israel imagined the dwelling place of the dead as an inhospitable land. "Hebrew Sheol is a collection and reflection of deadly perils, dangerous regions, and dark situations on earth: the scenery consists of treacherous marshes, threatening seas, impetuous rivers, and engulfing deeps."[2] Homer mentions four rivers and a lake in Hades.[3] The specifics vary in later Greek authors, but the fact of geographical description is common.

Despite their use of geographical features in describing hell, it seems likely that the authors of these texts did not have a clear map of hell either at hand or in mind, for it is often difficult to tell whether each mention of a river means a new river or whether the many mentions can be reduced to

---

1. See, e.g., E. A. W. Budge, ed. and trans., *The Book of the Dead: The Chapters of Coming Forth by Day* (London: Kegan Paul, Trench, Trübner, 1896).
2. N. J. Tromp, *Primitive Conceptions of Death and the Nether World in the Old Testament* (Rome: Pontifical Biblical Institute, 1969), 140. Tromp relies heavily on Job and Psalms for his description.
3. S. Eitrem, "Phlegethon," PW.

one or two rivers. Further, punishment is piled on top of punishment, often resulting in impossible combinations.[4]

This is in keeping with the impression made by the confused directions of most of the tours. Compared to them, the description of Enoch's journey in the Book of the Watchers is a model of clarity. Most of the tours do not even attempt to provide directions. In Apoc. Paul 32 the seer looks to the north, while in chapter 42 he looks toward the west. In Eth. Apoc. Mary (61) Mary is once said to go west. In the Greek Apocalypse of Mary, Mary travels west (chap. 3), south (chap. 5), and then to the left side of paradise (chaps. 22–23), which is placed in opposition to the east.[5] In other texts with fewer geographical details, like the Vision of Ezra and *Gedulat Moshe*, the direction of travel is downward. The Apocalypse of Ezra combines compass directions and descending steps in a most confusing fashion.

From Mire to Fire

The Sheol in which the Hebrew Bible places the dead to lead their shadow existence is often conceived as a pit or a bog. Pit, בור, is a common synonym for Sheol, particularly in Isaiah, Ezekiel, and Psalms.[6] Sheol is damp and dank, miry rather than fiery.[7] Miry bog, טיט היון (Ps. 40:3), and pit of the grave, באר שחת (Ps. 55:24), later appear in rabbinic literature as names for levels of hell.[8]

Although Hades is frequently thought of as subterranean, abyss and pit are not prominent features in the Greek literature describing the underworld.[9] Mire and mud, however, are important for the ideas about Hades associated with Orphism.[10] They provide a sort-of measure-for-measure punishment: the impure wallow in impurity.

---

4. See, e.g., Apoc. Paul 39, where homosexuals were "covered in dust, and their faces were like blood, and they were in a pit of tar and brimstone, and they were running in a river of fire" (HSW).

5. "Left" means west in another context in Greek. According to Liddell and Scott, *A Greek-English Lexicon*, "ἀριστερόν," augurs looked north. Omens from the left were unlucky, hence the extended meaning of ἀριστερόν. When one faces north, the left is west.

6. Tromp, *Death and the Nether World*, 66–71.

7. Ibid., 54–58.

8. Ginzberg, *Legends of the Jews*, 5:11, n. 25.

9. Plutarch is one writer who does place pits in Hades (*Face on the Moon* 944b–c, "*Live Unknown*" 1130d–e).

10. Plato (*Republic* 363c–d) refers the idea to "Musaios and his son," names associated with Orphism. When Plutarch refers to this passage from the *Republic* (*Cimon and Lucullus* 521),

Mud and mire have left their traces in the tours of hell,[11] but the most striking feature of the infernal terrain as depicted in these tours is the fire that seems to burn everywhere. When a true hell emerges in early Judaism, it is not usually called Sheol, which was the resting place of righteous and wicked alike, but rather Gehinnom (Gk., Gehenna), after the valley in Jerusalem.[12] While Sheol is a pit, Gehinnom is a valley; thus the imagery of depth is retained. Paul (Rom. 10:7) uses "abyss" to mean hell, and the abyss of Revelation is more or less equivalent to hell. In the detailed landscapes of the tours of hell, pits, valleys, and abysses are only some of the features of the geography.

Unlike the dark and dank Sheol, Gehinnom is fiery.[13] Fire has a long history of association with retribution—and theophanies[14]—in the Hebrew Bible. Most of these instances of retribution, in keeping with the concerns of the Bible, are national. Israel's desolation, present or threatened, is described as the work of fire,[15] as is God's vengeance on the wicked nations.[16] Thus it is not surprising that Joel associates fire with the day of God's judgment.[17] This association continues in apocalyptic literature.

The fiery associations of Gehinnom precede its development into hell. The earthly Gehinnom achieved notoriety in the Bible as the place where Jerusalemites burned their children as offerings to Moloch.[18] Thus Gehinnom is a place of both fire and disgrace. It is first designated a place of punishment by Jeremiah (7:30–34), who threatens that the valley of the sons of Hinnom will come to be called the valley of slaughter: God will strike the idolatrous people so that birds and beasts will feed on the corpses that lie uncovered in the valley for lack of burial space.

The earliest evidence for the belief in Gehinnom as the place of eternal punishment is 1 Enoch 27, part of the cosmic tour in the Book of the

---

he says that Plato calls this belief Orphic. Plato (*Phaedo* 69c) quotes those involved in the mysteries as saying that the uninitiated lie in the mud of Hades.

11. Gk. Apoc. Pet. 23, 24, and 31 contain references to "mire" (βόρβορος); both versions of the Apocalypse of Peter mention pits or places of discharge, excrement, and filth. Acts Th. 56 also speaks of a chasm full of mire (βόρβορος).

12. For variations on the names in the Bible and elsewhere see J. Jeremias, "γεέννα," *TDNT* 1(1964):657–58.

13. Fire and darkness need not be mutually exclusive: 1 Enoch 103:8 contains "darkness and chains and burning fire." I would like to thank G. W. E. Nickelsburg for pointing out this passage to me.

14. E.g., Gen. 15:17; Exod. 3:2; 19:18.

15. E.g., Isa. 1:7; Jer. 11:16; Amos 2:5; Lam. 4:11.

16. E.g., Gen. 19:24; Isa. 30:27, 30; Amos 1:4, 7, 10, 12, 14.

17. Joel 2:1–3.

18. 2 Kings 23:10; Jer. 7:30–34; 19:6; 32:35.

Watchers.[19] Although Gehinnom is not named, this section of the tour reflects the geography of Jerusalem, and it is clear that the "accursed valley" that Enoch sees is none other than the valley of Hinnom. There is no reference here to the fiery character of Gehinnom.

That character is well established in later literature.[20] The transition from fire as punishment on earth to the fire of Gehinnom can be followed by tracing the influence of a particularly important passage for the Jewish and Christian conception of hell, Isa. 66:24: "And they shall go forth and look on the dead bodies of the men that have rebelled against me; for their worm shall not die, their fire shall not be quenched, and they shall be an abhorrence to all flesh." This gruesome scene seems to be located in the earthly Jerusalem. The worms may well be a survival of the older pit imagery of Sheol (see below, under worms and other beasts).

Fire and worm show up together in Judith and Sirach, probably under the influence of this passage. In Judith (16:17) they are features of a biblical-style judgment on the wicked nations. "Woe to the nations that rise up against my people. . . . fire and worms he will give to their flesh. . ." (RSV).

In the Greek text of Sirach, on the other hand, the punishment of fire and worms is applied to the individual. "Humble yourself greatly, for the punishment of the ungodly is fire and worms" (7:17, RSV). The Hebrew reads, "for the expectation of man is worms." This version is more in keeping with the tone of Sirach as a whole, where there is little indication of belief in individual afterlife.[21]

At the beginning of the common era the fire and worms of Isaiah have been unambiguously placed in hell. The correspondence of details makes it clear that Mark 9:47–48 alludes to Isaiah: "It is better for you to enter the kingdom of God with one eye than with two eyes to be thrown into hell [Gk., Gehenna], where their worm does not die and the fire is not quenched" (RSV). Nor is Mark the only text to understand Isaiah as referring to hell. B. 'Eruvin 19a is another, although here the verse from Isaiah is not used to describe the nature of the punishments, but rather to prove the continued sinfulness of the dead, even in hell. Two of the tours of hell,

---

19. See above, p. 50, for dates of Book of the Watchers.

20. See Jeremias, "γέεννα," for fiery Gehenna in apocalyptic literature, rabbinic literature, and the New Testament.

21. M. Z. Segal (*Sefer ben Sirah haShalem*, 2d ed. [Jerusalem: Mosad Bialik, 1958], 46) thinks that the grandson misread תקוה, "expectation," as נקמה, "punishment," and that the end of the verse was influenced by Isa. 66:24. This would also account for the Greek "ungodly" in place of the Hebrew "man."

the Joshua b. Levi fragment (*Reshit Ḥokhmah*) and *Ged. Mosh.* 18, quote the passage in relation to the scene in hell.

In "apocalyptic" literature[22] "fire" is more common than "Gehinnom," and often the fiery punishments of the wicked are not specifically designated as punishments of Gehinnom.[23] Yet most punishments consist of being "cast" into fire, which requires, or at least suggests, a valley or pit of fire. Conversely, many of the references to Gehinnom indexed by Charles in his *Apocrypha and Pseudepigrapha of the Old Testament* do not specifically mention fire. At Qumran the term "Gehinnom" does not appear, at least not in the texts published in time for K. G. Kuhn's concordance,[24] but the fire of hell is mentioned several times.[25]

In the New Testament the concept of a fiery hell has been firmly established. The word γέεννα appears twelve times in the New Testament. Twice it forms part of the phrase γέεννα τοῦ πυρός (Matt. 5:22; 18:9), and three times the context clearly indicates fire (Mark 9:43, 47; James 3:6).

Rivers of Fire

Fire appears in Greek conceptions of the underworld in the form of a river. In the *Odyssey* 10.513, Pyriphlegethon, the fiery storm, is the name of one of the four rivers of Hades. Although the names of the other rivers vary from author to author, Pyriphlegethon or Phlegethon is a stable element of the later descriptions.[26]

In the description of the underworld in the *Phaedo* (114a), patricides and matricides are tormented in Pyriphlegethon, while the murderers float in the Kokytos, which is not fiery. Usually, however, the fiery river is more a

---

22. By this term, F. Lang ("πῦρ," *TDNT* 6[1968]:937–38) seems to mean roughly the contents of Charles' *APOT* 2.

23. See the instances cited in ibid., 938, under "eternal torment in hell" and "eternal fire."

24. K. G. Kuhn, *Konkordanz zu den Qumrantexten* (Göttingen: Vandenhoeck & Ruprecht, 1960). Other names for the land of the dead do appear. "Sheol" occurs eight times, always in the Thanksgiving Psalms. "Abaddon" appears five times, three times in the Thanksgiving Psalms. These frequencies probably result from the modeling of the Thanksgiving Psalms on the canonical Psalms. "Abaddon" occurs only five times in the Bible, once in Psalms. "Sheol" occurs sixteen times in Psalms, more often than in any other book.

25. Lang, "πῦρ," 939, refers to 1QS 2:8, 4:13; 1QH 17:13.

26. Eitrem, "Phlegethon." He suggests that the idea of a fiery river in Hades derives from the Greek practice of cremating the dead. This is particularly interesting in light of Tromp's comment (*Death and the Nether World*, 191), "Most descriptions of Sheol are borrowed from the grave. . . ." He points to the bed of worms in Isa. 14:1 and to the undying worm of Isa. 66:24.

geographical phenomenon than an instrument of punishment.[27] The descriptions of the underworld in Plato and Aristophanes indicate that mud rather than fire is the primary feature of the popular picture of Hades in the classical period.[28]

Among the Greeks Lucian in the second century C.E. is more or less alone in referring to fiery tortures in hell.[29] His hell scapes frequently include Pyriphlegethon.[30] In addition, he mentions the "wails of those roasting on the fire" (*Menippus* 14) and lists punishments including burning (*True Story* 2.31, *Funerals* 8). But nowhere in Lucian is fire a particularly prominent form of punishment. It seems possible that Lucian's attention to fire indicates influence from Jewish or Christian quarters, perhaps indirectly.

In 1 Enoch 17 : 5 a river of fire flows to the western end of the earth, near the mountains of darkness. It is not a river of punishment. R. H. Charles unhesitatingly identifies this river as Pyriphlegethon and assumes that the "great rivers" mentioned in 17 : 6 are the other traditional rivers of Greek Hades.[31] Charles views this part of the tour as a mixture of Greek and Babylonian motifs; the mountains of darkness for him are Babylonian. In his treatment of the passage J. T. Milik does not object to this cultural pastiche and even suggests some parallel Ugaritic imagery.[32] Given the mixed nature of Enochic geography, one should perhaps be a little more hesitant than Charles in identifying the origins of each motif.

Fiery rivers appear in a context more closely related to punishment in 1QH 3 : 28–34.[33] These rivers are agents of the eschatological conflagration in which the foundations of the earth are consumed.

The only river of fire in the Hebrew Bible is found in Dan. 7 : 10. It is not a river of punishment, but the stream that issues forth from the throne of the Ancient of Days.[34] Nevertheless, this river comes to be associated with hell. In b. Ḥagigah 13b and 3 Enoch 33 it is said to pour forth onto the

---

27. Eitrem, "Phlegethon."

28. Plato, *Republic* 363d and *Phaedo* 69c; Aristophanes, *Frogs* 145–46, 273. Dieterich, *Nekyia*, 81–83 offers other references, as does M. P. Nilsson, *Geschichte der griechischen Religion*, Handbuch der Altertums Wissenschaft (Munich: C. H. Beck, 1941), 1 : 651–52.

29. Dieterich, *Nekyia*, 199. See also *Phaedo* 114a for punishment in Pyriphlegethon.

30. *True Story* 2.30; *Menippus* 10; *Funerals* 3; *Lover of Lies* 24.

31. Charles, *Book of Enoch*, ad. loc.

32. J. T. Milik, *Books of Enoch*, 38–40.

33. I would like to thank G. W. E. Nickelsburg for calling this passage to my attention.

34. Similar streams of fire come forth from under God's throne in 1 Enoch 14 : 19. This section of 1 Enoch is older than the book of Daniel, but both texts probably reflect a more ancient tradition. The river of fire comes to the Babylonian Talmud and 3 Enoch from the canonical text, Daniel.

heads of sinners in hell.[35] While G. Scholem dates 3 Enoch to the end of the Talmudic period,[36] the participants in the discussion in Ḥagigah are R. Jeremiah b. Aba and R. Zuṭra b. Ṭuvyah, third-century Babylonian amoraim and students of Rav. R. Zuṭra attributes his statement that the river falls on the heads of sinners to Rav. If this attribution is correct, the statement goes back to the early third century.

C.-M. Edsman contends that the fiery river as punishment goes back even further. He points to a passage in Clement of Alexandria's *Excerpta Ex Theodoto* 38.

A river goes from under the throne of Space (τόπος) and flows into the void of the creation which is Gehenna, and it is never filled, though the fire flows from the beginning of creation. And Space itself is fiery. Therefore, he says, it has a veil in order that the things may not be destroyed by the sight of it. And only the archangel enters it, and to typify this the high priest every year enters the holy of holies.[37]

Edsman argues that Theodotus, a second-century Valentinian, here drew on a Jewish source.[38] Scholem, who does not seem to have known Edsman's work, also refers to the *Excerpta*. He considers this passage to be "soaked with Merkabah mysticism."[39] In nearby passages Space (τόπος = מקום) and the demiurge (δημιουργός = יוצר בראשית) are identical, most unusual for a Christian Gnostic text, but perfectly normal in a merkavah text. The passage quoted above contains other examples of merkavah terminology in the "throne" of Space and the veil.[40]

Thus, while the fiery river is well established in Hellenistic usage, the presence of such a river in the *Excerpta* suggests that the tours of hell may have known it from other sources as well. The author of the Apocalypse of Peter and Theodotos of the *Excerpta* were roughly contemporaries, and both lived in Egypt. It is not implausible that the kinds of Jewish traditions that appear later in the Babylonian Talmud and 3 Enoch were available to them in second-century Egypt.

---

35. All references to 3 Enoch refer to the edition of H. Odeberg (*3 Enoch or the Hebrew Book of Enoch* [Cambridge: Cambridge University, 1928; repr. with a prolegomenon by J. C. Greenfield, New York: KTAV, 1973]). C.-M. Edsman, *Le baptême de feu* (Uppsala: Almquist & Wiksells, 1940), 19–31, mentions these texts and many rabbinic parallels, which do not take the river to hell.

36. G. Scholem, *Jewish Gnosticism, Merkabah Mysticism, and Talmudic Tradition*, 2d ed. (New York: Jewish Theological Seminary, 1965), 7, n. 19.

37. Edsman, *Baptême de feu*, 28–29. R. Casey, ed. and trans., Clement of Alexandria, *Excerpta ex Theodoto*, Studies and Documents 1 (London: Christophers, 1934), 67.

38. Edsman, *Baptême de feu*, 28–29.

39. Scholem, *Jewish Gnosticism*, 34, n. 10.

40. Ibid., 34–35.

By-products of Fire

In addition to the other tortures to which they are subjected, the inhabitants of the infernal regions must tolerate a level of air pollution that the Environmental Protection Agency would surely rate unacceptable, for with fire come various chemical by-products: sulfur, brimstone, pitch, smoke.

All these words appear in contexts of destruction in the Hebrew Bible. Brimstone, גפרית, serves as a punishment for Sodom and Gomorrah (Gen. 19:24) and elsewhere.[41] It is always translated in the LXX as θεῖον. In the Vulgate it is *sulfur*. Thus sulfur and brimstone should probably be considered a single substance here.

The hapax כפר, the pitch Noah uses for his ark (Gen. 6:14), which is probably from a related root, is translated by the LXX as ἄσφαλτος. In the Vulgate it is *bitumen*.

Pitch, זפת, appears in Isa. 34:9, where it is paired with גפרית: "And her streams shall be turned to pitch and her soil to brimstone."[42] It is translated by the Greek as πίσσα, by the Vulgate, as *pix*. Pitch was used as a punishment in the Greco-Roman world, as Lucretius, *On the Nature of Things* 3.1017,[43] and Lucian, *Runaways* 33, indicate. These texts do not suggest any associations with afterlife.

Smoke, עשן, serves as a sign of God's anger and destruction in the Hebrew Bible.[44] It is interesting that none of these terms is particularly important in the New Testament except in the Revelation of John. There both brimstone and smoke figure prominently.[45]

Fire and Geography in the Tours of Hell

As Table 6 indicates, environmental punishments in general, and fire, rivers, and pits in particular, appear primarily in the Apocalypse of Paul, its descendants, and other relatively late Christian texts. For their length the two Ezra apocalypses have few such punishments, with plain fire playing a more important role than geographic features. The Jewish texts, with the

---

41. E.g., Deut. 29:22; Isa. 30:33; 34:9; Ezek. 38:22.

42. זפת appears twice in this verse from Isaiah and only one other time in the Bible, in Exod. 2:3 as one of the materials for Moses' basket.

43. Dieterich, *Nekyia*, 140–41, refers to this passage.

44. E.g., 2 Sam. 22:9 (=Ps. 18:9); Isa. 14:31; 65:5; Nah. 2:14; Ps. 68:3.

45. Brimstone appears once in Luke (17:29) in relation to the story of Sodom and several times in Revelation (9:17, 18; 14:10; 19:20; 20:10; 21:8), always in relation to the punishment of the wicked. Smoke appears once in Acts (2:19) in a quotation from Joel, and several times

Table 6. FIRE AND GEOGRAPHY

Text	Plain Fire	Rivers —	Rivers Fiery	Abysses/ Pits/ Gorges/ Valleys —	Abysses/ Pits/ Gorges/ Valleys Fiery	Brimstone/ Pitch	Smoke	Fiery Devices
Apoc. Pet. (Eth.)	6	1	1	2	1	—	—	5
Apoc. Pet. (Gk.)	4	—	—	—	—	—	—	3
Acts Th.	1	—	—	—	—	1	1	1
Apoc. Zeph.	—	—	3	4	1	1	—	2
Apoc. Paul	6	4	2	3	1	2	—	7
Eth. Apoc. Mary	3	2	1	5	5	2	—	15
Eth. Apoc. Bar.	5	1	—	5	—	2	—	11
Apoc. Gorg.	5	2	2	—	—	2	—	8
Gk. Apoc. Mary	2	2	—	1	—	1	—	2
Apoc. Ezra	4	2	—	—	—	—	—	2
Vis. Ezra	—	1	1	2	—	2	1	5
T. Isaac	—	1	1	1	1[a]	—	1	1[b]
L. Pach.	—	1	—	1	1	—	—	2
Dar. Tesh.	—	—	—	—	—	—	—	1
Isa. frag.	—	—	—	—	—	—	1	—
Josh. frag.	—	—	—	—	—	—	—	1
Ged. Mosh.	1	—	—	—	—	—	—	4
Elij. frag.	—	—	—	1	1	1	—	1

[a] Bohairic.
[b] Sahidic.

exception of *Gedulat Moshe*, lack fire and geographic features almost completely; even *Gedulat Moshe* contains relatively few.

The course of development of the environmental punishments is different from that of the hanging punishments. The earliest Christian texts, the Apocalypse of Peter, the Acts of Thomas, and the Apocalypse of Paul, like the Jewish texts, contain several hanging punishments, while the later Christian texts, despite signs of relation to the tradition found in the Apocalypse of Peter, have relatively few. On the other hand, the number of environmental punishments increases from the Apocalypse of Peter to the later Christian texts. The geography of the Apocalypse of Paul and its descendants is far more developed than that of the Apocalypse of Peter. Several punishments in the Apocalypse of Peter are set in "places."[46] This vague term rarely appears in the later texts, where greater geographic specificity has become the rule. Another aspect of the development of the environmental punishments, as we have seen, is that mud and mire, which coexist with the fire in the Apocalypse of Peter, have given way to the dominance of fire in the later texts. In fact, in some texts fire comes to permeate all features of hell. In the Ethiopic Apocalypse of Baruch, for example, there appear not only a fiery stream, a fiery sea, several fiery abysses, mountains of fire, and fire by itself, but also fiery dogs, serpents, vipers, angels, charcoal, rocks, trees, cauldrons, and robes. A similar list could be drawn up for other texts. It seems more reasonable to assume that, as fire comes to dominate, some authors set all the elements of hell ablaze, than to seek the pedigree of each blazing instrument of torture individually. In some cases the fire is a natural feature of the torture, as for the burning coals of *Darkhei Teshuvah*, for example.

Smoke in the Isaiah Fragment

The smoke of the fifth compartment of the Isaiah fragment requires some special discussion. Because all the other punishments of the Isaiah fragment are measure-for-measure (the middle three obviously so, the first less obviously; see chap. 3, above, under water-carriers in the Isaiah fragment), Lieberman insists that the smoke must also be understood as measure-for-

---

in Revelation (8:4; 9:2, 3, 17, 18; 14:11; 15:8; 18:9, 18; 19:3) in contexts similar to the ones in which brimstone appears, and often together with it.

46. The Ethiopic has ten "places" in the HSW translation (chaps. 7–11). The Greek text contains six (chaps. 21, 25–27, 30, 33). The translation in HSW calls the "narrow places" of chaps. 25 and 26 "gorges."

measure.[47] He argues that its explanation lies in the Latin idiom *fumum vendere*, literally "to sell smoke," used of officials who make false promises.[48]

This ingenious theory poses some interesting questions about the date of the Isaiah fragment, questions that Lieberman does not resolve. Lieberman's claim that the Isaiah fragment is influenced by the wording of the passage in the Palestinian Talmud rather than by its contents alone indicates a date in the fifth century at the earliest. Ginzberg, who edited the versions of the Isaiah fragment from the Geniza, considers it post-Talmudic.[49] What, then, is to be made of the use of the Latin idiom? Latin is not common in rabbinic materials;[50] it is quite surprising this late when the influence of Latin in the East is generally at low ebb. Nevertheless, whatever one might make of them separately, the conjunction of the first house with its water-carriers and the fifth house with, perhaps, a Latin idiom suggests that the date of the Isaiah fragment is a subject of interest and importance. Full discussion of this issue will be postponed to the next chapter (see chap. 5 under the date of the Isaiah fragment).

Worms and Other Beasts

A variety of beasts torture the inhabitants of hell in several of the texts (Table 7). Dieterich wished to understand the beasts of the Apocalypse of Peter as part of a Greek tradition of devourers that express the truth that death is a devourer, that men rot in the grave: Eurynomos, the demon of Polygnotos' painting at Delphi (described by Pausanias [10.28.7]); Cerberos, the dog-guardian of hell; and the snakes and beasts of Hades in the *Frogs* of Aristophanes (143, 278).[51]

Unfortunately for Dieterich, the Greek version of the Apocalypse of Peter contains only worms and reptiles. His argument would have been more appropriate in relation to other tours of hell. Worms, however, are absent from the Greek tradition, and snakes are as close as Dieterich is able to get to them. Thus he admits the importance of Isa. 66:24 for the worms in the Apocalypse of Peter.[52] Yet worms are so easily associated with the grave

---

47. Lieberman, "Sins," 44–45.

48. Lieberman (ibid., 45, n. 93) cites Martial 4.5.7; *Scriptores Historiae Augustae: Antonius Pius* 11.1; ibid. *Alexander Severus* 23.8; "and elsewhere."

49. Ginzberg (*Genizah Studies*, 191) assumes that the fragment is an abbreviation of a vision containing seven courts. Thus he considers the fragment late since the idea of seven compartments of hell is relatively late.

50. H. Fischel, "Greek and Latin Languages, Rabbinic Knowledge of," *EJ*.

51. Dieterich, *Nekyia*, 46–54.

52. Ibid., 223.

Table 7. Worms, Beasts, Angels

Text	Isaianic Worm	Worms	Snakes	Lions	Dogs	Dragons/ Vipers/ Scorpions/ Reptiles	Beasts	Others	Angels of Torment
Apoc. Pet. (Eth.)	pl., 1	1	—	—	—	—	2	1	2
Apoc. Pet. (Gk.)	pl., 1	1	—	—	—	1	—	—	2
Acts Th.	—	1	—	—	—	—	—	—	—
Apoc. Zeph.	—	—	—	—	—	—	—	—	3
Apoc. Paul	—	3	—	—	—	1	1	1	3
Eth. Apoc. Mary	—	1	2	1	1	1	—	—	6
Eth. Apoc. Bar.	—	—	2	—	2	1	—	—	1
Apoc. Gorg,	2	1	1	—	—	1	—	—	4
Gk. Apoc. Mary	—	1	—	—	—	—	5	—	—
Apoc. Ezra	1	—	—	—	—	—	1	—	—
Vis. Ezra	1	—	1	2	2	—	1	—	4
T. Isaac	pl., 1	—	—	1	1	—	—	3	—
L. Pach.	—	—	—	—	—	—	—	—	3
Dar. Tesh.	—	—	—	—	—	—	—	—	—
Isa. frag.	—	—	—	—	—	—	—	—	—
Josh. frag.	—	1	—	—	—	—	—	—	—
Ged. Mosh.	—	2	—	—	—	1	—	—	2
Elij. frag.	—	—	—	—	—	—	—	—	—

that more than simply their presence is needed to prove the influence of the passage from Isaiah.

Isa. 66:24 in the Massoretic text reads תולעתם, literally, "their worm." Brown-Driver-Briggs, *A Hebrew and English Lexicon of the Old Testament*, understands תולעתם here as a collective noun. The Greek of Isaiah translates it literally as ὁ σκώληξ αὐτῶν, a singular.[53] The entry in Liddell and Scott, *A Greek-English Lexicon*, offers no reason to regard σκώληξ as collective in normal usage.

Above, echoes of this passage from Isaiah in Sirach and Judith were discussed. The Greek of Sir. 7:17 preserves the singular σκώληξ,[54] while the phrase in Judith reads σκώληκας, the plural. Mark 9:47–48, which seems to be quoting Isaiah, uses the singular. The singular is not the natural form to use in this context in Greek, and thus it seems likely that when the singular appears in the tours of hell, it is a conscious echo of Greek Isaiah or Mark.

Many of the worms preserve another idiosyncrasy of Isaiah's worm, undyingness. Isaiah's verb "to die" is echoed only in Vis. Ezra 34, where the worm is described as *immortalis*,[55] and of course in the quotations in the Joshua b. Levi fragment and *Ged. Mosh.* 18. (In *Ged. Mosh.* 18 the relevant part of the verse is the unquenchable fire, for the torture described is by fire, not worms.) Elsewhere in the tours of hell the worm is called "unwearying" or "never sleeping." These changes in wording are perhaps intended to make Isaiah's point clearer: what Isaiah means is that the corpses experience constant gnawing, not that the worms are immortal.

In Eth. Apoc. Pet. 9 there appears a worm that never sleeps; in the Greek (chap. 27) there are worms that never rest. Apoc. Paul 42 contains a worm that never rests of great size and with two heads. (More ordinary worms also appear in the Apocalypse of Paul; see below.) In Gk. Apoc. Mary 18 and 23 a worm that never rests is mentioned. The same creature appears in Apoc. Ezra 4:20. Vis. Ezra 34 offers a worm similar to that of the Apocalypse of Paul, undying and immense. The Testament of Isaac has worms, in the plural, that sleep not.[56] Finally, although the worms that

---

53. No variants are noted in J. Ziegler, ed., *Septuaginta 14: Isaias* (Göttingen: Vandenhoeck & Ruprecht, 1939).

54. The Hebrew of Sirach here differs substantially from the Greek (see above, p. 109). The term for "worm" is not תולע, but רימה.

55. MS V: *immortalis*; MSS L and H: *inextinguibilis*.

56. The plural is found in both the Sahidic and Bohairic versions of the Testament of Isaac. Both Sahidic and Bohairic of Mark 9:48 have retained the singular. (See *The Coptic Version of the New Testament in the Northern Dialect* [Oxford: Oxford University, 1896] and *The Coptic Version of the New Testament in the Southern Dialect* [Oxford: Oxford University, 1911].) The relevant verse in Isaiah has not been published in either dialect as far as I know. Neither the Ethiopic nor the Arabic version of the Testament of Isaac contains any worms.

Joshua b. Levi sees in hell are not described, in the version of the fragment in *Reshit Ḥokhmah* Elijah quotes the relevant part of Isa. 66 : 24. As Ezra's immense worm and Paul's immense two-headed worm indicate, the careful preservation of the singular in Greek, where it is not natural, has turned Isaiah's poetic expression, which probably means "countless worms," into a monster.

Worms whose sleeping habits are not mentioned are also found in several texts. In Eth. Apoc. Mary (64) some are fiery, while in *Ged. Mosh.* 14 some are black and five hundred parsangs long. Finally, several texts include ordinary worms. It is impossible to know whether the ordinary worms are influenced by the Bible or are simply the natural companions of death.

As the table shows, the texts offer in addition to worms a wide assortment of unfriendly creatures: snakes, lions, dragons, dogs, panthers, vipers, and beasts generally, including a three-headed one. Are the other beasts of the underworld more likely to live up to Dieterich's expectations?

Only a few of these beasts are part of the Greek picture of Hades. What is more, beasts other than worms appear in texts that are unlikely to have felt any direct non-Christian influence. For example, dogs appear in the Ethiopic Apocalypse of Mary and the Ethiopic Apocalypse of Baruch, but it seems unlikely that they were suggested to the authors of these works by Cerberos, the hound of Hades in classical sources.

Most scholars believe that the picture of the netherworld in Coptic texts is Christian, but that it shows the influence of ancient Egyptian beliefs about the land of the dead.[57] Many animals are imagined as tormenters in hieroglyphic texts describing the netherworld. Fire-spitting snakes, crocodiles, birds, and dogs are particularly common. All but crocodiles appear at least once in the tours of hell.[58]

It is worth noting that two of the texts containing beasts, the Apocalypse of Peter and the Testament of Isaac, are probably of Egyptian origin. The demons of the Coptic versions of the Testament of Isaac have animal faces; the human body with animal head is well known in ancient Egypt.

Another tempting conjecture about the beasts is that they develop under the influence of the Acts of the Martyrs.[59] These texts frequently describe

---

57. J. Zandee, *Death as an Enemy* (Leiden: Brill, 1960), 297–307. Zandee does not convince me with his claim that the demotic texts, of which he treats only the Setme tale, differ little from the hieroglyphic texts. But the Egyptian coloring of later Egyptian Christian literature is generally acknowledged.

58. Ibid., 192–97. Perhaps crocodiles equal dragons.

59. Lieberman, "Sins," 48–51, argues that the punishments of the tours of hell were shaped by the tortures of the martyrs.

beasts devouring Christians in the arena.[60] Beasts appear most often in those tours of hell that can be assumed to have felt the influence of the Acts of the Martyrs, later Christian works like the Ethiopic Apocalypse of Mary, the Greek Apocalypse of Mary, and the Ethiopic Apocalypse of Baruch.

But the correspondence between the beasts of the tours of hell and the beasts of the accounts of the martyrs is not particularly close. For example, Eusebius (*Ecclesiastical History* 8.7) mentions bears, boars, and bulls, none of which appear in the tours of hell. One might argue that once the idea of beasts suggested itself to the authors of the tours, from whatever source, it acquired a life of its own. This is certainly the easiest way to account for the three– and ten–headed beasts (Gk. Apoc. Mary 17, 20) and perhaps for the others.

Angels of Torture

Wild beasts are not the only evil creatures whom the inhabitants of hell must face. Angels of torture also contribute to the suffering of sinners. A few of the angels are named, but most are anonymous.[61]

Dieterich understands these angels as the Hellenistic Jewish version of the Furies of Greek literature. While, as often, Dieterich overstates his case,[62] he does adduce a number of plausible parallels to torturing angels in later classical literature.[63] Certainly the punishing angels of the Hebrew Bible are of an entirely different nature. They perform missions of punishment at God's command in this world, but they do not enjoy torturing

---

60. See E. LeBlant, *Les persécuteurs et les martyrs aux premiers siècles de notre ère* (Paris: E. Leroux, 1893), 242–46; and, e.g., Eusebius, *Ecclesiastical History* 5.1; 8; Martyrs of Palestine; Acts of SS. Perpetua and Felicitas.

61. A torturing angel named Ezrael is mentioned in the Apocalypse of Peter. The name of a torturing angel in the Testament of Isaac varies from version to version.

62. Dieterich (*Nekyia*, 54–62) argues for an unbroken development from the Furies of Hades to the torturing angels of our texts. (See von Dobschütz, review of *Nekyia*, 345–46, for a critique of this claim.) To do so he blurs the distinctions between the Furies and other demonic figures. Thus, while originally the Furies were charged with avenging murder, broken oaths, and a few other specific crimes, Dieterich argues that their function expanded to include punishment and torture of all the wicked dead. E. Wüst ("Erinys," PW suppl. 8:118–20), however, argues that the Furies are the products of literature rather than popular imagination. In writers from Aristophanes to Clement of Alexandria, "a Fury from a tragedy" means an overdrawn, melodramatic character. Thus, while there are links between, say, the tormentors of Lucian's Hades and Homer's Furies, the unbroken chain Dieterich describes would have been rejected by members of Lucian's audience.

63. E.g., Virgil, *Aeneid* 6.570; Ovid, *Metamorphoses* 4.451–52; Seneca, *Hercules Furens* 982 (not 989 as in *Nekyia*, 59, n. 1).

their victims as do the angels of the tours of hell. Nor are the fiery angels of Revelation much like the angels of hell; they are not cruel demons, but God's agents in the final drama.

Dieterich follows R. Heinze in considering Philo the first to make the identification of Furies and angels.[64] The evil "angels" of Philo's *On Giants*, however, are not angels of punishment, despite the use of Ps. 78:49 (chap. 17), but rather souls. There are better parallels in Jewish (or Christian) literature.[65]

In the Parables of Enoch, Enoch sees "angels of punishment . . . preparing all the instruments of Satan" (1 Enoch 53:3) and "hosts of the angels of punishment" holding "scourges and chains of iron and bronze" (56:1). In the third heaven of 2 Enoch, Enoch finds "angels cruel and brutal, carrying weapons" (chap. 5). In T. Levi 3:2–3, unarmed angels of punishment are found in the heavens.

None of these texts can be dated and located without controversy. It is likely, however, that more than one is roughly contemporary with the Apocalypse of Peter. It appears, then, that a new class of angels, not to be found in the Bible, was emerging in Judaism and Christianity in the early part of this era, probably under the influence of Greek ideas.

With a few exceptions the presence of angels of torment in the tours of hell is correlated to the presence of environmental punishments. Thus such angels appear in the Apocalypse of Peter, the Apocalypse of Paul and its descendants, later Christian texts, and *Gedulat Moshe*. They appear also in the Apocalypse of Zephaniah, which contains little fire or infernal geography, and in the Vision of Ezra, which has little geography, although some fire. Their almost complete absence from the Ethiopic Apocalypse of Baruch is surprising.

Conclusions About Environmental Punishments

The environmental punishments discussed here do not as a rule appear in significant numbers in those texts where measure-for-measure hanging punishments figure prominently. In the Apocalypse of Peter, the two types of punishment are of more or less equal importance; in the Apocalypse of Paul, environmental punishments dominate, but measure-for-measure hanging punishments also play a role.

---

64. R. Heinze, *Xenokrates* (Leipzig: Teubner, 1892), 112; Dieterich, *Nekyia*, 61.

65. Dieterich (*Nekyia*, 202, n. 3) cites the passage from Sib. Or. 2:287–90. If James ("New Text," 576) is correct, however, this passage merely reflects the Apocalypse of Peter.

Unlike measure-for-measure punishments, environmental punishments are not associated with particular sins, and often a single punishment contains several of the elements discussed above. Texts do not seem to borrow specific punishments from each other. It is the fact of environmental punishments that is transmitted; the development of the various motifs seems to be the work of the individual authors.

Sins and Punishments of the Apocalypse of Paul Family

There are several groups of sins and punishments that are important for understanding the relations among the Apocalypse of Paul, its descendants, and the other Christian texts.

Immersion in the Fiery River

One such punishment, found in Apoc. Paul 31, Eth. Apoc. Mary (61–62), and Grk. Apoc. Mary 5–8, consists of several groups of sinners immersed in a fiery river to different depths. In Eth. Apoc. Bar. (71) sinners are immersed in an abyss of fire. Apoc. Gorg. (87) contains a set of punishments that may be a development of this punishment: sinners are covered to different heights by fire, but there is no indication that it is a single body of fire.

In the Apocalypse of Paul the principle of talion is operating, more obviously in some cases than in others. One group of sinners is immersed to the navel in punishment for fornication, while another group is covered to the lips for slander. The Ethiopic Apocalypse of Mary copies the sins and punishments of the Apocalypse of Paul with some additions. The Greek Apocalypse of Mary retains the principle of talion, but the sins are different. Some of the sins in the Ethiopic Apocalypse of Baruch go back to the Apocalypse of Paul, but the depth of immersion is unrelated to the sin. Both the sins of the Apocalypse of Paul and the principle of talion have disappeared in the Apocalypse of Gorgorios.

One characteristic shared by most of the sins punished in this fashion in the Apocalypse of Paul is their relation to church. Slander is a sin anywhere, but the sin of the slanderers immersed in the river is slander in church. The crime of the fornicators is apparently worse than simple fornication, for they are charged with fornicating even after having partaken of the Eucharist. The attempt to relate ethical sins to the institutions of Christianity can be detected in this punishment in the Ethiopic Apocalypse of Mary and the Ethiopic Apocalypse of Baruch as well, but not in the Greek Apocalypse of Mary or the Apocalypse of Gorgorios.

Sinful Church Officials

This concern for the institutions of Christianity also finds expression in the sinful church officials who figure prominently in Apoc. Paul 34–36, Eth. Apoc. Mary (62–64, 66–67), Eth. Apoc. Bar. (73), and Gk. Apoc. Mary 15–20. The Apocalypse of Paul describes four such figures: a presbyter, a bishop, a deacon, and a lector. In the Ethiopic Apocalypse of Mary and the Greek Apocalypse of Mary the lists are similar, but longer.[66] Eth. Apoc. Bar. (73) contains sinful hermits, deacons, and priests, but also priests and high priests (70), whose presence seems to reflect Falasha editing. The sins committed by these officials of the church are specified, but a component of the sin implicit in all cases is having failed to live up to the office. This is explicit in the Apocalypse of Paul, where, for example, a presbyter "who did not execute his ministry properly" (chap. 34) or a lector who "read to the people but . . . did not keep the commandments of God" (chap. 36) is punished.

Vis. Ezra 45–46 contains what may be a related group, doctors of the law who "mixed up baptism and the law of God." This mysterious sin is not explicated any further. Unlike the titles of the sinful church officials of the other texts, "doctor of the law" does not represent an actual office.

Kings and Princes of the World

Several of the descendants of the Apocalypse of Paul share with one another sins and punishments that do not appear in the Apocalypse of Paul itself. The Ethiopic Apocalypse of Mary, the Ethiopic Apocalypse of Baruch, and the Apocalypse of Gorgorios all contain kings and princes punished in various ways, although no such figures appear in the Apocalypse of Paul. In Eth. Apoc. Mary (64) "kings, leaders, and princes of the earth," charged with pride and the oppression of orphans and widows, hang in fire, bound by fiery chains. In Eth. Apoc. Bar. (72–73) the sins of the

---

66. The Ethiopic Apocalypse of Mary includes a pope (62), a deacon (62–63), a patriarch (63), a priest (63), another deacon (63–64), more priests (66), another priest (66–67), another deacon (67), and monks (67). The Greek Apocalypse of Mary contains a steward (chap. 15), a presbyter (chap. 16), a lector (chap. 17), patriarchs and bishops (chap. 18), female presbyters (chap. 19), and a deaconess (chap. 20).

"kings, governors, and princes"[67] are described at great length, and the description is followed by what appears to be a brief doublet of the punishment.[68] Crimes against orphans and lack of charity are specified among the sins of the first section. In both sections the punishment of the rulers is immersion in a cauldron of fire. In Apoc. Gorg. (86) the kings of the earth are punished with immersion in a fiery river; they hold fiery pails in their hands. In a separate section "the mighty who afflicted the homes of the poor and the strangers with cold and frost" are fittingly punished with cold (87).

The kings and princes of this world[69] appear also in Vis. Ezra 48–49, where they are punished in an enormous furnace. Poor people watch the punishment and accuse them of persecuting the poor and enslaving free men.

The continuity in these texts, then, is in the description of the sin rather than of the punishment. The phrase "of this world" or "of the earth," which describes the kings and princes in the Ethiopic Apocalypse of Mary, the Apocalypse of Gorgorios, and the Vision of Ezra, further suggests a relationship among the texts.[70] Although the punishments in the Ethiopic Apocalypse of Baruch and in the Vision of Ezra are quite close, this is probably coincidence.

The biblical language used to describe the sins of the rulers in the Ethiopic Apocalypse of Mary and the Ethiopic Apocalypse of Baruch links these sinners to the "mighty" of the Apocalypse of Gorgorios and to sinners in two other texts, those who trusted in riches and persecuted widows and orphans (Apoc. Pet. Eth. chap. 9; Gk. chap. 30) and those who persecuted widows, orphans, and the poor and did not hope in the Lord (Apoc. Paul 39).[71] Not hoping in the Lord may be the opposite side of trusting in riches. The punishments are not particularly close. In the Apoc-

---

67. I rely on translations here. I suspect that the middle terms, "*duces*" in Chaîne's Latin translation of the Ethiopic Apocalypse of Mary and "governors" in Leslau's English translation of the Ethiopic Apocalypse of Baruch, represent the same Ethiopic word.

68. The second version contains no independent details that would justify its inclusion. Similar repetition occurs in relation to the church officials.

69. "Princes of this world" according to MSS VH. MS L reads simply "princes."

70. Vision of Ezra: *huius mundi*. Chaîne translates the phrase in the Ethiopic Apocalypse of Mary "*terrae*"; Leslau translates "of the earth" for the Apocalypse of Gorgorios.

71. In Exod. 22:21, the children of Israel are commanded not to oppress widows and orphans. God is described as "father of orphans and judge of widows" in Ps. 68:6. The combination "widows and orphans" is frequent, and it occurs most often in descriptions of God's role as their protector, commandments that Israel not oppress them, and rebukes of Israel for oppressing them.

alypse of Peter the sinners wear filthy rags and are tortured with fiery stones, while in the Apocalypse of Paul their hands and feet are wounded and they stand naked in the cold while worms feed on them. It is tempting to connect the punishment in the Apocalypse of Paul to the punishment of the mighty in the Apocalypse of Gorgorios, but the Apocalypse of Gorgorios so rarely employs details from other texts that I hesitate to do so.

The crucial transformation of persecutors into kings and princes takes place after the Apocalypse of Paul or at least in a form of the Apocalypse of Paul that has not come down to us. It is interesting that the Vision of Ezra shares a detail with the Ethiopic descendants of the Apocalypse of Paul. As will appear below, this is not a unique instance of such sharing.

Finally, in this context reference should be made to the fifth court of the Isaiah fragment, where the "governors, rulers, and treasurers" and Pharaoh himself are punished with smoke (see the discussion of smoke in the Isaiah fragment above).[72] While the status of the sinners is similar, there is nothing in the phrasing of their titles or the description of their sins to suggest a connection with the kings and princes of the world.

Fiery Seats

Eth. Apoc. Mary (62), Eth. Apoc. Bar. (70), and Gk. Apoc. Mary 13 share with the two Ezra apocalypses a punishment that does not appear in the Apocalypse of Paul. This is a fiery seat, used in the Ethiopic Apocalypse of Mary to punish the pope and in the Ethiopic Apocalypse of Baruch to punish priests and high priests. In the Ezra apocalypses (Apoc. Ezra 4: 9–12; Vis. Ezra 37–39), it is Herod who is seated on a fiery throne. The thought in all four texts seems to be that a fiery (official) seat is a fitting punishment for those who abused power.

In the Greek Apocalypse of Mary the fiery seat is put to different use. Those who failed to rise before the presbyters are seated on fiery benches in a different sort of measure-for-measure. As in some of the hanging punishments, the instrument of sin becomes the means of punishment.

In Deut. 24's laws of social justice, the laws about widows and orphans (here linked with sojourners, Deut. 24:17–22) follow the laws about the poor (Deut. 24:14–15). Zech. 7:10 explicitly links the poor to widows and orphans (and again, sojourners): "Do not oppress the widow, the orphan, the sojourner, or the poor. . . ." The Apocalypse of Gorgorios' "strangers" are probably equivalent to sojourners.

72. "Governors, rulers, and treasurers" is the reading of the Geniza fragments. The other versions contain different titles without any obvious difference in sense.

Conclusions About the Sins and Punishments of the Apocalypse of Paul Family

What emerges from these sins and punishments is further confirmation for the view presented above in Chapter 1 that the Ethiopic Apocalypse of Mary stands closest of the descendants to the Apocalypse of Paul. The independence of the Apocalypse of Gorgorios in its descriptions is confirmed. The Ethiopic Apocalypse of Baruch, which shows contact with the Apocalypse of Paul and the Ethiopic Apocalypse of Mary in other areas, reworks the sins and punishments with relative freedom. There are too many striking contacts between the Greek Apocalypse of Mary and the others to dismiss as coincidence, yet the Greek Apocalypse of Mary is a far more independent work than the Ethiopic Apocalypse of Mary or the Ethiopic Apocalypse of Baruch. The absence from the Apocalypse of Paul of the sinful rulers and the fiery seat that appear in the descendent texts may point to a form of the Apocalypse of Paul in which such motifs did appear. Their appearance in the Ezra apocalypses, which requires further clarification, will be discussed in Chapter 5.

THE DEVELOPMENT OF THE TRADITION

In the preceding chapters I argued that both formal features and content indicate that the tours of hell form a tradition. Here I would like to use the evidence accumulated in those chapters to attempt a sketch of the history of the tradition.

THE APOCALYPSE OF PETER AND THE JEWISH TEXTS

Such an attempt must begin with the Apocalypse of Peter, the earliest datable tour of hell. Yet despite its date, there are a number of reasons for suggesting that it is not the fountainhead of the tradition, but only the earliest surviving member. The picture of hell in the Apocalypse of Peter is highly developed, not impossible at the beginning of a tradition, but certainly unexpected. Further, the sins and punishments of the apocalypse suggest that its author drew on preexistent sources.

The presence of very similar or identical sins of speech in two different groups of sins is one hint of the Apocalypse of Peter's use of such sources. At the beginning of the description of hell in the Apocalypse of Peter,[1] three hanging punishments appear: men and women hang by their tongues for blaspheming the way of righteousness, women hang by their hair for fornication,[2] and men hang by their thighs (Gk., feet) for the same sin (Eth. chap. 7; Gk. chaps. 22–24).

---

1. In the Greek text, a general description of the place of punishment precedes the hanging punishments.

2. Before this in both Ethiopic and Greek there appears a fiery punishment for those who denied righteousness (Eth.) or turned away from it (Gk.).

Later in both Ethiopic and Greek there appear several sins of speech with measure-for-measure punishments that do not involve hanging (Eth. chap. 9; Gk. chaps. 28–29). In the Greek text blaspheming the way of righteousness appears for a second time among these sins. In the Ethiopic text the equivalent sin is doubting God's righteousness.

When the measure-for-measure hanging punishments of the Apocalypse of Peter are compared to the similar punishments in the Jewish tours of hell and other Christian tours of hell, the case for the use of sources becomes compelling. (Table 4 in chap. 3 gives a complete picture of the distribution of these punishments.) The closest parallels to the punishments in the Apocalypse of Peter appear in some of the Jewish texts.

We have seen that Jewish texts more or less contemporary with the Apocalypse of Peter, like the Mishnah, had perfected measure-for-measure rewards and punishments in this world, but paid little attention to their usefulness for the next world. The Jewish tours of hell, where measure-for-measure is applied to the dead, are later than the Apocalypse of Peter. In order to explain the relationship between the earliest Christian tour of hell and the Jewish tours, we need to reconstruct the development of the Jewish tours.[3]

Lieberman's Reconstruction of the Development of the Jewish Tours of Hell

Lieberman offers the following picture:[4]

The story in the Palestinian Talmud discussed above is the earliest of the Jewish texts. It is set at the time of Simeon b. Sheṭaḥ, and the amoraim no longer know the meaning of Miriam's punishment; this shows that it is very early indeed.[5] The lack of measure-for-measure in the two versions of Miriam's punishment is another sign of earliness: in the Apocalypse of Peter the punishment does not always fit the crime; in the later tours of hell such correspondence is more prevalent.[6]

---

3. M. Gaster's claim ("Hebrew Visions," 571–72) that the Hebrew texts are the ancestors of even the earliest Christian works, offered without any supporting argument, cannot be taken seriously. The unstated presupposition is that Christian literature of this kind can borrow from Jewish literature, but that Jewish literature cannot borrow from Christian. This is not an uncommon point of view, but it is demonstrably false. Gaster is sensible enough to admit that Hebrew texts like *Gedulat Moshe* are probably not at present in their original, Second Temple form.

4. "Sins." Lieberman summarizes his family tree for the Jewish texts on 48. See Figure 1.

5. Ibid., 34.

6. Ibid., 36.

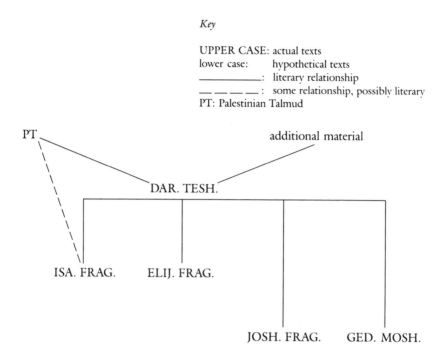

Key

UPPER CASE: actual texts
lower case: hypothetical texts
————————: literary relationship
— — — — : some relationship, possibly literary
PT: Palestinian Talmud

PT

additional material

DAR. TESH.

ISA. FRAG.   ELIJ. FRAG.

JOSH. FRAG.   GED. MOSH.

Figure 1. Lieberman's Family Tree for Jewish Texts

This last argument is based on a false premise. The Apocalypse of Peter has relatively as many or more measure-for-measure punishments than most of the later Christian texts. (See Table 2.)

For Lieberman, the "unknown midrash" on which R. Meir of Rothenburg drew in *Darkhei Teshuvah* is the next stage of development after the Palestinian Talmud. It contains the Palestinian Talmud's story and additional material. The sin of the woman with the pivot through her ear has been transformed to make it measure-for-measure, as has the sin of the women who hang by their breasts.

Both the Elijah fragment and the Isaiah fragment drew on this unknown midrash. The first court of the Isaiah fragment contains a variation on the punishment of the tax collector in the Palestinian Talmud and the unknown midrash: the punishment of the water-carriers of hell. In place of a pivot in the ear for gossip in the unknown midrash, the Isaiah fragment has men hanging by their tongues in the second court. The fifth court differs more significantly from the fifth compartment of the unknown midrash. The unknown midrash punishes those whose chatter leads them away from Torah, while in the Isaiah fragment the court is occupied by the princes of the world.[7]

Further, Lieberman argues, the Isaiah fragment shows a clear instance of dependence on the Palestinian Talmud. The first Geniza manuscript of the Isaiah fragment has women hanging by the "threads of their breasts," as does the Chronicles of Yeraḥme'el. The other texts of the Isaiah fragment omit the difficult "threads" altogether; perhaps it was confusing. Lieberman shows that "threads" is either a scribal error for or a misunderstanding of the rare word for "nipples" in the passage from the Palestinian Talmud where Miriam is said to be hanging by the nipples of her breasts. The word is so rare that, for Lieberman, it must have come to the Isaiah fragment from the Palestinian Talmud.[8] Lieberman does not make it clear whether he believes that this rare phrase was once found in the unknown midrash, which he has identified as the immediate source of the Isaiah fragment, or whether he assumes that the author of the Isaiah fragment knew both the passage in the Palestinian Talmud and the unknown midrash.

The dependence of the Elijah fragment on the unknown midrash is shown by the recurrence of the hanging punishments and by the similarity of the morals of the two stories: "By the limb with which each man sinned, by the same limb will he be punished" (Elijah fragment) and "The limbs that committed the sin are punished in Gehenna more than the other limbs" (*Darkhei Teshuvah*).[9] The latest descendants of the Palestinian Talmud through the unknown midrash are the Joshua b. Levi fragment and *Gedulat Moshe*.[10]

A difficulty in Lieberman's interpretation of the "threads" of the breasts in the Isaiah fragment has already been noted: Lieberman seems to make the fragment depend directly on the Palestinian Talmud for the threads, but not for the rest of its contents. The situation could be explained by suggesting that a scribe who copied the fragment was familiar with the passage in the Palestinian Talmud and added the word. A learned Jew in the Middle Ages might have known such a passage, since the Palestinian Talmud achieved normative status, although of a limited kind. But it is also possible that both the Palestinian Talmud and the Isaiah fragment drew on an earlier text that contained the unusual word.

---

7. Ibid., 37–45. I am spelling out the reasoning implicit in Lieberman's arguments.

8. Ibid., 38–39. Lieberman refers only to the reading of the first Geniza MS. For the Chronicles of Yeraḥme'el, see Stone's transcription of the MS (*Elijah*, 21, 23). Gaster ignores the difficulty, translating simply "breasts" (*Chronicles of Jerahmeel*, 36).

9. Lieberman, "Sins," 47.

10. Ibid., 48, n. 108.

Another objection to Lieberman's theory is that the parallel between the story from the Palestinian Talmud and the Setme tale suggests that hanging by the breasts may not be an integral part of the story from the Palestinian Talmud. Gressmann even argued that Miriam herself was not part of the original story and that the pivot was at first in the tax collector's ear.[11]

A third weakness in Lieberman's argument is his claim that the morals drawn by the Elijah fragment and *Darkhei Teshuvah* indicate literary dependence. The two sentences make somewhat different points, both rather obvious, which certainly do not constitute grounds for a claim of literary dependence (see the discussion of the Elijah fragment in chap. 1, above).

Fourth, Lieberman views the punishment of the first court of the Isaiah fragment as close enough to the tantalization of the Palestinian Talmud and *Darkhei Teshuvah* to be literarily dependent on them. (See chap. 3, above, on water-carriers in the Isaiah fragment for a discussion of the first court of the Isaiah fragment.) In fact, the punishments are quite different in their specifics. In the Palestinian Talmud and *Darkhei Teshuvah* a wicked man stands near water, thirsting, and yet is unable to drink. In the Isaiah fragment people carry pitchers in an attempt to fill a bottomless well, but "are not permitted" to drink. It is difficult to see why these two forms of tantalization imply any sort of relationship between the texts in which they appear.[12]

An Alternate Reconstruction

Against Lieberman's picture of almost linear development from the Palestinian Talmud to the unknown midrash to the Elijah fragment and the Isaiah fragment (Figure 1), I prefer to suggest the existence of a source or sources earlier than the Palestinian Talmud (see Figure 2). This source contributed the hanging punishments to the Apocalypse of Peter and the Isaiah fragment; some of those in the Elijah fragment; perhaps through the Isaiah fragment, those of *Darkhei Teshuvah*; and perhaps the punishment of hanging by the breasts to the Palestinian Talmud. This source

---

11. Gressmann, *Armen Mann*, 17.

12. Lieberman, "Sins," 38–40. Lieberman himself seems to have second thoughts. While "it is possible that the kernel of the vision in the first house is found in the Palestinian Talmud," the language in which the punishment is described in the Isaiah fragment "reminds us very well" of Apoc. Paul 39 (41). But in his summary of his genealogy for the texts he discusses (48), Lieberman does not pursue his own suggestion about the source used by *Darkhei Teshuvah* in addition to the Palestinian Talmud (40), nor does he develop the possibility that the Isaiah fragment drew on the Apocalypse of Paul.

would have contained the core of sins and punishments discussed above: men hanging by their genitals and women hanging by their hair or breasts for sexual sins[13] and those who sinned in word hanging by their tongues.

According to this theory the Elijah fragment is quite independent of the Palestinian Talmud. The Palestinian Talmud would have contributed the first two punishments of *Darkhei Teshuvah* and perhaps have influenced the Isaiah fragment's first court, but more likely not.

It is difficult to decide whether the other measure-for-measure punishments found in the Elijah fragment and in two early Christian texts, the Acts of Thomas and the Apocalypse of Paul, represent developments of this core group or different traditions. The Elijah fragment contains all three of the measure-for-measure hanging punishments common to the Apocalypse of Peter and the other Jewish texts; some of its additional measure-for-measure hanging punishments have parallels in other tours of hell (see chap. 3, above, under hanging in hell).

Despite the view of some scholars that it is directly dependent on the Apocalypse of Peter for its sins and punishments (see chap. 1, above), the Acts of Thomas shares only two combinations of sin and punishment with the Apocalypse of Peter and the Jewish texts: women hanging by their hair for immodesty, and people hanging by their tongues for sins of speech. The Acts of Thomas also contains men hanging by their feet for rushing to do evil. The adulterers who hang by their loins in the Ethiopic version of the Apocalypse of Peter and by their genitals in the Jewish texts hang by their feet in the Greek version of the Apocalypse of Peter. It seems possible that "rushing to do evil" implies sexual sin and that this combination of sin and punishment in the Acts of Thomas is derived from the more clearly expressed combination found in the other texts. The fourth hanging punishment of the Acts of Thomas is hanging by the hands for stealing and lack of charity. The only parallel to this combination appears in *Gedulat Moshe*; the parallel is probably coincidental.

It is not impossible that the Acts of Thomas took its four hanging punishments from the three of the Apocalypse of Peter, modifying one considerably and adding another. But if the Apocalypse of Peter drew on Jewish traditions from the turn of the era used also by the Jewish tours of hell, the Acts of Thomas too might have drawn on such traditions. Both the simi-

---

13. I do not know how to explain Christian use of hair where the Jewish texts have breasts as the sinful limb for women's sexual offenses (see above, pp. 73–74). It is possible that the difference is an accident. Perhaps there existed two Jewish traditions, one of which happens to have been preserved by Jews while the other was preserved by Christians. But the consistency of the Jewish use of breasts and the Christian use of hair suggests that a real preference is involved.

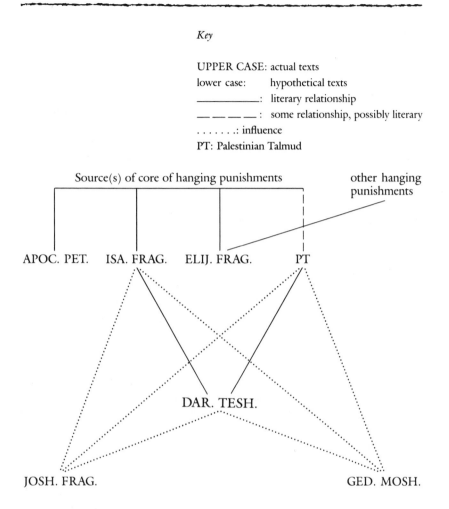

Key

UPPER CASE: actual texts
lower case: hypothetical texts
_____: literary relationship
_ _ _ _ :   some relationship, possibly literary
. . . .: influence
PT: Palestinian Talmud

Source(s) of core of hanging punishments   other hanging punishments

APOC. PET.   ISA. FRAG.   ELIJ. FRAG.   PT

DAR. TESH.

JOSH. FRAG.   GED. MOSH.

Figure 2. My Family Tree for Jewish Texts

larities and the differences between the Acts of Thomas and the Apocalypse of Peter are easier to understand as the result not of literary dependence but of the use of the same traditions.[14]

Nor does the Apocalypse of Paul draw its hanging punishments from the Apocalypse of Peter, although it shows other signs of relationship to

14. A. F. J. Klijn (*Acts of Thomas*, 251–53) makes much the same argument in his discussion of the question of which version of the hell passage in the Acts of Thomas is prior. He does

the earlier work. The sinful limb of the male adulterers in the Apocalypse of Paul is the eyebrow. This choice of limb is not without parallel (see the discussion of hanging in hell in chap. 3, above), and it probably represents another tradition available in the early centuries of this era.

The picture of the situation in those centuries that emerges from this discussion is as follows: The sins and measure-for-measure hanging punishments shared by the Apocalypse of Peter and the Jewish tours of hell had been brought together, perhaps as a part of an early Jewish tour of hell. Other sins and measure-for-measure punishments were known, but there is no clear evidence that they circulated in groups.

Jewish Texts Borrowing from Christian?

A competing explanation for the material the undoubtedly early and Christian Apocalypse of Peter has in common with later Jewish texts is that the Jewish texts borrowed from contemporary Christian texts that drew directly on the Apocalypse of Peter. This seems at first a more plausible explanation than the one I have just proposed. It was my expectation when I began my work that it would prove to be the best explanation. After all, medieval Jewish political apocalypses show close contacts with the Christian apocalypses of their times. The relationship between these Jewish and Christian texts and their sources has not been worked out in detail, but books like W. Bousset's *Antichrist Legend*, written almost a century ago, or K. Berger's recent study of a medieval Greek Daniel apocalypse, *Die griechische Daniel-Diegese*, make it clear that the relationship is more than the use of some of the same canonical texts would ensure.[15] The apocalyp-

---

not view the similarities of the Acts of Thomas and the Apocalypse of Peter as demonstrating the dependence of the Acts on the apocalypse. He argues, as I have, that both texts drew on Jewish traditions. In doing so, however, he accepts uncritically the claims of M. Gaster, quoting approvingly (252 n. 4) Gaster's statement "All these Christian Revelations are based directly upon those Hebrew visions" ("Hebrew Visions," 571). Klijn notes A. Marmorstein's caution ("Jüdische Parallelen zur Petrus Apokalypse," *Zeitschrift für die neutestamentliche Wissenschaft* 10[1909] : 297–300) about the late dates of the Jewish texts cited by Gaster, but argues, "It is . . . hardly possible that Jewish apocalypses borrowed from Christian sources" (252, n. 3). The a priori nature of this claim, which is demonstrably wrong, should be obvious. (See, e.g., below, n. 15, on medieval Daniel apocalypses.)

15. W. Bousset, *The Antichrist Legend*, prologue and trans. A. H. Keane (London: Hutchinson & Co., 1896), 101–12. K. Berger, *Die griechische Daniel-Diegese* (Leiden: Brill, 1976). Stone and Strugnell, *Elijah*, collect texts that indicate the existence of a tradition of description of the appearance of the antichrist, widely diffused in Jewish and Christian materials.

tic traditions of medieval Islam also show ties to contemporary Christian works.[16]

The Isaiah fragment and the Elijah fragment, however, look very little like the visions of hell that proliferate in the Christian Middle Ages: the redactions of the Apocalypse of Paul and a series of more innovative visions in the West, the Ethiopic descendants of Paul, the visions of the Life of Pachomios and the Testament of Isaac in Egypt, or the Ezra apocalypses and the Greek Apocalypse of Mary in the Greek East. None of these texts preserves even the two measure-for-measure hanging punishments found in the Apocalypse of Paul, although the Apocalypse of Ezra and the Greek Apocalypse of Mary contain one relevant hanging punishment each.

Another possibility is that the later Jewish texts drew on the Muslim visions of hell. This solution seems particularly appropriate for the Isaiah fragment, which we know to have been transmitted in Muslim countries because it appears in the Cairo Geniza. Yet while hanging is not absent as a punishment in the Muslim texts, it is not particularly prominent. The measure-for-measure hanging punishments that do appear are the same core found in the Jewish and Christian texts. In one text (Asín's 2B), immodest women hang by their hair, false witnesses hang by their tongues, and adulterous women hang by their breasts. In another text (*Book of the Ladder*, chap. 79), men and women hang by their genitals for adultery.[17] But the relative lack of importance of hanging in these texts and the failure of the three types of hanging characteristic of the Jewish tours to appear in any one text make it unlikely that the Jewish tours are borrowing from the Muslim. The presence of women hanging by their hair and women hanging by their breasts in a single text may suggest the use of both Jewish and Christian traditions by the Muslim text.

For a moment, let us assume that the Apocalypse of Peter was readily available in the Middle Ages. (As far as can be determined, it was not; see

---

Striking evidence of literary borrowing, pointed out to me by Stone, is the epithet ἐπτάλοφος, "seven-hilled," for Rome in both the Greek Daniel apocalypse published by Berger (see his index) and, transliterated in Hebrew characters, in the Hebrew Vision of Daniel (ed. Y. ibn Shmuel, *Midreshei Geulah* [Jerusalem and Tel Aviv: Mosad Bialik, 1954], 252, line 32). While Rev. 17:9 refers to the seven hills of the wicked city, it does not use the term ἐπτάλοφος. The term does, however, appear in classical sources, according to Liddell and Scott, *A Greek-English Lexicon*.

16. A. Abel, "Changements politiques et littérature eschatologique dans le monde musulman," *Studia Islamica* 2(1954):23–43.

17. In Asín's text 1A, two hanging punishments, by the knees and by the legs, appear; the hanging itself is not measure-for-measure. One nonmeasure-for-measure hanging punishment, hanging by the feet, appears in Asín's 2B in addition to the three measure-for-measure hanging punishments. Asín's texts 1B and 3 contain no hanging punishments at all.

under the Apocalypse of Peter in chap. 1, above.) In addition to hanging punishments and in greater quantity, the Apocalypse of Peter contains fiery punishments. Above (chap. 1) it was argued that the gridiron of the Elijah fragment may not be original. Granting that it is, the Jewish texts contain fire only there and in the burning valley of the Elijah fragment, the smoke of the fifth court of the Isaiah fragment, and the fire-and-snow punishment of the Joshua b. Levi fragment. Fire is an important form of punishment only in *Gedulat Moshe*. Yet the dominant image of hell in classical rabbinic literature and the medieval midrashim is fiery.[18] Thus it is difficult to understand why a medieval Jewish author borrowing from the Apocalypse of Peter or a related text would fail to borrow some fire as well. The theory of medieval Jewish borrowing, for all its inherent plausibility, simply does not work in this case. Instead it appears that the Apocalypse of Peter, the other early Christian texts, and the Jewish texts drew on a tradition that predated them all.

The Date of the Isaiah Fragment

In this regard it is interesting to note that the Isaiah fragment, in content, if not in form, shows signs of being much earlier than the fact that it first appears in the Cairo Geniza might suggest. Three of its five punishments belong to the core of hanging punishments just discussed. One of the punishments in the first court is that of the water-carriers of Hades known from classical sources, a common motif on sarcophagi. (See chap. 3, above.) If Lieberman is correct, the punishment of the fifth court relies on a Latin wordplay for its effect. (See the discussion of smoke in the Isaiah fragment in chap. 4, above.) Neither punishment, then, is likely to derive from a period or location in which Greco-Roman paganism had been completely submerged and Latin was no longer a language with which Jews were likely to have contact.

The form of the Isaiah fragment, on the other hand, shows signs of lateness. In the Geniza manuscripts and the Chronicles of Yeraḥme'el, the first

---

18. See Blau, "Gehenna," *JE*, and B. Kedar, "Netherworld: In the Aggadah," *EJ*. The picture of hell is more developed in the medieval midrashim than in classical rabbinic sources. The difference between the Isaiah fragment or the Joshua b. Levi fragment and the other descriptions is well illustrated by a glance at the other short works found with the Joshua b. Levi fragment in the "Tractate of Gehenna" (*Bet ha-Midrasch* 1:147–49). One describes the five kinds of fire in Gehenna in some detail. The next describes how the wicked are tortured with both fire and snow. The last describes seven fiery levels of hell and rivers of fire.

three courts contain proof texts in good rabbinic fashion.[19] These proof texts are missing in the version of the Isaiah fragment in *Bet ha-Midrasch*. It seems likely that the Geniza manuscripts are the earliest forms of the fragment that have survived. The absence of the proof texts in *Bet ha-Midrasch* almost certainly does not indicate an earlier form of the work. Probably the absence is best explained as a scribe's abbreviation.

The Isaiah fragment, then, may be a rare phenomenon, the remnant of a Jewish apocalypse that originated in Second Temple times and that was transmitted in Hebrew by Jews. The history of the Elijah fragment, preserved in a Latin Christian document of perhaps the fifth century, is more typical of early Jewish apocalypses. James at the beginning of the century and Stone and Strugnell more recently suggest that a tour of hell was part of a now lost Elijah apocalypse of the Second Temple period.[20] Stone and Strugnell include the Isaiah fragment in their collection of Elijah apocrypha; it is related to them both by content and by the attribution to Seder Eliyyahu in the first Geniza manuscript. But it does not seem implausible that a tour of hell was once found in an Isaiah apocalypse as well. The Ascension of Isaiah, preserved in Ethiopic, Latin, and Slavonic in a Christian form, could be descended from a Jewish Isaianic tour that included hell. (See the discussion below on ascent apocalypses and merkavah mysticism.)

The Transmission of Literature of the Second Temple Period into the Middle Ages

The Isaiah fragment presents a puzzle. How do early Jewish traditions survive outside the mainstream of rabbinic literature during the period of the formation of the Talmud to reemerge in the post-Talmudic Middle Ages? The Isaiah fragment is not the only example of such traditions. The midrashim of the school of R. Moses the Preacher of Narbonne in the eleventh century, for example, know traditions found otherwise only in 1 Enoch, Jubilees, and the Testaments of the Twelve Patriarchs.[21] Yet none of these

---

19. For Chronicles of Yeraḥme'el, see Stone's transcription of the MS (*Elijah*, 21,23). Gaster omits the prooftexts from his English translation (*Chronicles of Jerahmeel*, 36–37), probably because he does not believe them to be original. (See his comments on prooftexts in "Hebrew Visions," 572.)

20. James, *LAOT*, 61; Stone and Strugnell, *Elijah*, 1.

21. H. Albeck, introduction to *Midraš Berešit Rabbati* (Jerusalem: Mekize Nirdamim,

three works was available in western Europe at that time as far as we know.

In the case of the Testaments of the Twelve Patriarchs, I believe that R. Moses must have had access to the Greek text (or a Hebrew translation of the Greek).[22] That is, he must have known the work in its final Christian form, rather than Jewish traditions from Second Temple times that were used in the Testaments. Since R. Moses' Christian neighbors did not yet have access to the Testaments of the Twelve Patriarchs, another avenue of transmission must be sought. A Byzantine–South Italian connection seems plausible in the light of contacts between the Jews of Provence and Italy.

But no such Byzantine solution will do for 1 Enoch and Jubilees;[23] neither was preserved for long in Greek. Could R. Moses have had access to a Hebrew version of Jubilees, as has been claimed with little evidence beyond the parallels,[24] or were these pseudepigrapha, preserved today primarily in Ethiopic, also translated into Arabic for Arabic-speaking Christians and then transmitted through Muslim channels to Spain and a European Jewish community? The fact that much of Ethiopic literature was translated from Arabic intermediaries lends plausibility to such a conjecture,[25] but in order to evaluate such a theory it would be necessary to engage in a close study of any reflexes of these pseudepigrapha that can be perceived in Arabic literature, both Christian and Muslim, of the early Middle Ages.[26]

While it is possible that Arabic sources and Muslim transmitters provide an answer to the puzzle of R. Moses the Preacher's knowledge of pseudepigraphic traditions, the available Muslim tours of hell do not explain the Isaiah fragment. The Muslim texts, as indicated above, contain many strictly Muslim peculiarities and few of the features that distinguish the Jewish texts.

Why are there no tours of hell preserved in classical rabbinic literature? Lieberman notes the puzzling fact that the measure-for-measure principle that the rabbis had perfected for this world is rarely employed for the

---

1940), 5, 17–18, for suggestions about knowledge of the pseudepigrapha. Albeck is certainly guilty of parallelomania here, but the parallels to the texts mentioned above are significant.

22. See M. Himmelfarb, "R. Moses the Preacher and the Testaments of the Twelve Patriarchs," *AJS review* 9 (forthcoming).

23. Himmelfarb, "A Report on Enoch in Rabbinic Literature," SBL Seminar Papers, 1978, 1:262–63, 266.

24. Ibid., 1:268–69, n. 24.

25. See chap. 1, n. 12, for references to the discussion of Ethiopic translation from Arabic.

26. Even someone well qualified to make such a study would be handicapped by the tremendous amount of Arabic literature that remains unpublished.

next.[27] I can go no further than the standard generalization that the rabbis were wary of apocalypses. One feature of the tours of hell might have made them particularly an object of disapproval: in order to serve their monitory purpose, their contents must be told publicly. Thus they differ from other apocalypses and from the merkavah literature not only tolerated but apparently propagated by the rabbis, which is intended to remain the private possession of a relatively small circle.

Conclusions

The demonstrative explanations of the Apocalypse of Peter suggest that it is best viewed in the context of Jewish apocalyptic literature. Its hanging punishments seem to derive from Jewish traditions that must have appeared in at least one Jewish apocalypse of the Second Temple period. The Apocalypse of Peter, then, is the successor of earlier Jewish tours of hell.

THE ENVIRONMENTAL PUNISHMENTS

The history of transmission of the environmental tortures that constitute the major part of the remaining punishments in the Apocalypse of Peter is relatively straightforward. After the Apocalypse of Peter, this type of punishment appears in the Apocalypse of Paul, its descendants, and other later Christian texts.

While the Apocalypse of Peter is the first tour of hell in which a picture of the geography of hell drawn from a range of Jewish and Greek sources appears, there is no reason to believe that the Apocalypse of Peter did not have predecessors in this respect as well, which, given its early date, may again be Jewish predecessors. It seems unlikely that the early works preserved in the Isaiah fragment and the Elijah fragment contained such punishments; if they did, it is difficult to understand why the hanging punishments were preserved, while the picture of a fiery hell, so much closer to the view that dominates medieval Jewish and Christian literature, was not.

It is primarily through the influence of the Apocalypse of Paul that these

---

27. "These earlier rabbinic sources and many others do not portray the topography of Gehenna in its details, its dimensions, compartments, divisions and subdivisions. They do not mention the refined tortures of Gehenna, their minutiae, and the ramified penal code which governs Hades. The rabbis certainly lacked neither the imagination nor the legal mind required for such descriptions" (Lieberman, "Some Aspects of After Life," 496).

environmental punishments reach later Christian texts. But how do they reach the Apocalypse of Paul? To phrase the question differently, it is clear that the Apocalypse of Peter and the Apocalypse of Paul are related, but what is the nature of that relationship?

THE APOCALYPSE OF PETER AND THE APOCALYPSE OF PAUL

In his introduction to the Apocalypse of Paul, James writes, "I have not marked the parallels with *Peter*: the reader cannot miss them. . . ."[28] In "The Revelation of Peter," however, James has provided a list of the correspondences that lead him to regard the Apocalypse of Paul as a descendant of the Apocalypse of Peter.[29]

Despite his immense learning and his usually sound judgment, James, who lived at the height of the era of parallel collecting (as, for example, in the introductions in *APOT*), was not immune to that tendency. Some of the parallels he enumerates are no more than similar phrases that occur in both texts: for example, "The light (of the city) was beyond the light of the world" (Gk. Apoc. Paul 23); and "exceeding bright with light" (Gk. Apoc. Pet. 15), of the fields of the blessed. Others are phrases so easily arrived at for a description of hell that they show little about dependence: for example, "being led away into a dark place" (Gk. Apoc. Paul 39); and "cast into a dark place" (Gk. Apoc. Pet. 27). But most problematic of all for the argument that the Apocalypse of Paul is the direct descendant of the Apocalypse of Peter are the parallels in the descriptions of sins and punishments. The parallels indicate a common stock of sins and methods of punishment, but for many of them the similarities turn out to be less striking than the differences. These supposed parallels are treated individually in an appendix below.

Significant Parallels

There are, however, several parallels significant enough to suggest that the Apocalypse of Paul knew the Apocalypse of Peter or a close relative. Some are noted by James, who was interested in verbal parallels rather than in parallels of content; others are not.

---

28. *ApNT*, 525, n. 2.

29. James's "The Revelation of Peter" appears in J. A. Robinson and M. R. James, *The Gospel According to Peter and the Revelation of Peter* (London: C. J. Clay & Sons, 1892). James (66–67) uses the Greek text of the Apocalypse of Paul rather than the Latin, either because he

Elements of the following appear on James's list:

1. The punishment of the women who committed infanticide in Apoc. Paul 40, fire and devouring beasts, is not unlike the second of the two punishments for abortion and infanticide in Eth. Apoc. Pet. 8, devouring beasts that spring from the congealed milk that flows from the mothers' breasts.

2. Punishments of wearing rags or dark clothing appear in both apocalypses. The crimes for which men and women wear rags (and suffer other tortures) in the Apocalypse of Peter (Eth. chap. 9, Gk. chap. 30) are trust in riches and cruelty toward widows and orphans. In Apoc. Paul 40, rags are part of the punishment for those who seemed to lead a monastic life but "showed no charity and had no pity on the widows and fatherless" (*ApNT*). Girls who lost their virginity wear dark clothing in both Eth. Apoc. Pet. 11 and in Apoc. Paul 39. (See chap. 3 above.)

3. In both texts people chew on their tongues in punishment for sins of speech. In Eth. Apoc. Pet. 9, the sin is slander and doubting God's righteousness; in Gk. Apoc. Pet. 29 the sin is false witness.[30] In Apoc. Paul 37 the sin has become ecclesiastical: mocking the word of God in church.

Two other parallels worth considering are not noted by James:

4. Women who engaged in fornication hang by their hair in the Apocalypse of Peter, while men hang by their loins (Gk., feet) (Eth. chap. 7, Gk. chap. 24). In Apoc. Paul 39, Paul sees men and women hanging by their eyebrows and their hair for adultery.[31]

5. The final punishment that the Apocalypse of Peter and the Apocalypse

---

wants to be able to compare the wording of two Greek texts, or because he believed the Greek to be more original; he does not make his reasons clear (65). Of course, in 1892 the only version of the Apocalypse of Peter known was the Greek. James uses the numeration of his own edition of the Apocalypse of Peter, published in this volume. It does not correspond to any other edition of the Akhmim text that I know. In what follows, I have substituted the more commonly used numeration for James's.

30. Eth. Apoc. Pet. 11 also mentions slaves who were not obedient to their masters chewing their tongues.

31. Silverstein, *Visio*, 31, points out that the Coptic version of the Apocalypse of Paul echoes the explanation for the punishment of the women found in the Apocalypse of Peter while altering the punishment. In the Apocalypse of Peter the punishment is explained thus: "These are they who plaited their hair, not to create beauty, but to turn to fornication, and that they might ensnare the souls of men to destruction" (HSW). The Coptic version of the Apocalypse of Paul reads, "And I saw some men and some women suspended head downwards; and great torches of fire were burning before their faces, and dragon-serpents were girt about their bodies and were devouring them. . . . 'These are the women who used to beautify themselves with the paints and unguents of the Devil, and then go to church to find occasions for committing adultery, and not [to seek] their lawful husbands . . .'" (Budge, *Coptic Texts*, 1063; Coptic 14a–14b).

of Paul have in common is blindness for hypocrisy or incomplete righteousness (Eth. Apoc. Pet. 12, Apoc. Paul 40) (see chap. 3, above). This punishment is particularly interesting because it appears also in the Apocalypse of Zephaniah. The Apocalypse of Paul seems to combine elements of the punishment of the Apocalypse of Peter with elements of the sin of the Apocalypse of Zephaniah. On other grounds it is likely that the Apocalypse of Paul knew both the Apocalypse of Zephaniah and the Apocalypse of Peter.

The Nature of the Relationship

The parallels between the Apocalypse of Peter and the Apocalypse of Paul suggest a relationship between the two texts closer than one would expect in unrelated works of the same genre, but they do not point decisively to literary borrowing. (By "literary" I mean that the author of one text actually had access to a copy of the other text.)

The episode of the infanticides is the most dramatic example. Is the version in the Apocalypse of Paul literarily dependent on the episode in the Apocalypse of Peter? Or is it a revision done from memory? This punishment is one of the most striking in the Apocalypse of Peter; perhaps the author of the Apocalypse of Paul had read the Apocalypse of Peter before commencing his own work and remembered the episode, but not all its details.

On the other hand, it is possible that the Apocalypse of Paul's version of the episode is in no way indebted to the Apocalypse of Peter. As an examination of the range of forms this punishment takes in other tours of hell demonstrates, the versions in these two apocalypses are not particularly close (see the discussion of punishment for abortion and infanticide in chap. 3, above). The authors of both texts may have drawn the raw materials for their versions of the episode from a third tour of hell, now lost, or from some other kind of source. This would help to explain the fact that the Ezra apocalypses, which do not otherwise show close contacts with the Apocalypse of Peter, know a form of the punishment very similar to Peter's; perhaps they drew on Peter's source.

But a textual source may be too concrete. Perhaps two authors drew independently on a well-known tradition or traditions, not necessarily written. The descriptions in the Apocalypse of Elijah and the Life of Shenouti of a torture particularly similar to the punishment of the infanticides in the Vision of Ezra show that the punishment, if not its application measure-for-measure, was known outside the tours of hell. The punishment of blindness raises similar questions. The sin and punishment as they appear in the Apocalypse of Paul combine features of the versions in the Apocalypse of Peter and the Apocalypse of Zephaniah. Is it reasonable to suggest that the author of the Apocalypse of Paul was consciously attempting to combine them? If so, why is there so little other evidence of literary borrowing from the Apocalypse of Peter? If not, how are the similarities to be explained? Again we must appeal to hypothetical common sources, texts and traditions.

Clarity about the range of possibilities for relationships among texts is of great importance for the study of the pseudepigrapha. All historians are limited to what has survived, but for the student of pseudepigrapha what has survived represents a small fraction of what once was, as James's *Lost Apocrypha of the Old Testament* and Stone and Strugnell's *Books of Elijah* demonstrate. The fact that important texts like the Assumption of Moses and 3 Baruch have survived in only one or two manuscripts is further confirmation of the high rate of loss of such texts. Many of the theological and social factors at work in consigning these texts to oblivion, particularly early in this era, have been the subject of scholarly examination; the mechanics of and motivation for transmission need to be studied in much more detail.[32]

In any case it is obviously wrong to proceed in the discussion of the relationship between texts like the Apocalypse of Peter and the Apocalypse of Paul as if all the pieces of the jigsaw puzzle were on the table and needed only to be put together. Many of the puzzle pieces are missing, and there is little hope of ever finding them. Thus it may be misguided to attempt to put all the extant pieces together. Large gaps in the puzzle may be the sign of an accurate reconstruction.

The analogy of the jigsaw puzzle is helpful in making the point about the evidence forever lost to us. It is also useful negatively, for in some ways the analogy of the jigsaw puzzle is misleading. While puzzle pieces can take an endless variety of shapes, there are only two possible relationships between pieces. Either they fit together or they do not. Texts can be related by direct literary dependence at one extreme or unconscious borrowing at the other, by use of common sources, written and oral, and by complicated

---

32. R. A. Kraft's paper, "The Pseudepigrapha in Christianity," read at the Studiorum Novi Testamenti Societas meeting at Duke University in August 1976, sets out the methodological problems that so many students of the pseudepigrapha have ignored and suggests some lines of research.

chains of influence. It is often impossible to specify the precise nature of the relationship between two texts. The examples considered above can reasonably be interpreted in a number of different ways.[33]

To return to the question of the relationship between the Apocalypse of Peter and the Apocalypse of Paul, three points need to be made. First, there is no compelling evidence of literary dependence. Second, there is no reason to assume that these two early Christian tours of hell stood alone. If other such tours had survived, a different picture of the development of the tradition might have emerged. Finally, it is safe to conclude that the similarities of the Apocalypse of Paul to the Apocalypse of Peter indicate that by the time of the Apocalypse of Paul a genre had come into existence.

APPENDIX: JAMES'S LIST OF PARALLELS OF THE APOCALYPSE OF PAUL
TO THE APOCALYPSE OF PETER

Here I intend to justify my dismissal of most of James's parallels by examining them one by one. I quote the phrase from the Apocalypse of Paul according to James's listing. Even when James cites the Greek version of the Apocalypse of Paul, as he does for all but the last several examples, I give the chapter numbers of the more widely available Latin text. I give references to the Apocalypse of Peter in Greek according to the more standard numeration. (See above, n. 29.) I do not quote the phrase from the Apocalypse of Peter at the beginning of the entry; it is provided in the course of the discussion.

1. "The place of the just" (Apoc. Paul 19; Gk. Apoc. Pet. 20). In both apocalypses the phrase is used of paradise. It does not appear in the Ethiopic version of the Apocalypse of Peter. It is hardly distinctive enough to suggest dependence.

2. "Trees planted, full of different fruits" (Apoc. Paul 22; Apoc. Pet. Eth. 16, Gk. 15). Again the phrase comes from the description of paradise. The description in the Apocalypse of Paul is more elaborate than that of the two versions of the Apocalypse of Peter, and it emphasizes supernatural fecundity.

3. "The light (of the city) was beyond the light of the world" (Gk. Apoc. Paul 23; Gk. Apoc. Pet. 15). The sentence does not appear in the Latin of the Apocalypse of Paul. Since there is no heavenly city in the Apocalypse of Peter, the phrase there, "exceeding bright with light," refers to a paradise filled with trees. (See above, [2].)

4. "When he passes out of the world" (Apoc. Paul 27; Gk. Apoc. Pet. 15). In the Apocalypse of Paul the phrase is used to describe the deaths of the hospitable heroes of the Hebrew Bible, who are rewarded by a river of wine. In the Greek ver-

---

33. Kraft, "Reassessing the 'Recensional Problem' in the Testament of Abraham" in *Studies on the Testament of Abraham*, 121–37, shows in relation to a somewhat different problem the inadmissibility of the assumption that the simplest hypothetical chain is the most likely to correspond to reality.

sion of the Apocalypse of Peter "outside this world" describes the location of paradise.

5. "'Great is your judgment'" (Apoc. Paul 16, 18; Apoc. Pet. Eth. 7, Gk. 25). In the Apocalypse of Paul "Righteous is your judgment" is the refrain of the angels as God condemns the souls of sinners to punishment in the section on the departure of souls from the body. (Why James translates "*Great* is your judgment" I do not know. The Greek of the Apocalypse of Paul reads δικαία ἡ κρίσις σου.) In the Apocalypse of Peter the souls of their victims watch the torture of murderers in hell and cry out, "O God, righteous is your judgment" (Gk.) or "Righteousness and justice is the judgment of God" (Eth.).

6. "The souls of the murdered are introduced" (Apoc. Paul 18; Apoc. Pet. Eth. 7, Gk. 25). In the Apocalypse of Paul the sinful soul is confronted with the soul he murdered as part of the judgment scene. In the Apocalypse of Peter, the murdered souls appear in hell, watching the torture of the murderer and acclaiming God's righteousness. The Ethiopic version is somewhat closer to the scene in the Apocalypse of Paul, for in it the angel Ezrael brings the murdered souls forward to watch the punishment of their murderers.

7. "'There was no light there, but darkness'" (Apoc. Paul 31; Gk. Apoc. Pet. 21). This is Paul's impression of the area before him as he is about to begin the tour of hell. There is no introductory description in the Ethiopic of the Apocalypse of Peter, but the Greek contains one, and it is to it that James alludes here, although the parallel is faint. I quote here James's translation (*ApNT*): "And I saw also another place over against that one . . . and the angels that punished them had their raiment dark, according to the air of that place."

8. "'A multitude of men and women *cast* therein'" (Apoc. Paul 31; Apoc. Pet. Eth. 7, Gk. 25). James seems to have made a mistake in referring to chap. 16 of the Greek text; there one soul is *cast* into the outer darkness (as in Latin chap. 16), but no multitude is cast anywhere. Chap. 31 in Greek contains precisely the phrase James quotes; Latin chap. 31 reads "submerged" rather than "cast." In chap. 31 of both versions, sinners stand in a fiery river to various levels. (See below [9].) In the Apocalypse of Peter the scene is quite different: "And the murderers and those who have made common cause with them are cast into the fire, in a place full of venomous beasts" (Gk., "cast into a narrow place full of evil beasts").

9. "'Some up to their knees'" (Apoc. Paul 31; Apoc. Pet. Eth. 10, Gk. 31). Paul sees sinners standing in a fiery river. According to the Latin, different sins lead to different depths of immersion. Those standing in the river up to their knees engaged in idle chatter after leaving church. The Greek text, while describing immersion to various depths, charges all the sinners with fornication and adultery. In the Apocalypse of Peter, on the other hand, men and women stand up to their knees in a lake of filth and mire for the sin of usury.

10. "'But trusted in the vanity of their wealth'" (Apoc. Paul 37; Apoc. Pet. Eth. 9, Gk. 30). This parallel is discussed above (p. 141); it is more impressive than most.

11. "'The widow and orphan he did not pity'" (Apoc. Paul 35, 40; Apoc. Pet.

Eth. 9, Gk. 30). Again, a parallel of some substance. In the Apocalypse of Paul this sin is one of the failings of the bishop who is thrown into the fiery river and otherwise tortured (chap. 35) or of hypocritical monks (chap. 40). In the Apocalypse of Peter the sin is linked to trusting in riches. (See above, p. 141.)

12. "'Eating their tongues'" (Apoc. Paul 37; Apoc. Pet. Eth. 9, Gk. 29). In the Apocalypse of Paul gnawing on one's tongue is part of the punishment for mocking the word of God in church. In the Ethiopic version of the Apocalypse of Peter those who chew on their tongues are slanderers; in the Greek they are false witnesses. (See above, p. 141.)

13. "'Being led away into a dark place'" (Apoc. Paul 39; Apoc. Pet. Eth. 9, Gk. 27). In the Apocalypse of Paul this is the punishment for defilement of virginity. In the Apocalypse of Peter being cast into a dark place is the punishment for persecuting and betraying the righteous.

14. "'Standing upon fiery spits'" (Apoc. Paul 40; Apoc. Pet. Eth. 9, Gk. 30). In the Apocalypse of Paul being impaled on a spit of fire is part of the punishment for infanticide. The Greek Apocalypse of Peter has "gravel stones sharper than swords" (*ApNT*) as part of the punishment for trusting riches and persecuting widows and orphans. The Ethiopic version speaks of a "pillar sharper than swords."

15. "'These are they that corrupted themselves and killed their children'" (Apoc. Paul 40; Apoc. Pet. Eth. 8, Gk. 26). This is the episode of the infanticides, discussed above (p. 141).

16. "'And worms devouring them'" (Apoc. Paul 37, 39; Apoc. Pet. Eth. 7, 9, Gk. 25, 27). In the Apocalypse of Paul worms are part of the punishment of usurers who trusted in riches (chap. 37) and of oppressors of widows, orphans, and the poor (chap. 39). In the Apocalypse of Peter worms eat at murderers like a "dark cloud" (Eth. 7, Gk. 25). In the Ethiopic version (chap. 9), a worm that never sleeps eats at the betrayers of the righteous. In the Greek version (chap. 27), there are plural worms that never weary going about the same task.

17. "'These are they that demanded interest on interest and trusted in their riches'" (Apoc. Paul 37; Apoc. Pet. Eth. 9, 10, Gk. 30, 31). In the Apocalypse of Paul the two sins are punished together. In the Apocalypse of Peter usury forms a separate sin (Eth. 10, Gk. 31), while trust in riches is linked to the oppression of widows and orphans. The punishment for usury in both texts involves immersion, but the details are not similar. (See above, [10] and [11] for trust in riches.)

18. "'Into this pit flow all the punishments'" (Apoc. Paul 38; Apoc. Pet. Eth. 8, Gk. 26). As he looks at the bloodlike pit in which sorcerers are submerged up to their lips, Paul is told by the angel that all punishments flow into the pit. The description of the pit in which women who have had abortions stand up to their throats is as follows in the Apocalypse of Peter: "Into it flow all kinds of things from everywhere" (Eth.) or "another gorge [literally, narrow place] in which the discharge and the excrement of the tortured ran down and became like a lake" (Gk.) (HSW).

19. "'And beasts tearing them'" (Apoc. Paul 40; Apoc. Pet. Eth. 7, Gk. 25). In the Apocalypse of Paul this is part of the punishment of the women who com-

mitted infanticide. In the Apocalypse of Peter beasts whose activity is described in rather different words eat at the murderers.

20. "'There was straitness, and the mouth of the well was strait'" (Apoc. Paul 41; Gk. Apoc. Pet. 25, 26). The deepest hell of the well of the Apocalypse of Paul is missing altogether in the Apocalypse of Peter; the "strait places" of the Greek Apocalypse of Peter contain the murderers and the women who procured abortions.

21. "'The worm that is restless'" (Apoc. Paul 42; Apoc. Pet. Eth. 9, Gk. 27). Paul's worm that never rests is a monster, a cubit in length with two heads. It tortures those who deny the resurrection. The worms that rest not in the Apocalypse of Peter are not nearly so impressive; they torture the persecuters and betrayers of the righteous. (See above, [16]).

22. "'Girls in black raiment,' 'Men and women clothed in rags full of pitch and sulphur'" (Apoc. Paul 39, 40; Apoc. Pet. Eth. 9, 11, Gk. 21, 30). The girls in black raiment have defiled their virginity. They are found in Apoc. Paul 39 and Eth. Apoc. Pet. 11; they are discussed above (p. 141). The rags full of pitch and sulfur are also discussed in the body of the text in relation to the sin of oppressing widows and orphans. (See above, [10] and [11].) In Gk. Apoc. Pet. 21, angels dressed in dark raiment appear. James cites the passage as a parallel to the passages in the Apocalypse of Paul, but its relevance is not clear.

Of the twenty-two parallels examined here only (10), (11), (12), (15), (17), and (22) suggest anything more than a common stock of phrases to describe paradise, sin, and punishment, and several of these exceptions are closely related to one another.

THE APOCALYPSE OF PAUL AND THE APOCALYPSE OF ZEPHANIAH

One important difference between the Apocalypse of Peter and the Apocalypse of Paul is the context in which the tours of hell appear. Unlike the Apocalypse of Peter, the Apocalypse of Paul is concerned exclusively with the fate of souls after death. While the Apocalypse of Peter includes a brief look at paradise, the tour of hell of the Apocalypse of Paul is complemented by a full tour of paradise, and the tours are preceded by a description of the deaths of a righteous man and a sinner and the reception of their souls. Features of this arrangement reappear in the Ethiopic descendants of the Apocalypse of Paul.

But the Apocalypse of Paul is not the first place that these new elements appear. They are found in a less developed form in the Apocalypse of Zephaniah. Some of the parallels between the two texts are quite striking.

M. R. James suggests that the opening of the Apocalypse of Zephaniah should be understood as describing the death of a righteous man.[34] It is

---

34. *ApNT*, 530, n. 3.

not implausible that the righteous man in question is the seer himself. This would be a parallel to the description of the exit of the souls from the body in Apoc. Paul 13–16.

Indeed, Zephaniah undergoes some of the same experiences as the dead souls of the Apocalypse of Paul. Like the righteous soul, Zephaniah has words of comfort addressed to him (see [5] below, p. 149). Like the wicked soul, he is confronted by an angel bearing a list of his sins (see [4] below, p. 149). On the other hand, at most points Zephaniah's role is like that of Paul in the Apocalypse of Paul. The difference in the roles of the two seers in the pleading on behalf of sinners toward the end of both texts (Apoc. Zeph. [16–17]; Apoc. Paul 43–44) is related to the differences already noted. Paul participates in the entreaties of the angels, while Zephaniah looks on as the righteous heroes of the Hebrew Bible beseech God, perhaps because Zephaniah is not as clearly differentiated as Paul from those on whose behalf mercy is being sought.

The verbal parallels between the texts are best represented schematically. Some are noted by James in his translation of the Apocalypse of Paul in *The Apocryphal New Testament*; others are mentioned by Duensing in his introduction to the Apocalypse of Paul in Hennecke-Schneemelcher, *New Testament Apocrypha*.

1. When the seer looks back at earth, it appears:

Apoc. Zeph.: "like a drop of water" (1, line 18).   Apoc. Paul: "as nothing" (chap. 13).[35]

2. Various angels in the two texts are described in similar terms:

Apoc. Zeph.: angels entrusted with the souls of the wicked—faces like panthers, *teeth stick out of mouth*, bloody eyes, hair loose, flaming scourges (4–5).
The accuser—face of a lion, *teeth stick out of mouth* like a bear, hair loose, body like serpent (8).

Apoc. Paul: angels entrusted with the souls of the wicked—faces full of fury, *teeth stick out of mouth*, eyes like morning star, hair and mouth give off sparks of fire (chap. 11).[36]

3. Good angels, the angel Eremiel in the Apocalypse of Zephaniah, the angels entrusted with the souls of the righteous in the Apocalypse of Paul, are described thus:

---

35. Ibid.
36. Ibid., 530, n. 1. James does not note the description of the accuser.

Apoc. Zeph.: *face shines like sun, golden girdle* on breast, feet like brass (9).	Apoc. Paul: *faces shine like sun, golden girdles* on loins, palms in hands, sign of God, clothing with name of son of God (chap. 12).

4. In the Apocalypse of Zephaniah, Eremiel confronts Zephaniah with a list of his sins; in the Apocalypse of Paul, the wicked soul is confronted by its angel with such a list. The lists are called:

Apoc. Zeph.: ⲭⲉⲓⲣⲟⲅⲣⲁⲫⲟⲛ (10–11).	Apoc. Paul: *Cirographon* (chap. 17); Coptic: ⲭⲉⲓⲣⲟⲅⲣⲁⲫⲟⲛ (26b).[37]

5. In the Apocalypse of Zephaniah, Zephaniah is encouraged by the angels; in the Apocalypse of Paul, first the righteous soul, and later Paul, is encouraged by the angels, thus:

Apoc. Zeph.: "Be strong and of good courage . . . for you conquer the accuser and come up from Amente and the abyss . . ." (12). "Strengthen yourself, you who have been strong; be of good courage, you who have been of good courage. For you have conquered the accuser, you have escaped from the abyss and Amente . . ." (13–14).	Apoc. Paul: "Be of good courage . . ." (2) (chap. 14). "Be of good courage and be strong . . ." (St. Gall text, chap. 14; cf. Syriac). "Be strong, you will conquer the accuser who will come in Amente" (Coptic, 35b).

A few words are in order here. The last exhortation from the Apocalypse of Paul comes from the long Coptic ending. While the other texts break off abruptly, the Coptic takes Paul on still another tour of paradise. It is unlikely that the ending of the Coptic is original. Thus one of the most striking parallels to the Apocalypse of Zephaniah in the Apocalypse of Paul is probably the work of a copyist or redactor.[38]

I have translated the passages in (5) in light of their relationship to the phrase חֲזַק וֶאֱמָץ: "Be strong and of good courage" (RSV), which appears four times in chapter 1 of Joshua. The only published Coptic manuscript of the first six chapters of Joshua contains too many lacunae to permit certainty, but it seems to indicate that the two verbs ⲭⲣⲟ and ⳓⲛ̄ⳓⲟⲙ, which appear in both the passages from the Apocalypse of Zephaniah, were used to translate חֲזַק וֶאֱמָץ in Joshua.[39]

---

37. Ibid., 534, n. 1; Duensing, HSW 2:757.

38. Duensing (HSW 2:757) argues that the exhortation, even if original, must have been copied from the Apocalypse of Zephaniah.

39. A. F. Shore, ed., *Joshua I–VI and Other Passages in Coptic Edited from a Fourth-Century Sahidic Codex in the Chester Beatty Library in Dublin*, Chester Beatty Monograph Series 9

The exhortation "Be of good courage" is *"viriliter age"* in the Latin of the Apocalypse of Paul; "Be of good courage and be strong" is *"viriliter age et confortare."* [40] The Latin version of the Apocalypse of Paul is translated from Greek, and *viriliter age et confortare* is a good translation of the Greek Bible's ἴσχυε καὶ ἀνδρίζου in the four verses in Joshua, although the order of the verbs has been reversed. Indeed, *viriliter age* is an etymologically equivalent translation of ἀνδρίζου, which derives from ἀνήρ, "man," as *viriliter* derives from *vir*, "man." [41]

6. In both texts, the seer gets into a boat while hosts of angels sing.

Apoc. Zeph.: boat; 1,000 × 1,000, 10,000 × 10,000 angels (13).

Apoc. Paul: golden boat; 3,000 angels (chap. 23). [42]

7. In the Apocalypse of Zephaniah, Zephaniah finds among the righteous in paradise several heroes of the Hebrew Bible. These six appear again in the paradise of the Apocalypse of Paul, although there they are only a few of the many heroes of both the Hebrew Bible and the New Testament.

Apoc. Zeph.: Abraham, Isaac, Jacob, Enoch, Elijah, David (14).

Apoc. Paul: Enoch and Elijah (chap. 20); Abraham, Isaac, Jacob, Lot, Job (chap. 27); David (chap. 29); Abraham, Isaac, Jacob (chap. 47); Elijah, Elisha, Enoch (chap. 51; Enoch in Coptic only; the other texts have broken off). [43]

These parallels make some kind of relationship between the Apocalypse of Paul and the Apocalypse of Zephaniah certain, although not necessarily

---

(Dublin: Hodges Figgis, 1963). Most of Josh. 1:6 is lost in a lacuna in this MS; in Josh. 1:7, the first verb is lost, but ϬⲘϬⲞⲘ is preserved. At Josh. 1:9 all the first verb ⲭⲣⲟ and the second part of the second verb [ϬⲘ]ϬⲞⲘ are preserved. Finally Josh. 1:18 offers the ⲟ of ⲭⲣⲟ, and ϬⲘϬⲞⲘ.

40. The second exhortation from the Apocalypse of Paul appears in Latin only in the St. Gall MS. It appears also in the Syriac version. The St. Gall MS is published by Silverstein, *Visio*, 131–47. He regards it as a particularly important text, dependent not on the Paris MS, the main witness to the long Latin of the Apocalypse of Paul, but on the source of the Paris MS (chap. 3, esp. 21, 33–35). Although he does not discuss the exhortation, he considers the St. Gall MS to preserve a better form of the incident of the departure of the souls from the body, in which the exhortation appears, than does the Paris MS (25).

41. The Vulgate translates the phrase in Josh. 1:6, 7, and 9 as *confortare et esto robustus*. In Josh. 1:18, however, it translates *confortare et viriliter age*.

42. *ApNT*, 538, n. 1.

43. Duensing, HSW 2:757.

a direct relationship. The Apocalypse of Paul is much more expansive than the Apocalypse of Zephaniah. The three sins and punishments of the Apocalypse of Zephaniah are only a small fraction of the many in the Apocalypse of Paul. The brief description of the places of the righteous in the Apocalypse of Zephaniah has become a full tour of paradise in the Apocalypse of Paul. The vision of souls leaving the body is more highly developed and carefully balanced in the Apocalypse of Paul than in the Apocalypse of Zephaniah. The incidents in the Apocalypse of Zephaniah that are without parallel in the Apocalypse of Paul are precisely the ones that one would expect to trouble later Christians—the seer's confrontation with the accuser and the angel Eremiel whom he mistakes for God. Thus the Apocalypse of Paul has all the marks of a later phase of the tradition.

THE PLACE OF THE APOCALYPSE OF ZEPHANIAH

The Apocalypse of Zephaniah and the Book of the Watchers

In Chapter 2 it was argued that all the tours of hell belong to a literary tradition of which the Book of the Watchers is the earliest surviving representative. This claim was made on the basis of the shared feature of demonstrative explanation. In addition, it was noted that there are certain similarities in content: the cosmic tour of the Book of the Watchers shares to some extent the interest of the tours of hell in the fate of souls after death.

Of all the tours of hell the Apocalypse of Zephaniah, which is perhaps the most idiosyncratic, shows the closest links to the cosmic tour of the Book of the Watchers. The name of the archangel who appears to Zephaniah at his moment of need is Eremiel. This is not a common angelic name, but similar names appear in a few other texts. In 2 Baruch 55:3 the angel Ramiel is in charge of true visions. In 4 Ezra 4:36 the angel Jeremiel converses with Ezra about the souls in the chambers; his function is not explicitly noted. The Syriac version of 4 Ezra calls this angel Ramiel, as in 2 Baruch, also a Syriac text. First Enoch 20:8 [44] mentions Remiel, the angel "whom God set over those who rise."

In both 1 Enoch and 4 Ezra, these similarly named angels are associated with the fate of the dead. This makes probable some relationship to the angel Eremiel in the Apocalypse of Zephaniah, who says of himself, "I am

---

44. This sentence with the name and function of Remiel is preserved only in the second of the Greek texts from Gizeh, and not in Ethiopic or Aramaic. Charles (*Book of Enoch*, ad loc.) argues that it is original because it is needed to reach the number seven, mentioned in both the Greek MSS.

the archangel Eremiel, the one who is down under over the abyss and Amente, in whose hand all souls have been sealed, from the end of the flood which was upon the earth until this very day" (10).[45]

A second and more important parallel to 1 Enoch occurs in Zephaniah's visit to the abode of the righteous at the beginning of the text. Zephaniah comes to water of some kind (2, line 1). The Coptic is ϣⲱⲧⲉ. Steindorff translates "*Brunnen*," spring; Houghton translates "spring (fountain)." Zephaniah asks the angel, Is there no darkness here at night? The angel replies that this is the place of the righteous and the holy ones, so that there is never darkness there, but always light (2, lines 6–8).

In 1 Enoch 22:2, Enoch is taken to see the hollows in which the souls of the dead are stored. "And there were four hollow places in it, deep and very smooth; three of them were dark and one bright and there was a fountain (πηγή) of water in its midst" (Charles).[46] The angel Raphael explains the sight: the "bright spring (πηγή) of water" indicates the abode of the righteous (22:9).[47]

The primary meaning of πηγή, according to Liddell and Scott, is running water. It can mean fount or source. The Coptic ϣⲱⲧⲉ, which both Steindorff and Houghton translate "spring," means, according to Crum, "well, cistern, pit."[48] But Crum does cite the Bohairic translation of Gen. 24:29, where ϣⲱⲧⲉ translates the Greek πηγή. The Hebrew here is עַיִן, "spring." Thus it seems likely that ϣⲱⲧⲉ in the Apocalypse of Zephaniah is equivalent to πηγή in the Book of the Watchers.

Yet the choice of words is not as important as the similarity of the pictures. Next to the place of light in the Apocalypse of Zephaniah is a place of punishment (2, lines 9–10). Similarly in the Book of the Watchers the place of the righteous is one hollow of four; the others contain the souls of sinners awaiting punishment.

What is striking about the parallels between the Book of the Watchers and the Apocalypse of Zephaniah is that they include features of the Book of the Watchers that are not common in later apocalypses. The Book of the Watchers' picture of the souls of the dead waiting in chambers until the last judgment is found also in 4 Ezra at the end of the first century C.E., and a similar belief may be implied in the Ethiopic of the Apocalypse of Peter,

---

45. I paraphrase Steindorff's German translation, with an eye to Houghton's literal English translation.

46. I quote the Greek; the Ethiopic does not include the description of the hollows as dark and bright. There are no Aramaic fragments for this verse.

47. The explanation appears in both Ethiopic and Greek. Again there are no Aramaic fragments.

48. W. E. Crum, *A Coptic Dictionary* (Oxford: Oxford University, 1939).

where the punishments Peter sees will not begin until the last judgment. All the other tours of hell, including the Apocalypse of Zephaniah, assume the present enactment of the punishments described. Yet despite the fact that the punishments are actually occurring, the Apocalypse of Zephaniah pictures a place for righteous souls with light and a spring as in the Book of the Watchers. Similarly, it preserves the angelic name Eremiel, which disappears elsewhere after the first century C.E.

The Apocalypse of Zephaniah and Merkavah Mysticism

The Apocalypse of Zephaniah also shows points of contact with the literature of merkavah mysticism. When Zephaniah enters the beautiful city, he has a strange experience.[49]

> I went with the angel of God. I looked before me. I saw gates. After that, when I had come closer, I found that they were gates of brass. The angel touched them. They opened before him. I went in with him. I found its whole street like a beautiful city. I went into its midst. After that the angel of the Lord changed his appearance before me on that spot. But I looked at them. I found that they were gates of brass, and locks of brass, and bolts of iron.
>
> But my mouth was closed. Yonder in there I saw before me again brass gates, how they threw forth fire for nearly fifty stades. Again I withdrew back. . . . I saw a great sea. I thought that it was a sea of water. I found that it was a sea of fire and slime that threw off much fire, whose waves glowed with sulfur and pitch. They threw themselves so as to come near me.

Zephaniah thinks that he sees God coming to save him, throws himself down, looks up to find the terrifying angel later identified as the accuser, and prays to God. Eremiel appears, explains that he is not God, and urges Zephaniah to repent.

What is the meaning of this passage? Zephaniah enters the beautiful city only to find his way blocked by obstacles that he misperceives. He notices the brass gates before entering the city, but not the brass locks and iron bolts. Have the gates changed, or has Zephaniah failed to see? Nor did he expect the gates to throw out fire. When he first sees the sea, Zephaniah thinks that it is a sea of water, but he quickly discovers that it is really a sea of fire and slime. Immediately after, Zephaniah mistakes two different angels for God.

An echo of a similar incident is preserved in the famous passage in b. Ḥagigah 14b: "Our rabbis taught: Four entered paradise, and they are b.

---

49. I paraphrase Steindorff's translation of the text, 6–7; translation, 45–47.

Azai and b. Zoma, Aḥer,[50] and Rabbi Aqiba. Rabbi Aqiba said to them, 'When you arrive at pure marble stone, don't say, "Water, water," as it is said, "None who speaks lies shall come into my presence"' (Ps. 101:7)." The text goes on to describe the fates of the four who entered.

To elucidate this difficult passage, Scholem draws on a passage from the Munich manuscript of the Lesser Hekhalot.

But if one was unworthy to see the King in his beauty, the angels at the gates disturbed his senses and confused him. And when they said to him: "Come in," he entered, and instantly they pressed him and threw him into the fiery lava stream. And at the gate of the sixth palace it seemed as though hundreds of thousands and millions of waves of water stormed against him, and yet there was not a drop of water, only the ethereal glitter of the marble plates with which the palace was tessellated. But he was standing in front of the angels and when he asked: "What is the meaning of these waters," they began to stone him and said: "Wretch, do you not see it with your own eyes? Are you perhaps a descendant of those who kissed the Golden Calf, and are you unworthy to see the King in his beauty?" . . . And he does not go until they strike his head with iron bars and wound him.[51]

Each of these texts is concerned with the visionary's inability to perceive accurately the heavenly realm. As Rabbi Aqiba's warning in Ḥagigah hints and as the Apocalypse of Zephaniah and the Lesser Hekhalot illustrate, this inability creates danger for the seer.[52] The similarity of details in the Lesser Hekhalot and the Apocalypse of Zephaniah is particularly striking: gates, iron bars, fire, waterless waves.

---

50. "*Aḥer*" means "other." This is the name the rabbis give to Elisha b. Abuya, who started out as one of their number, after he had become a heretic. In some traditions, as in b. Ḥagigah, his heresy is attributed to dire misunderstanding of what he saw during his ascent to heaven.

51. G. Scholem, *Major Trends in Jewish Mysticism*, 3d ed. (New York: Schocken, 1954), 52–53. In *Jewish Gnosticism* (15), Scholem quotes from the unpublished Jewish Theological Seminary MS of the Lesser Hekhalot a similar passage in which iron bars are tossed at b. Azai.

Scholem's views about the dating of the hekhalot texts have undergone some change since *Major Trends*, when he tended to date them to the talmudic period or later, although he insisted on the earliness of some of the traditions preserved in them (40–48). More recently in *Jewish Gnosticism* (chap. 1) and in his article "Kabbalah" in *EJ*, Scholem has preferred earlier dates. The Lesser Hekhalot has yet to be edited and published, except for a small section, so that more precise conclusions are impossible. For an introduction to the Lesser Hekhalot, see Gruenwald, *Apocalyptic and Merkavah Mysticism*, 142–49. Gruenwald also discusses the passage in question on 82–92.

52. J. Maier ("Das Gefärdungsmotiv bei der Himmelsreise in der jüdischen Apokalyptik und 'Gnosis,'" *Kairos* 5[1963]:33–38), discusses the texts from Ḥagigah and the Lesser Hekhalot and others in relation to their use of water. The article includes a discussion of the biblical and ancient Near Eastern background of fire and water as sources of danger.

Another episode in the story of the four who entered paradise provides a parallel to Zephaniah's next trial, his encounter with the accuser and Eremiel. The amoraim offer the following account of the experience that turned Elisha b. Abuya into Aḥer, the heretic (b. Ḥagigah 15a). "He looked at Metatron who was given permission to sit and write down the merits of Israel. He said, It is taught that in heaven there is neither sitting nor contention, neither separation nor combination.[53] Perhaps, God forbid, there are two powers in heaven." The same tradition appears in 3 Enoch 16.[54]

Like Metatron, who writes down the merits of Israel, the archangel Eremiel appears in the Apocalypse of Zephaniah with a scroll in his hand. On it are written all of Zephaniah's sins. In both texts the visionary mistakes a lesser being for God, although the results of this mistake are not as dire for Zephaniah as they are for Elisha b. Abuya.

Ascent Apocalypses and Merkavah Mysticism

While he never worked out the details of his view, Scholem always argued that there is an unbroken line of development from prerabbinic visionary literature like 1 Enoch 14, some of the other early apocalypses, and some of the literature from Qumran, to the merkavah mysticism of rabbinic literature and the hekhalot texts.[55] The vocabulary, motifs, and ideas common to the Apocalypse of Zephaniah and merkavah texts are drawn from that tradition; there is no need to take the parallels assembled above as indicating a direct literary relationship between the Apocalypse of Zephaniah on the one hand and the Lesser Hekhalot and b. Ḥagigah on the other.

Indeed, I suspect that further study would encourage us to view the ascents of hekhalot literature as only one crystallization of themes that appear in a wide range of Jewish and Christian literature. Several Jewish and Christian apocalypses that describe ascents through the seven heavens contain merkavah motifs (see the discussion on the extent of the form in chap.

---

53. The last phrase is problematic. The two main options are the one suggested by Maimonides in his commentary to Sanhedrin chap. 10, which is offered above, and Rashi's interpretation in his commentary ad loc., "no back and no weariness."

54. See A. F. Segal, *Two Powers in Heaven* (Leiden: Brill, 1977), 60–67, for a discussion of the meaning of these passages in relation to the issue of two powers.

55. Scholem, *Major Trends*, 40–44; most recently, "Kabbalah," *EJ* 10:495–503. Gruenwald has tried to work out some of the details of the relations between the apocalypses and merkavah literature (*Apocalyptic*, chaps. 1–2). He does not seem to know the Apocalypse of Zephaniah.

2, above). A number of these are motifs that appear in the Apocalypse of
Zephaniah as well. For example, an incident of confusing an angel with
God appears in the Ascension of Isaiah. When Isaiah attempts to worship
the angel who is the ruler in the second heaven, he is rebuked by his guide,
who tells him not to worship any of the inhabitants of the six heavens, but
only the supreme ruler in the seventh heaven (Asc. Isa. 7:21).[56] This incident lacks the shared details of the incidents in b. Ḥagigah and the Apocalypse of Zephaniah; it is completely undeveloped. Yet it points to similar
concerns.

Another example of such a motif is the special garment that figures in
the Apocalypse of Zephaniah, the Ascension of Isaiah, and also in 2
Enoch. As he steps into the boat that transports him to paradise,
Zephaniah dons a garment that allows him to understand the language of
the angels (13, line 5). In the Ascension of Isaiah garments are linked to
thrones and crowns as the reward of the righteous (8:26). Isaiah discovers
that the righteous in heaven have received only their garments, while
thrones and crowns must await the return of Christ (9:10–13). These garments, Charles suggests quite reasonably, are spiritual bodies.[57] The righteous whom Isaiah beholds in heaven are "stript of the garments of the
flesh"; they wear instead "their garments of the upperworld" (9:9). Although the text is not clear, it seems that Isaiah dons his garment on entering the seventh heaven, as does Enoch in 2 Enoch.[58] As Enoch stands before the divine throne, God orders Michael to remove his terrestrial
garments, to anoint him with oil, and to dress him in a garment of glory
(chap. 9).

Finally, such a garment is mentioned in a hekhalot text. Scholem points
to a passage in 3 Enoch (Sefer Hekhalot) 18, where the angel Azbuga's

---

56. Little attention has been given to the parallels between the ascent of the Ascension of
Isaiah and hekhalot texts. It may be that the obviously Christian content of this section of the
Ascension of Isaiah discourages such observation. Yet there are similarities both of structure—the ascent through seven heavens filled with angels—and of specific elements. Gruenwald, *Apocalyptic*, 57–62, treats the Ascension of Isaiah as a Jewish text and compares it to
hekhalot texts, but never argues explicitly for its Jewish origins. In relation to the obviously
Christian passage in 9:11–18, he writes, "There are good reasons to believe that the book as a
whole is of Jewish origin and that all the clear Christian references belong to a later editor or
interpolator" (62, n. 119).

57. See Charles's note to Asc. Isa. 4:16 for parallels from the pseudepigrapha and New
Testament.

58. At the beginning of the ascent (7:25) Isaiah says, "The glory of my appearance was
undergoing transformation as I ascended to each heaven in turn." In the seventh heaven,
when Isaiah's presence is challenged, a voice says, "It is permitted to the holy Isaiah to ascend
hither; for here is his garment" (9:2). Is the garment already on Isaiah, or is it awaiting him
in the seventh heaven?

name is explained (incorrectly) as meaning, "In the future he will gird (clothe) the righteous and pious of the world with the garments of life and wrap them in the cloak of life that they may live in them an eternal life."[59]

Clement of Alexandria quotes a description of the fifth heaven from an Apocalypse of Zephaniah (*Stromateis* 5.11.77). In the section on the Apocalypse of Zephaniah in Chapter 1, it was argued that this passage could not have been taken from the Greek original of the Coptic Apocalypse of Zephaniah, which nowhere alludes to more than one heaven. But the recognition of elements of merkavah tradition in the Coptic apocalypse points to a connection between it and the lost Greek work, for as Scholem notes, the Greek fragment contains several examples of merkavah motifs and vocabulary.[60]

The phrase "temples (ναοί) of salvation," Scholem argues, is an example of merkavah terminology; ναός, "temple," is the equivalent of היכל, "temple," or more often in this literature, "palace."[61]

The passage quoted by Clement also mentions the hymns sung by the angels, the crowns on the head of each angel, and the thrones in which the angels sit. These elements have parallels in the ascent apocalypses and the hekhalot texts, although in hekhalot texts angels do not have their own thrones, and all interest is centered on the divine throne.[62]

The Coptic Apocalypse of Zephaniah and Clement's fragment share few details. What they do have in common are links to the merkavah tradition. I hesitate to make any suggestions about relationship between the two works on this basis alone, but it is not unlikely that at some early stage in

---

59. G. Scholem, "The Paradisic Garb of Souls and the Origin of the Concept of *Haluka de Rabbanan*" (Hebr.), *Tarbiz* 24(1955):290. The article is concerned primarily with the development of the concept in the Zohar. Scholem shows that this motif appears in later aggadot influenced by the hekhalot literature. In *Jewish Gnosticism*, chap. 8, Scholem discusses the role of the garment of God in hekhalot literature. This concept does not, as far as I know, appear in the pseudepigrapha, although the raiment of the one on the throne is sometimes alluded to in merkavah visions, as in Daniel 7, 1 Enoch 14:20, and 1 Enoch 71:10, as Gruenwald notes (*Apocalyptic*, 64).

The translation of the passage from 3 Enoch is Odeberg's.

60. Scholem, *Jewish Gnosticism*, 18–19.

61. Ibid. The Greater Hekhalot contains examples of hekhalot of silence, holiness, and purity. The Lesser Hekhalot mentions "gates of salvation."

62. For enthroned angels, Scholem, ibid., 19, refers to Odeberg, *3 Enoch*, Intro., 142, for a list of references from the pseudepigrapha and the New Testament.

For crowns, Scholem, *Jewish Gnosticism*, refers to 3 Enoch 12:3, 16:1, chap. 18. See also Odeberg's note, *3 Enoch*, text, 52–53. As we saw above, crowns appear with garments in the Ascension of Isaiah.

For hymns, 2 Enoch 9, Asc. Isa. 7:15 and passim, Apoc. Abr. 17, Apoc. Paul 23, the Angelic Liturgy from Qumran (4Q Shir Shab), 3 Enoch 34–35, Greater Hekhalot (examples quoted by Scholem, *Jewish Gnosticism*, 20–30), etc.

their histories they go back to a common source. Zephaniah, after all, is not the most common hero in apocalyptic literature, and it may be that the text on which Clement drew represents a reworking in light of a seven-heavens schema of an earlier Zephaniah apocalypse now preserved in Coptic, as 2 Enoch seems to represent a reworking of the Book of the Watchers.

For a variety of reasons linked to the history of scholarship, the cosmological concerns so central to many apocalypses have usually been downplayed in relation to apocalyptic eschatology.[63] With the publication of the Qumran fragments of 1 Enoch, M. E. Stone in particular has insisted on the importance of these cosmological interests for an understanding of the genre apocalypse.[64] While the secrets of the hekhalot literature, the Apocalypse of Zephaniah, and other texts, on the one hand, and cosmological secrets, on the other hand, are not unrelated, and while both kinds of interests can appear in a single text like 2 Enoch, there are significant differences between them. Do they grow out of a common stock and then diverge, or are they originally different ways of conceiving of the heavens? Can the relatively well attested *Sitz im Leben* of the hekhalot texts in the talmudic period tell us anything about the setting of the Book of the Watchers with its ascent *and* cosmic tour? The origins of cosmological speculation and the meaning of its emergence in third-century Judaism are most important questions for any student of the apocalypses. The relation of angelological speculation to this trend should also be put on the agenda.

THE DESCENDANTS OF THE APOCALYPSE OF PAUL

The Apocalypse of Paul was undoubtedly the most popular and influential of the early tours of hell in the Middle Ages. The Latin redactions were described briefly in Chapter 1 in the discussion of related texts. In the East, the published descendants of the Apocalypse of Paul consist of one Greek and three Ethiopic works; in all, Paul has been replaced by other figures.

Ethiopic Texts

The dependence of the three Ethiopic texts, the Ethiopic Apocalypse of Mary, the Ethiopic Apocalypse of Baruch, and the Apocalypse of Gorgo-

---

63. Stone, "Lists of Revealed Things in Apocalyptic Literature," 439–43.

64. Stone's "Lists" was written before Milik's evidence for the early dates of the Astronomical Book of Enoch and the Book of the Watchers was available, but its conclusions about

rios, on the Apocalypse of Paul, and their relations to one another were discussed in a preliminary fashion in Chapter 1, above. All shared certain structural features with the Apocalypse of Paul. An examination of some of the common sins and punishments (see under sins and punishments of the Apocalypse of Paul family in chap. 4, above) confirmed the view that the Ethiopic Apocalypse of Mary stands closest to the Apocalypse of Paul, while the Apocalypse of Gorgorios treats the parent text the most freely. The Ethiopic Apocalypse of Mary usually adapts the sins and punishments of the Apocalypse of Paul, while the Ethiopic Apocalypse of Baruch and especially the Apocalypse of Gorgorios invent their own sins and punishments, drawing on the elements available in the Apocalypse of Paul and perhaps other texts—fire, environmental punishments, hanging (but not by the sinful limb), hypocritical ecclesiastical officials, for example—but arranging them in new configurations.

An interesting problem is raised by the fact that the three Ethiopic texts sometimes share motifs absent from the Apocalypse of Paul with the Greek Apocalypse of Mary and the Ezra apocalypses. Does this suggest that the Ethiopic texts had access to a source in addition to the Apocalypse of Paul, a source known also to the Greek Apocalypse of Mary and the Ezra apocalypses? Or does it suggest a version of the Apocalypse of Paul that contained these features?

A serious attempt to date these texts and to place them in the context of Ethiopic literature has not yet been made. Such a project might shed new light on the development of the tours of hell and on their sources.

The Greek Apocalypse of Mary

The Greek Apocalypse of Mary shares a number of elements with the Apocalypse of Paul and one or more of the Ethiopic texts: pleading for Sabbath rest for the sinners, the punishment of immersion to various depths in a fiery river, and ecclesiastical sinners. It also shares with the Ethiopic texts the fiery-seat punishment, which does not appear in the Apocalypse of Paul itself. It does not share the Ethiopic texts' structural similarities to the Apocalypse of Paul: it contains no departure of souls from the body and no description of paradise.

In the Greek Apocalypse of Mary the ecclesiastical concerns of the

---

the importance of the speculative wisdom in Jewish apocalypses were given great support by those early dates. For Stone's views since he was able to take account of the early dates, see "The Book of Enoch and Judaism in the Third Century B.C.E."

Apocalypse of Paul are highly developed, but most of the sins and punishments are quite independent of the Apocalypse of Paul, more independent than those of the Ethiopic Apocalypse of Mary or the Ethiopic Apocalypse of Baruch. The Greek Apocalypse of Mary shows no clear links to any texts outside the Apocalypse of Paul family, however, and is probably best understood as the work of an author familiar with the Apocalypse of Paul, but with no intention of producing a mere adaptation.

THE EZRA APOCALYPSES

Sins and Punishments Appearing in Both Texts

The tour of the Vision of Ezra is longer than the tour of the Apocalypse of Ezra; the Apocalypse of Ezra includes large sections of other kinds of material. Almost all the punishments in the Apocalypse of Ezra have parallels in the Vision. Below I have listed the punishments common to both texts, following their order of appearance in the Apocalypse of Ezra, with comments about their relationship.

1. In Apoc. Ezra 4:9–12 Herod is tortured on a fiery throne for killing the babies. The sin and punishment are the same in Vis. Ezra 37–39, but Herod's advisers are tortured along with him. A punishment of a fiery seat is assigned to sinful church officials in several texts related to the Apocalypse of Paul (see chap. 4, above).

2. In Apoc. Ezra 4:13–14 Ezra sees a crowd of sinners in seething fire. "I heard their noise, but I did not see their forms." In Vis. Ezra 28–29 Ezra says of sinners who are submerged in fire, "A noise was heard, but no flesh was seen because of the fire and the torture." In the Apocalypse of Ezra no sin is specified, but the Vision offers a long list: greed, rapaciousness, inhospitability, uncharitableness, taking what belongs to others, evil desires (vv. 31–32). Greed in various forms is a common sin in the tours of hell. The punishment found in the Ezra texts belongs to the store of fiery punishments that appear in the Apocalypse of Peter, the Apocalypse of Paul, and later Christian texts, but it is not found anywhere else in this precise form.

3. In Apoc. Ezra 4:20 Ezra sees "the worm that does not sleep and fire burning the sinners." No details about the sinners are provided. In Vis. Ezra 34–36 Ezra sees an enormous "worm that dies not," eating sinners who are "full of all evil." The Isaianic worm is a common punishment in the tours of hell (see chap. 4, above).

4. In Apoc. Ezra 4:22–24 Ezra sees a man hanging by his eyelids while

angels whip him because he slept with his mother. In Vis. Ezra 19–20 Ezra sees both men and women hanging in fire, no limb specified, while angels strike them for sleeping with their mothers. The version in the Vision is somewhat confused; it seems likely that women are not among the original group guilty of sleeping with their mothers. In the discussion of hanging by the sinful limb above (see discussion of hanging in hell in chap. 3), it was suggested that hanging by the eye is a measure-for-measure punishment for sinful desires. Incest is not a major interest of the tours of hell. Incest of fathers with daughters appears in a list of sexual sins punished by submerging in an abyss in Eth. Apoc. Mary (62); in Eth. Apoc. Bar. (71) the same kind of incest figures in a similar list with a similar punishment. Incest with sisters is mentioned in *Ged. Mosh.* 18, where it is punished with snow and fire, worms, and torturing angels. Incest of mothers and sons appears nowhere else in these texts.

5. In Apoc. Ezra 5:2–3 Ezra sees a woman punished for infanticide. She is hanging while four beasts suck at her breasts. Her sin is described by the angel thus: "This one begrudged giving her milk and instead threw the infants into rivers." The Vision of Ezra contains two punishments for infanticide. In the first, women are sent into a burning furnace while their children accuse them before God (vv. 51–53). The second (vv. 53a–54) is close to the punishment in the Apocalypse of Ezra. In the extended discussion of the punishments for abortion and infanticide in Chapter 3, above, these two versions were discussed in some detail, and it was argued there that the two punishments of the Vision of Ezra are likely to be original.

6. In Apoc. Ezra 5:24–25 Ezra sees a man who removed boundaries hanging by his head. In Vis. Ezra 57a–57c those who changed boundaries and gave false testimony are torn apart by beasts. The sin of changing boundaries is unparalleled in the other tours of hell.

These are the punishments common to both Ezra apocalypses. The order of the punishments in the Vision of Ezra differs from that in the Apocalypse of Ezra at two points: Herod's punishment in the Vision comes after the immortal worm, and the punishment of those who committed incest is the first of the six in the Vision. This degree of correspondence seems to represent more than a common stock of sins and punishments arranged separately by each author.

In general the Vision of Ezra provides more detail in its versions of the punishments than does the Apocalypse. The Vision's longer readings are as follows: It includes Herod's advisers with him (1); provides a long list of the sins of those whose noise was heard, but who were not seen (2); offers a sin, if vague, for those tortured by the worm (3); gives two versions of the punishment for infanticide (5); and mentions a second sin of the remover of boundaries (6).

The two punishments for abortion/infanticide of the Vision of Ezra are probably original, but the other longer readings of the Vision give the impression of additions, although it is difficult to make an air-tight case for this impression in most instances. The overabundance of sins, all of the same kind, in (2) and the lack of specificity of the sins in (3) suggest that they are not integral parts of the text. The advisers in (1) also seem superfluous, especially since the angel's explanation of the punishment mentions only Herod. Bearing false witness, the second sin in (6), seems to be a gloss on the difficult "removing boundaries," which is unparalleled in the tours of hell but which may refer to Deut. 19:14 and 27:17. (The Greek of Apoc. Ezra 5:25 is close to the LXX of Deut. 27:17, where the verb for "remove" is also $\mu\epsilon\tau\alpha\tau\iota\vartheta\eta\mu\iota$. "Boundary" in the LXX is ὅριον; in the Apocalypse of Ezra it is ὅρος.)

In the punishment for incest (4), the single shared punishment for which it contains more detail than the Vision, the Apocalypse of Ezra probably preserves the original form. The eyelid by which the sinner hangs in the Apocalypse of Ezra is idiosyncratic enough that its elimination is easily understood, yet it makes sense in the context of measure-for-measure punishments for sexual sins which focus on seductive appearance and desire.

It appears, then, that with the exception of the punishments for infanticide the Apocalypse of Ezra preserves the punishments in more nearly their original forms. This position is supported by the evidence of the punishments that are found in only one of the two texts.

Sins and Punishments Appearing Only in the Apocalypse of Ezra

There is only one true punishment in the Apocalypse of Ezra that has no parallel in the Vision: in Apoc. Ezra 4:16–18 eavesdroppers are punished with fiery pivots in their ears. This punishment resembles one version of the punishment of Miriam in the Palestinian Talmud and of the rich man in the Setme tale, although the sin is different. (See the section on tantalization and the pivot punishment in chap. 3, above.)

The twelve-plagued abyss (4:21) of the Apocalypse of Ezra does not function as a punishment. A seven-sealed well into which various heretics are forced appears in Apoc. Paul 41 and some of its descendants. In the medieval redactions of the Apocalypse of Paul, a furnace with six or seven plagues appears. The plagues are sometimes enumerated: snow, ice, fire, blood, serpents, lightning, stench, for example.[65] Redaction 8 has a twelve-

---

65. Silverstein, *Visio*, 52. This list comes from Redaction 4; other versions differ.

plagued furnace. Silverstein suggests that the number twelve is the result of a misreading, XII for VII.[66] On the other hand, both seven and twelve are commonly used round (and magical) numbers.

The Vision of Ezra lacks the description of the antichrist in chains (Apoc. Ezra 4:25–43), but similar descriptions of the antichrist in quite different contexts show that the antichrist tradition is not inextricably linked to tours of hell.[67]

Sins and Punishments Appearing Only in the Vision of Ezra

There are eight punishments in the Vision of Ezra that do not appear in the Apocalypse of Ezra.

1. Those who deny God and sin with women before mass on Sunday are torn apart by beasts (and burned, according to MSS VH) (vv. 8–11). Fornication is one of the most common sins of the tours of hell; no special genealogy is required for this sin or its punishment. What is noteworthy, however, is the ecclesiastical element. The sin is not simple fornication, but fornication before mass on Sunday. This type of concern is characteristic of the Apocalypse of Paul and its descendants.

2. Angels torture adulterers and adulteresses (vv. 13–18). Again, a standard sin and an unexceptional punishment.

3. Sinners (no specifics given) attempt to cross a bridge that some of the righteous have just traversed, but the bridge becomes so narrow that they fall into the fiery river below (vv. 36c–36e). The bridge that sinners cannot cross appears in several of the medieval redactions of the Apocalypse of Paul, including Redaction 6, the most influential. These texts, however, contain a detail not found in the Vision of Ezra: when the sinners have fallen off the bridge, they are grouped according to the nature of their sin. Silverstein traces the entrance of this motif, so important in Zoroastrian eschatology, into western Europe back to Gregory the Great's *Dialogues*, book 4. There the detail of grouping by sins is also to be found.[68]

The Vision of Ezra describes the bridge as narrow as a thread for sinners. No such detail appears in the Latin redactions of the Apocalypse of Paul, but the narrowness of the bridge is described in some of the vernacular versions of the Apocalypse of Paul and other medieval visions. One Italian version of the Apocalypse of Paul describes the bridge as "narrow as a single hair." Silverstein suggests a Muslim source for this image.[69]

---

66. Ibid., 57; 116, n. 79.
67. For other such descriptions, see Stone and Strugnell, *Elijah*, 27–39.
68. Silverstein, *Visio*, 77–79.
69. Ibid., 77.

4. Angels stick thorns in the eyes of those who "showed foreign ways to those who go astray" (vv. 40–42). This sin is unparalleled in the tours of hell discussed here, but the punishment is perhaps remotely related to the pivots in ears and eyes, including the pivot in the ear of the eavesdropper of the Apocalypse of Ezra (see above, p. 94), or to the hot iron in the eyes of those who blasphemed and slandered the way of righteousness (Gk. Apoc. Pet. 28; the Ethiopic text is somewhat different). Punishments involving piercing the eyes of the sinners appear in Redaction 6 (chaps. 3 and 10) of the Apocalypse of Paul.[70]

5. Girls who lost their virginity before marriage bear some sort of heavy burden, probably chains (vv. 43–44). The text is corrupt here. The relation of the punishment that appears in the Vision of Ezra to the form found in the Apocalypse of Peter and the Apocalypse of Paul and its descendants was discussed above (see chap. 3); it was argued that the form of punishment in the Vision of Ezra is related to that of the Apocalypse of Paul.

6. Burning iron and lead are poured over doctors of the law who "mixed up baptism and the law of God" (vv. 45–47). The possibility of a relationship between these doctors and the sinful church officials of the Apocalypse of Paul family was raised above (p. 123). Even if the doctors are not derived from the Apocalypse of Paul, their presence reflects similar interests.

7. Kings and princes of the world are punished in a fiery furnace while poor people accuse them of having made free men into slaves (vv. 48–49). There sinners appear in several of the texts descended from the Apocalypse of Paul although not in the Apocalypse of Paul itself. They were discussed above (see the section on kings and princes of the world in chap. 4, above), where it was argued that the Vision of Ezra probably shows contacts with these other texts.

8. Those who raised their hands against their parents[71] and insulted them are punished in another furnace with those who denied God and did not pay fair wages to their servants (vv. 50–50a). While the punishments are not particularly similar, the sin of failing to honor parents appears in Eth. Apoc. Pet. 11 and in Redaction 6 (chap. 2) of the Apocalypse of Paul.[72]

The influences that can be discerned in the sins and punishments found in the Vision of Ezra but not in the Apocalypse of Ezra confirm the picture of the Vision of Ezra as a later reworking of the material common to the

---

70. Ibid., 82–84; text, 215–17. On Redaction 6 and its relation to Irish works and to the Apocalypse of Peter, 89–90.

71. I read "manus miserunt" with MSS VH.

72. Silverstein, *Visio*, 58; text, 215. Silverstein is not aware of the parallel in the Apocalypse of Peter, perhaps because this sin appears only in the Ethiopic version, not in the Greek.

two Ezra texts, a picture that had already begun to emerge from the examination of that common material. Of the eight sins and punishments found only in the Vision of Ezra, one (2) did not show any special affinities to other texts. Two, (1) and (6), reflected the sort of ecclesiastical interests found in the Apocalypse of Paul and its descendants, even if they are not actually dependent on the other texts. Two others, (5) and (7), may well depend respectively on the Apocalypse of Paul and on its descendants. Another, (3), is very close to a punishment found in the Latin redactions of the Apocalypse of Paul and elsewhere in the medieval West, while two more, (4) and (8), can perhaps be linked to Redaction 6 of the Apocalypse of Paul or to the Apocalypse of Peter. It is worth noting that the extra material of the Vision of Ezra appears in three blocks: (1) and (2) in verses 8–18 before the first common sin, (3) in verses 36c–36e, and (4)–(8) in verses 40–50a between Herod and the infanticides. Such blocks may suggest the use of sources where these elements were already grouped together.

The links to Redaction 6 of the Apocalypse of Paul or to the Apocalypse of Peter are particularly intriguing in light of the close parallel between the Vision of Ezra's punishments for abortion/infanticide and those of the Apocalypse of Peter. Further, the Vision of Ezra seems to show the influence of both the Apocalypse of Paul and its descendants with some punishments that must be related to the Apocalypse of Paul itself and others that appear only in the descendants. Again it is worth noting that one of the elements common to the Vision and the Apocalypse of Ezra, Herod on the fiery throne, finds parallels in the family of the Apocalypse of Paul but not in the Apocalypse of Paul itself.

The main source for the special elements of the Vision of Ezra, then, is the family of the Apocalypse of Paul, although the question of a geographical location is difficult to resolve. The relation to the redactions of the Apocalypse of Paul suggests the West; the relation to the descendants, the East. The Vision of Ezra itself survives in Latin, translated from Greek. Perhaps the parallels to the Latin redactions of the Apocalypse of Paul entered the Vision after it had been translated into Latin; a study of the language of the parallels as compared to the rest of the text might yield helpful results. The parallels to the Apocalypse of Peter probably reached the Vision through an intermediate later source, like Redaction 6 of the Apocalypse of Paul.

The Vision must have been quite selective in its borrowings from other texts. While fire, worms, tormenting angels—all part of the stock of punishments of these later texts—are abundant in the Vision, geographic features, equally common in the later texts, are almost entirely lacking. This is true also for the material that the Vision shares with the Apocalypse of Ezra.

In light of this examination of the Vision of Ezra, the position of A.-M. Denis, who argues that the Vision of Ezra is older than the Apocalypse of Ezra, the Apocalypse of Sedrach, the Apocalypse of Paul, the Apocalypse of Ps.-John, and the Apocalypse of Mary (I assume he means the Greek apocalypse) because of its relative freedom from Christian elements and New Testament references, is difficult to maintain.[73]

The Question of Interpolations and the Prehistory of the Ezra Apocalypses

Some scholars have considered these Ezra texts to be Jewish works with Christian interpolations. Riessler, for example, included them in his *Altjüdisches Schriftum ausserhalb der Bibel* in 1928,[74] and U. Müller in a 1976 German translation still refers to a "*jüdische Grundschrift*" of the Apocalypse of Ezra.[75]

There are certainly cases that can usefully be considered interpolation. The words "my son Jesus" in the Latin of 4 Ezra 7:28 where the other versions read "my son the Messiah" or "the Messiah of God" are a good example. The addition to the Latin version is a limited one that has not affected the content or tone of the text as a whole. In the Vision of Ezra, however, the amount of material so clearly Christian that it must be regarded as interpolated is so large and its influence on the tone and message of the text so far-reaching, that it is difficult to imagine that it was added by the scissors-and-paste method that interpolation suggests. It seems more reasonable to suppose that an overall reworking has taken place and that the Jewish core, if one ever existed, is no longer recoverable simply by excising the patently Christian passages.[76]

The same is true for the Apocalypse of Ezra. The text does not read smoothly, and this may suggest several not very well integrated sources. But to separate out the Christian parts as secondary requires radical surgery based on the premise that Christians would neither attribute their compositions to heroes of the Hebrew Bible nor draw on Jewish themes. In fact, it should be noted that several of the sins and punishments common to the Apocalypse and the Vision of Ezra, the punishments for abortion/infanticide and Herod's throne, show definite links to other Christian

---

73. A.-M. Denis, *Introduction aux pseudépigraphes grecs de l'ancien testament*, SVTP 1 (Leiden: Brill, 1970), 93. Mercati, "Anecdota," 65–68, makes a similar argument.

74. (Augsburg: B. Filser, 1928).

75. U. Müller, "Die griechische Esra-Apokalypse," in *Jüdische Schriften aus hellenistisch-römischer Zeit V* (Gütersloh: Gerd Mohn, 1976), 88.

76. Mueller and Robbins, in "Vision of Ezra," are quite clear that the work is "thoroughly Christian."

texts. Fire is an important element of the common punishments, again suggesting a Christian background.

This does not mean that the Apocalypse of Ezra does not preserve some "Jewish" elements. The connection to 4 Ezra is much stronger in the Apocalypse of Ezra than in the Vision. The punishment for incest as described in the Apocalypse of Ezra, hanging by the eyelids, finds parallels in one Christian text and two Jewish texts: adulterers hang by their eyebrows in the Apocalypse of Paul, and men hang by their eyes for sexual sins in the Elijah fragment and *Gedulat Moshe*. The Apocalypse of Ezra is like the other Christian texts in containing fiery punishments, but unlike them in lacking geography. Further, the Apocalypse of Ezra is the only one of the Christian texts not demonstrably as early or earlier than the Apocalypse of Paul that does not seem particularly indebted to it.

It seems plausible that the Apocalypse and the Vision of Ezra derive from a Christian tour of hell written relatively early in the development of the genre, before the dominance of the Apocalypse of Paul had been established. This Ur-Ezra tour was influenced by, perhaps even modeled on, 4 Ezra.[77] The Apocalypse of Ezra preserves more of this early tour than does the Vision, which has lost many of the links to 4 Ezra and has gained many new punishments under the influence of later texts. Yet we have seen that there are clearly Christian elements among the sins and punishments that must have formed part of Ezra's tour of hell before the Vision and the Apocalypse of Ezra separated. The punishments for abortion/infanticide are clearly early (see chap. 3, above); the presence in both Ezra apocalypses of the fiery seat may indicate that this punishment is earlier than its absence from the Apocalypse of Paul would suggest. Although usually the Apocalypse of Ezra preserves the earlier form of common material, the Vision occasionally seems to be more original, as in the punishments for abortion/infanticide.

THE TESTAMENT OF ISAAC AND THE LIFE OF PACHOMIOS

Both the Testament of Isaac and the Life of Pachomios are Egyptian texts.[78] The dates of the manuscripts provide both with a *terminus ad quem* in the ninth century.

---

77. The existence of 2 Baruch, an eschatological apocalypse, and 3 Baruch, a tour of the heavens, shows that both types of apocalypse could be attributed to a single hero.

78. Some scholars would consider the Testament of Isaac a Jewish text and thus would assume a lost Greek original. I argued above (see the Testament of Isaac in chap. 1) that there is every reason to regard the Testament of Isaac as the work of Egyptian monks.

Both tours emphasize fire as a medium of punishment, and neither is obviously dependent on any other text. The authors seem to have drawn on well-known motifs of the kind common in the Apocalypse of Paul and the later tours, arranging them freely.

The angel in charge of punishments in the Testament of Isaac is called Abdemerouchos in the Sahidic, Abtelmolouchos in the Bohairic. This name must ultimately go back to the caretaking, $\tau\eta\mu\epsilon\lambda o\hat{u}\chi os$, angel of the Apocalypse of Peter. It seems likely, however, that the names in the Testament of Isaac, which are quite close to the form Aftemelouchos of the Coptic version of the Apocalypse of Paul, go back not to the Apocalypse of Peter but to a version of the Apocalypse of Paul.

CONCLUSIONS

The Tours of Hell and the History of Tour Apocalypses

The first point that can be charted in the history of the tours of hell is the Book of the Watchers in the third century B.C.E., which contains both the demonstrative explanations so important in the tours of hell and a description of the fate of souls after death. The tours of hell represent one stream in the development of tour apocalypses in the centuries after the Book of the Watchers.

In the late Second Temple period tours with a particular interest in the punishment of the wicked after death must have circulated. Hanging by the sinful limb was probably the dominant method of punishment; the heroes were probably Isaiah and Elijah.

At about the same time the Apocalypse of Zephaniah was being written. It contains demonstrative explanations and shows an interest in reward and punishment, but the brief tours of hell and paradise make up a relatively small part of the text. Its contribution to the development of the tours of hell came primarily through the scenes of departure of souls from the body and the elements of the picture of paradise that the Apocalypse of Paul drew from it (or a closely related text). With its relationship to the merkavah tradition, the Apocalypse of Zephaniah stands at the edge of the tradition of tours of hell.

Early in the Christian era the author of the Apocalypse of Peter drew on a Jewish tour or tours with hanging punishments and added to it fiery punishments and geographical features, perhaps known from other Jewish apocalypses. In the third century the author of the Apocalypse of Paul combined a tour of hell of the kind found in the Apocalypse of Peter with a tour of paradise indebted to the Apocalypse of Zephaniah but expanded to match the style of the tour of hell, and with a description of the departure of souls from the body, also indebted, as we have seen, to the Apocalypse of Zephaniah or at least to the same tradition. The relationship of the Apocalypse of Paul to the Apocalypse of Peter is probably indirect; several such tours of hell may have been available to the author of the Apocalypse of Paul.

At about the same time as the Apocalypse of Paul, an Ezra apocalypse that is no longer extant but that stands behind the Apocalypse of Ezra and the Vision of Ezra was being written. Its author probably drew on 4 Ezra as well as on the various hell traditions available to him. The Apocalypse of Ezra is closer to this early Ezra apocalypse than is the Vision.

In the succeeding centuries the Apocalypse of Paul became far more widely known than the Apocalypse of Peter and the Ezra apocalypse. The Ethiopic Apocalypse of Mary, the Ethiopic Apocalypse of Baruch, and the Apocalypse of Gorgorios are all descendants of the Apocalypse of Paul, as is the Greek Apocalypse of Mary. The tours of hell in both the Life of Pachomios and the Testament of Isaac show the influence of the Apocalypse of Paul or its descendants, although they do not take over specific details. In the West, a number of medieval redactions of the Apocalypse of Paul circulated. The Apocalypse of Paul and its descendants also had a significant influence on the Vision of Ezra.

While the early Jewish tours of hell on which the Apocalypse of Peter drew have been lost, fragments were preserved by Jews and by Christians. The Elijah fragment was preserved by the Christian author of the Epistle of Titus; the Isaiah fragment survived in Hebrew, undoubtedly transformed to some degree. This text together with a story found in the Palestinian Talmud that drew on some similar traditions contributed to the midrash quoted by R. Meir of Rothenburg in *Darkhei Teshuvah*. The amora Joshua b. Levi, already associated with otherworldly journeys by the Babylonian Talmud, became the hero of a tour of hell that seems to show the influence of these texts and perhaps other such sources. Finally, *Gedulat Moshe* integrated elements of these earlier tours with other views of hell. (See Figure 3 for a schematic and somewhat simplified representation of the development of the tours of hell.)

The history of the tours of hell is part of the history of tour apocalypses more generally, and the results of this study can be used to illumine that broader history in a preliminary way. The demonstrative explanations so central to the tours of hell do not appear in all tour apocalypses, nor are they distributed in a random manner. They appear in tours with special ties to the Book of the Watchers or with a strong interest in reward and punishment after death. The tours of hell should perhaps be treated as a

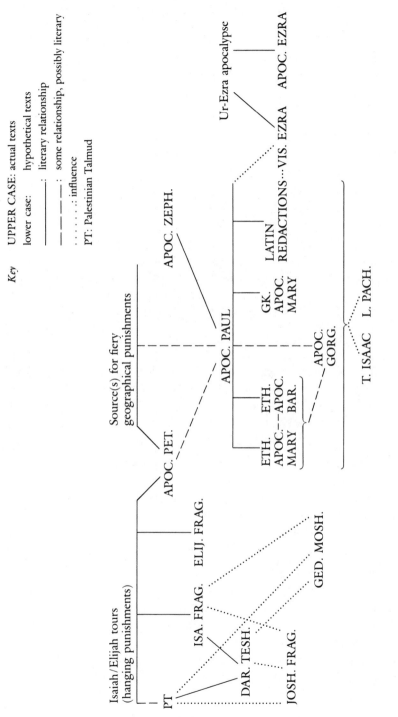

Figure 3. Family Tree for Tours of Hell

Key

UPPER CASE: actual texts

lower case: hypothetical texts

————— : literary relationship

— — — : some relationship, possibly literary

· · · · · · : influence

PT: Palestinian Talmud

Isaiah/Elijah tours (hanging punishments)

Source(s) for fiery geographical punishments

Ur-Ezra apocalypse

PT

DAR. TESH.

ISA. FRAG. ELIJ. FRAG.

JOSH. FRAG.

GED. MOSH.

APOC. PET.

APOC. ZEPH.

APOC. PAUL

ETH. APOC. MARY — ETH. APOC. BAR.

APOC. GORG.

GK. APOC. MARY

LATIN REDACTIONS · · · VIS. EZRA

APOC. EZRA

T. ISAAC L. PACH.

subdivision of this second category, which also includes 3 Baruch and the tour of the Testament of Abraham.

On the whole demonstrative explanations do not appear in the tours in which the seer is conducted through seven heavens full of angels. These apocalypses draw on the merkavah tradition that finds expression in rabbinic literature and the hekhalot texts and are perhaps more indebted to 1 Enoch 14 than to 1 Enoch 17–36; the relationship of these apocalypses to each other and to the merkavah tradition requires further study. For example, the hekhalot texts seem to be the work of a sociologically distinct group, however difficult it is to define the membership of that group. A little is known from the texts themselves about how the hekhalot literature functioned for the mystics who produced it; perhaps the function of other tour apocalypses can be illumined by the hekhalot texts.

This breakdown of the tour apocalypses into tours of the seven heavens and tours concerned with reward and punishment is crude and preliminary. Texts like the Apocalypse of Zephaniah and 2 Enoch span the categories, and attention must be given to the cosmological concerns that appear in a variety of tour apocalypses and to the relationship of the tours to history and collective eschatology.

Another central theme of this study has been a question of great importance for ancient literature generally and for the "pseudepigrapha" specifically, the question of transmission: how it was accomplished and what motivated it. One aspect of the question, the dynamics of transmission, has been touched on throughout the study. The relations among the various tours of hell offer examples of direct literary dependence, general influence, and many intermediate possibilities.

A particularly puzzling problem of transmission presents itself in relation to the medieval Jewish tours of hell, which contain early Jewish traditions ignored by or unknown to classical rabbinic literature. How did these traditions reach the Middle Ages? Despite the fact that a figure like R. Meir of Rothenburg, perhaps the leading German rabbi of the thirteenth century, could include such a tour in his responsa, the Hebrew tours of hell (except *Gedulat Moshe*) seem unaffected by the picture of hell in the classical rabbinic sources and in turn seem not to have affected that picture. The Isaiah fragment and the Joshua b. Levi fragment are copied with midrashim that contain descriptions of hell indebted to the classical rabbinic sources, and even so little cross-fertilization has occurred.

Further, texts of the type on which the medieval Hebrew fragments of tours of hell seem to draw, apocalypses of the Second Temple period, in general have not survived in Hebrew; that is, they have not been transmitted by Jews. The importance of the question of who in the Jewish world had access to these ancient works or traditions and how they were preserved goes beyond the tours of hell, for the same questions need to be raised about other medieval Jewish works that show evidence of knowledge of traditions found otherwise only in Second Temple texts no longer extant in Hebrew.

One result of the study of a long-lived tradition like that of the tours of hell is that it allows us to see how interests change. The examination of the later tours of hell contributes to a picture of the concerns of medieval Judaism and Christianity. The development of such a picture aids the study of early Judaism and Christianity, for while most scholars regard certain texts preserved only in medieval Christian manuscripts as Jewish works dating from the turn of the era, there has been little careful argument to justify these views. At least in part the absence of argument can be attributed to the paucity of data on which to base it. One remedy for this situation is the development of a clear picture of characteristic medieval concerns with which to compare the interests of texts of uncertain date and provenance.

Second Enoch is one example of such a text. While citations suggest that a Greek form survived into the thirteenth century, the earliest preserved copy of 2 Enoch is found in a Slavonic manuscript of the fifteenth century.[1] Yet 2 Enoch is most often treated as a Jewish apocalypse of the late Second Temple period.[2]

When 2 Enoch is placed alongside the tours of hell, its contents are seen to differ sharply from those of the medieval works among the tours but to show some similarities to those of the earlier works. Thus such a comparison provides another piece of evidence for an early origin for 2 Enoch.

The differences between 2 Enoch and the medieval texts are not proof that 2 Enoch is early. It would be quite circular to build up a picture of what constitute the concerns of medieval apocalypses based on a selected group of texts and then to determine that any apocalypse that failed to exhibit those concerns is earlier (or later). The broader the base on which the picture draws, the more useful it is.

Indeed, since 2 Enoch is not primarily concerned with hell, it would be more appropriate to compare it to a range of ascents through the seven heavens. This brings us back to the history of the tour apocalypses as a whole. To make that comparison possible would be the completion of the task begun here.

---

1. Vaillant, *Le livre des secrets d'Hénoch*, v, viii.

2. For this view, Charles, *APOT* 2 : 425–30, and Charlesworth, *Pseudepigrapha*, 104. There are, however, some voices in favor of medieval Christian origin; Milik (*Books of Enoch*, 107–12) presents his own version of this position and discusses some earlier formulations.

BIBLIOGRAPHY

This bibliography has two parts. The first is a Select Bibliography of the Tours of Hell. For each tour it lists editions, translations, bibliographies, and particularly significant secondary literature. There has been no attempt at completeness. In cases where other editions and translations exist, those listed have been chosen on the basis of quality and especially availability.

The second part of the bibliography is a listing of Sources Consulted. Classical texts and Philo are cited according to the Loeb Classical Library editions when available.

SELECT BIBLIOGRAPHY OF THE TOURS OF HELL

THE APOCALYPSE OF PETER

Ethiopic Text
Grébaut, S. "Littérature éthiopienne pseudo-clémentine." *Revue de l'orient chrétien* 15(1910) : 198–208, 307–8. (French translation, 208–14, 316–17.)

Greek Text
Klostermann, E. *Apokrypha I: Reste des Petrusevangeliums, der Petrusapokalypse und der Kerygma Petri.* Kleine Texte für Theologische Vorlesung und Übingen 3.1. Bonn: A. Marcus & E. Weber, 1903. 8–11.

Translation
HSW 2 : 663–83. Ethiopic trans. by H. Duensing; Greek trans. by C. Maurer. (Where the two versions correspond to each other, the translations are printed in parallel columns.)

Bibliography
Maurer, C. HSW 2 : 667–68.

Selected Studies
Dieterich, A. *Nekyia: Beiträge zur Erklärung der neuentdeckten Petrusapokalypse.* 2d
ed. annotated by R. Wünsch. Leipzig and Berlin: Teubner, 1913.
James, M. R. "The Recovery of the Apocalypse of Peter." *Church Quarterly Review*
159(1915):1–36. (A review of the new discoveries for the "reading public," still
useful today.)

THE ACTS OF THOMAS

Greek Text
Bonnet, M. *Acta Apostolorum Apocrypha* 2.2. Leipzig: H. Mendelssohn, 1903.
99–288.

Translation of the Greek Text
Bornkamm, G. HSW 2:425–531.

Syriac Text and Translation
Wright, W. *Apocryphal Acts of the Apostles* I:172–333 (text); II:146–298 (translation).

Bibliography
Bornkamm, G. HSW 2:425–26.

Selected Studies
Bornkamm, G. *Mythos und Legende in der apokryphen Thomas-Akten.* FRLANT,
n.s. 31. Göttingen: Vandenhoeck & Ruprecht, 1933.
Klijn, A. F. J. *The Acts of Thomas.* Novum Testamentum Supplements 5. Leiden:
Brill, 1962. (This is a translation of the Syriac text with a long introduction and
commentary.)

THE APOCALYPSE OF ZEPHANIAH

Text and German Translation
Steindorff, G. *Die Apokalypse des Elias, eine unbekannte Apokalypse und Bruchstücke
der Sophonias-Apokalypse.* TU, n.f. 2.3a. Leipzig: J. C. Hinrichs, 1899. 34–65.

English Translations
Houghton, H. P. "The Coptic Apocalypse." *Aegyptus* 39(1959):76–83, 87–91. (A
word-for-word translation.)
Wintermute, O. S. "Apocalypse of Zephaniah." In *The Old Testament Pseudepigrapha.* Edited by J. H. Charlesworth. Garden City, N.Y.: Doubleday, forthcoming.

Bibliography
Charlesworth, J. H. *The Pseudepigrapha and Modern Research with a Supplement.* SCS 7S. Chico, Calif.: Scholars Press, 1981. 220–23, 307.

Selected Studies
The Apocalypse of Zephaniah has been more or less ignored by students of early Judaism and Christianity. The very brief but suggestive remarks offered by Harnack and James remain the most significant comments on this apocalypse.

Harnack, A. von. *Geschichte der altchristlichen Literatur bis Eusebius.* 2d ed. Introduction by K. Aland. Leipzig: J. C. Hinrichs, 1958; 1st ed. 1893–1904. Part 2.1, 572–73.
James, M. R. *ApNT* 530, nn. 1, 3; 534, n. 1; 540, n. 1.
———. *LAOT* 73–74.

THE APOCALYPSE OF PAUL

Texts

Paris MS: James, M. R. *Apocrypha Anecdota.* Texts and Studies 2.3. Cambridge: Cambridge University, 1893. 11–42.
St. Gall MS: Silverstein, T. *Visio S. Pauli.* Studies and Documents 4. London: Christophers, 1935. 131–47.

Translations

James, M. R. *ApNT* 526–55. (Based on Paris MS, with readings and passages drawn from the Coptic, Greek, and Syriac versions.)
Duensing, H. *HSW* 2:755–803. (Based on Paris MS, with readings and passages drawn from the St. Gall MS, and the Coptic, Greek, and Syriac versions.)

Bibliography

Duensing. *HSW* 2:758–59.
Silverstein: *Visio.* 219–29.

Selected Studies

Casey, R. "The Apocalypse of Paul." *JTS* 34(1933):1–32. (The best summary treatment.)
Silverstein, *Visio.* (The main interest of this study is the development and interrelations of the medieval Latin redactions; it also offers the most complete discussion of the relations among the versions.)

THE ETHIOPIC APOCALYPSE OF MARY

Text and Latin Translation
Chaîne, M. "Apocalypsis seu Visio Mariae Virginis." In *Apocrypha de B. Mariae Virginis.* Corpus Scriptorum Christianorum Orientalium. Scriptores Aethiopici 1/7 (1909). Ethiopic section 51–80; Latin section 43–68.

Bibliography
Collins, A. Y. "Early Christian Apocalypses." In *Apocalypse: The Morphology of a Genre (Semeia* 14[1979]). Edited by J. J. Collins. 115.

Selected Studies
Chaîne's introductions (in Latin) to both the Latin and Ethiopic sections of his edition are the most extended discussions of this little-studied text.

THE ETHIOPIC APOCALYPSE OF BARUCH

Text and French Translation
Halévy, J. *Tě'ězāza Sanbat (Commandements du sabbat).* Bibliothèque de l'École des Hautes Études 137. Paris: É. Bouillon, 1902. 80–96 (text); 196–209 (translation).

English Translation
Leslau, W. *Falasha Anthology.* Yale Judaica Series 6. New Haven: Yale University, 1951. 57–76.

Bibliography
Leslau, W. *Falasha Anthology.* 64.

Selected Studies
Very little has been written about this text. Leslau provides an introduction, and his remarks about the Book of the Angels (50–52), another work included in the *Falasha Anthology,* are also relevant.

THE APOCALYPSE OF GORGORIOS

Text and French Translation
Halévy, J. *Tě'ězāza Sanbat (Commandements du sabbat).* Bibliothèque de l'École des Hautes Études 137. Paris: É. Bouillon, 1902. 97–107 (text); 210–19 (translation).

English Translation
Leslau, W. *Falasha Anthology.* Yale Judaica Series 6. New Haven: Yale University, 1951. 77–91.

Bibliography
Leslau, W. *Falasha Anthology*. 81.

Selected Studies
Very little has been written about this text. Leslau provides an introduction.

THE GREEK APOCALYPSE OF MARY

Text
James, M. R. *Apocrypha Anecdota*. Texts and Studies 2.3. Cambridge: Cambridge
  University, 1893. 115–26.

Translation
Rutherford, A. *Ante-Nicene Fathers* 9. New York: Scribner's, 1899. 169–74.

Bibliography
Collins, A. Y. "Early Christian Apocalypses." In *Apocalypse: Morphology of a Genre*
  (*Semeia* 14[1979]). Edited by J. J. Collins. 116.

Selected Studies
Very little has been written about this text. James, M. R. *Apocrypha Anecdota*,
  111–15, is probably the most useful introduction.

THE APOCALYPSE OF EZRA AND THE VISION OF EZRA

Texts
Wahl, O. *Apocalypsis Esdrae. Apocalypsis Sedrach. Visio Beati Esdrae*. PVTG 4.
  Leiden: Brill, 1977.

Translation—Apocalypse of Ezra
Walker, A. *Ante-Nicene Fathers* 8. New York: Scribner's, 1899. 571–74.

Translations—Vision of Ezra
Riessler, P. *Altjüdisches Schrifttum ausserhalb der Bibel*. Augsburg: B. Filser, 1928.
  350–54.
Mueller, J., and Robbins, G. "Vision of Ezra." In *The Old Testament Pseudepigrapha*.
  Edited by J. H. Charlesworth. Garden City, N.Y.: Doubleday, forthcoming.

Bibliography
Wahl, O. *Apocalypsis Esdrae*. 9–11.

Selected Studies
James, M. R. Introduction to R. L. Bensly, *The Fourth Book of Ezra*. Texts and Studies 3.2. Cambridge: Cambridge University, 1895.
Stone, M. E. "The Metamorphosis of Ezra: Jewish Apocalypse and Medieval Vision." *JTS* n.s. 33(1982):1–18.

THE TESTAMENT OF ISAAC

Sahidic Text
Kuhn, K. H. "The Sahidic Version of the Testament of Isaac." *JTS* n.s. 8(1957): 225–39.

Bohairic Text
Guidi, I. *Il Testamento di Isaaco e il Testamento di Giacobbe*. Rendiconti della Reale Accademia dei Lincei. Classe di scienze morali, storiche e filologiche 5/9. Rome: Accademia, 1900. 223–64.

Translation of the Sahidic Text
Kuhn, K. H. "An English Translation of the Sahidic Version of the Testament of Isaac." *JTS* n.s. 18(1967):325–36.

Translation of the Bohairic Text
Chaîne, M. in M. Delcor, *Le Testament d'Abraham*. SVTP 2. Leiden: Brill, 1973.

Bibliography
Charlesworth, J. H. *The Pseudepigrapha and Modern Study with a Supplement*. SCS 7S. Chico, Calif.: Scholars Press, 1981. 123–25, 305.

Selected Studies
James, M. R. *The Testament of Abraham*. Texts and Studies 2.2. Cambridge: Cambridge University, 1892. 153–61. (James's comments, with Kuhn's remarks in his introductions to the text and translation, seem to me the best things written on the Testament of Isaac.)

THE LIFE OF PACHOMIOS

Text
Lefort, L. T. *S. Pachomii Vita bohairice scripta*. Corpus Scriptorum Christianorum Orientalium. Scriptores Coptici 3/7 (1925).

Translation
Lefort, L. T. *Les vies coptes de Saint Pachôme et de ses premiers successeurs*. Bibliothèque du *Muséon* 16. Louvain: *Muséon*, 1943.

THE MIDRASH FROM DARKHEI TESHUVAH

Text and German Translation
Gressmann, H. *Vom Reichen Mann und Armen Lazarus*. Abhandlungen der königlichen preussischen Akademie der Wissenschaften, Phil.-hist. Klasse. Berlin: Akademie, 1918. 79–83.

Selected Studies
Lieberman, S. "On Sins and Their Punishments." In *Texts and Studies*. New York: KTAV, 1974.

THE ISAIAH FRAGMENT

Texts and Translations
1. Chronicles of Yeraḥme'el: Stone, M. E., and Strugnell, J. *The Books of Elijah, Parts 1 and 2*. Texts and Translations 18; Pseudepigrapha Series 8. Missoula, Mont.: Scholars Press, 1979. 20–23. (Hebrew text with facing English translation.)
2. "A Description of Judgment in the Grave": Jellinek, A., ed. *Bet ha-Midrasch*. Reprint ed. Jerusalem: Wahrmann, 1967. 1st ed. 1853–78. 5:50–51. (Hebrew text; no translation of this version is available.)
3 and 4. Geniza texts: Ginzberg, L. *Ginze Schechter: Genizah Studies in Memory of Dr. Solomon Schechter*. Vol. 1: *Midrash and Haggadah* (Hebr.). Texts and Studies of the Jewish Theological Seminary of America 7. New York: Jewish Theological Seminary, 1928. 196–98, 204–5. (Hebrew texts; no translation of these versions is available.)

Selected Studies
Lieberman, S. "On Sins and Their Punishments." In *Texts and Studies*. New York: KTAV, 1974.

THE JOSHUA B. LEVI FRAGMENT

Texts and Translations
1. Chronicles of Yeraḥme'el: Stone, M. E., and Strugnell, J. *The Books of Elijah, Parts 1 and 2*. Texts and Translations 18; Pseudepigrapha Series 8. Missoula, Mont.: Scholars Press, 1979. 16–18. (Hebrew text with facing English translation.)
2. *Reshit Ḥokhmah*: Stone and Strugnell, *Books of Elijah*. 18–20. (Hebrew text with facing English translation.)

GEDULAT MOSHE

Text
Wertheimer, S. A. *Batei Midrashot.* 2d ed. Jerusalem: Mosad ha-Rav Kook, 1954. 1:273–85. (Wertheimer publishes a Yemenite MS entitled "Like an Apple Tree Among the Trees of the Forest." According to A. J. Wertheimer, the work was first published in Salonika in 1726–27 as *Gedulat Moshe* and it has been printed many times since under that title. In the second edition of *Batei Midrashot*, A. J. Wertheimer notes differences between the printed version and the Yemenite MS.)

Translation
Gaster, M. "Hebrew Visions of Hell and Paradise." *Journal of the Royal Asiatic Society* 23(1893):572–82. Reprinted in Gaster, M. *Studies and Texts in Folklore, Magic, Medieval Romance, Hebrew Apocrypha, and Samaritan Archeology.* London: Maggs Bros., 1925–28.

Selected Studies
Lieberman, S. "On Sins and Their Punishments." In *Texts and Studies.* New York: KTAV, 1974.

THE ELIJAH FRAGMENT

Text and Translation
Stone, M. E., and Strugnell, J. *The Books of Elijah, Parts 1 and 2.* Texts and Translations 18; Pseudepigrapha Series 8. Missoula, Mont.: Scholars Press, 1979. 14–15. (Latin text with facing English translation.)

Selected Studies
Lieberman, S. "On Sins and Their Punishments." In *Texts and Studies.* New York: KTAV, 1974.

SOURCES CONSULTED

Abel, A. "Changements politiques et littérature eschatologique dans le monde musulman." *Studia Islamica* 2(1954):23–43.
Amélineau, E., trans. "Vie arabe de Schnoudi." *Memoires de la mission archéologique française au Caire* 4 (1888): *Monuments pour servir à l'histoire de l'Egypte chrétienne aux IV⁰ et V⁰ siècles.*
Asín Palacios, M. *La escatalogía musulmana en la Divina Comedia.* 2d ed. Madrid-Granada: Escuelas de Estudios Arabes, 1943.

————. *Islam and the Divine Comedy.* Trans. H. Sunderland. London: John Murray, 1926.

Becker, E. J. *A Contribution to the Comparative Study of the Medieval Visions of Heaven and Hell with Special Reference to the Middle English Versions.* Baltimore: J. Murphy, 1899.

Bensly, R. L. *The Fourth Book of Ezra.* Introduction by M. R. James. Texts and Studies 3.2. Cambridge: Cambridge University, 1895.

Berger, K. *Die griechische Daniel-Diegese.* Leiden: Brill, 1976.

Bertram, G. "κρέμαννυμι." *TDNT* 3(1964):918.

Blau, L. "Gehenna." *JE.*

Bornkamm, G. *Mythos und Legende in den apokryphen Thomas-Akten.* FRLANT, n.s. 31. Göttingen: Vandenhoeck & Ruprecht, 1933.

Bousset, W. *The Antichrist Legend.* Prologue and trans. A. H. Keane. London: Hutchinson & Co., 1896.

Boyce, M. "Middle Persian Literature." In *Iranistik* 4.2.1. Handbuch der Orientalistik I. Leiden: Brill, 1968.

Bruyne, D. de. "Epistula Titi, Discipuli Pauli, de Dispositione Sanctimonii." *Revue bénédictine* 37(1925):47–72.

————. "Nouveaux fragments des Actes de Pierre, de Paul, de Jean, d'André et de l'Apocalypse d'Élie." *Revue Bénédictine* 25(1908):318–35.

Budge, E. A. W., ed. and trans. *The Book of the Dead: The Chapters of Coming Forth by Day.* London: Kegan Paul, Trench, Trübner, 1896.

————. *Coptic Texts* vol. 5. (Reprint of *Miscellaneous Coptic Texts in the Dialect of Upper Egypt* [1915].) New York: AMS, 1977.

Casey, R. "The Apocalypse of Paul." *JTS* 34(1933):1–32.

Cerulli, E. *Il "Libro della scala" e la questione delle fonti arabo-spagnole della Divina Commedia.* Studi e Testi 150. Rome: Vatican, 1949.

Chaîne, M. "Apocalypsis seu Visio Mariae Virginis." *Apocrypha de B. Mariae Virginis.* Corpus Scriptorum Christianorum Orientalium. Scriptores Aethiopici 1/7 (1909). Ethiopic section 51–80; Latin section 43–68.

Charles, R. H. *The Apocrypha and Pseudepigrapha of the Old Testament.* Oxford: Oxford University, 1913.

————. *The Ascension of Isaiah.* London: A. & C. Black, 1900.

————. *The Book of Enoch.* Oxford: Oxford University, 1912.

Charlesworth, J. H. *The Pseudepigrapha and Modern Study with a Supplement.* SCS 7S. Chico, Calif.: Scholars Press, 1981.

Clement of Alexandria. Ed. and trans. R. Casey. *Excerpta ex Theodoto.* Studies and Documents 1. London: Christophers, 1934.

Cohn, H. H. "Talion." *EJ.*

Collins, J. J. *The Apocalyptic Vision of the Book of Daniel.* Harvard Semitic Monographs 16. Missoula, Mont.: Scholars Press, 1977.

————. "Jewish Apocalyptic Against Its Hellenistic Near Eastern Environment." *Bulletin of the American Schools of Oriental Research* 220(1975):27–36.

Collins, J. J., ed. *Apocalypse: The Morphology of a Genre* (*Semeia* 14 [1979]).

Cross, F. L., and Livingstone, E. A. *The Oxford Dictionary of the Christian Church.* 2d ed. London: Oxford University, 1974.

Cumont, F. *Lux Perpetua.* Paris: P. Geuthner, 1949.

Danby, H., trans. *The Mishnah.* London: Oxford University, 1933.

Delcor, M. *Le Testament d'Abraham.* SVTP 2. Leiden: Brill, 1973.

Denis, A.-M. *Introduction aux pseudépigraphes grecs de l'ancien testament.* SVTP 1. Leiden: Brill, 1970.

Dieterich, A. *Nekyia: Beiträge zur Erklärung der neuentdeckten Petrusapokalypse.* 2d ed., annotated by R. Wünsch. Leipzig and Berlin: Teubner, 1913. First ed., 1893.

Dinzelbacher, P. "Die Vision Alberichs und die Esdras-Apokryphe." *Studien und Mitteilungen zur Geschichte des Benediktiner-Ordens und seiner Zweige* 87(1976): 435–42.

Dobschütz, E. von. Review of A. Dieterich, *Nekyia. Zeitscrift für Kulturgeschichte,* 1894, 340–48.

Easton, B. S. "NT Ethical Lists." *Journal of Biblical Literature* 51(1932): 1–12.

Edsman, C.-M. *Le baptême de feu.* Uppsala: Almquist & Wiksell, 1940.

Eissfeldt, O. *The Old Testament: An Introduction.* Trans. from the 3d Ger. ed. of 1964 by P. R. Ackroyd. New York: Harper & Row, 1976.

Eitrem, S. "Phlegethon." PW.

Elbaum, J. "Tanna de'vei Eliyahu." *EJ.*

Epstein, L. *Sex Laws and Customs in Judaism.* New York: Bloch, 1948.

Fischer, U. *Eschatologie und Jenseitserwartung im hellenistischen Diasporajudentum.* Berlin: De Gruyter, 1978.

Fishbane, M. "Accusations of Adultery: A Study of Law and Scribal Practice in Numbers 5:11–31." *HUCA* 45(1974): 25–45.

———. "The Qumran Pesher and Traits of Ancient Hermeneutics." *Proceedings of the Sixth World Congress of Jewish Studies* (Jerusalem, 1977), 97–114.

Gaster, M. "Hebrew Visions of Hell and Paradise." *Journal of the Royal Asiatic Society* 23(1893): 571–611. Reprinted in Gaster, M. *Studies and Texts in Folklore, Magic, Medieval Romance, Hebrew Apocrypha, and Samaritan Archeology* 1: 124–64. London: Maggs Bros., 1925–28.

Gaster, M., ed. and trans. *The Chronicles of Jerahmeel.* 2d ed. Prolegomenon by H. Schwarzbaum. New York: KTAV, 1971.

Ginzberg, L. "Baruch, Apocalypse of (Greek)." *JE.*

———. *The Legends of the Jews.* Philadelphia: Jewish Publication Society, 1909.

Ginzberg, L. ed. *Ginze Schechter: Genizah Studies in Memory of Dr. Solomon Schechter.* Vol. 1: *Midrash and Haggadah* (Hebr.). Texts and Studies of the Jewish Theological Seminary of America 7. New York: Jewish Theological Seminary, 1928.

Gowers, E. *A Life for a Life?* London: Chatto & Windus, 1956.

Grébaut, S. "Littérature éthiopienne pseudo-clémentine." *Revue de l'orient chrétien* 12(1907): 139–51, 285–97; 15(1910): 198–214, 307–23, 424–39.

Greenberg, J. "Crimes and Punishments." *Interpreter's Dictionary of the Bible.* New York and Nashville, Tenn.: Abingdon, 1962.

Greenberg, M. "Ezekiel." *EJ*.

Greenfield, J. C., and Stone, M. E. "The Enochic Pentateuch and the Date of the Similitudes." *Harvard Theological Review* 70(1977):51–66.

Gressmann, H. *Vom reichen Mann und Armen Lazarus*. Abhandlungen der königlich preussischen Akademie der Wissenschaften, Phil.-hist. Klasse. Berlin: Akademie, 1918.

Griffith, F. L., ed. and trans. *Stories of the High Priests of Memphis*. Oxford: Oxford University, 1900.

Gruenwald, I. *Apocalyptic and Merkavah Mysticism*. Leiden: Brill, 1980.

Harnack, A. von. "Der apokryphe Brief des Paulusschülers Titus 'De dispositione sanctimonii'." *Sitzungsberichte der preussischen Akademie der Wissenschaften*, Phil.-hist. Klasse 17(1925):180–213.

———. *Geschichte der altchristlichen Literatur bis Eusebius*. 2d ed. Introduction by K. Aland. Leipzig: J. C. Hinrichs, 1958. 1st ed. 1893–1904.

———. *Die Petrusapokalypse in der alten abendländischen Kirche*. TU 13.1. Leipzig: J. C. Hinrichs, 1895.

Harrison, A. R. W. *The Law of Athens: Procedure*. Oxford: Oxford University, 1971.

Hauck, F. "μοιχεύω." *TDNT* 4(1967):729–35.

Hauck, F., and Schulz, S. "πορνή." *TDNT* 6(1968):579–95.

Haug, M. *The Book of Arda Viraf*. Assisted by E. W. West. Text prepared by Destur Hoshangji Jampaspji Asa. Bombay: Government Central Book Depot; London: Trübner, 1872.

Hennecke, E. *New Testament Apocrypha*. Edited by W. Schneemelcher; English translation edited by R. McL. Wilson. Philadelphia: Westminster, 1963–65.

Herdlitczka. "Talio." PW.

Himmelfarb, M. "A Report on Enoch in Rabbinic Literature." SBL Seminar Papers 1978, vol. 1, 259–69.

———. "R. Moses the Preacher and the Testaments of the Twelve Patriarchs." *AJS review* 9. Forthcoming.

Houghton, H. P. "The Coptic Apocalypse." *Aegyptus* 39(1959):40–91, 170–210.

Hylén, J. E. *De Tantalo*. Uppsala: Almquist & Wiksell, 1896.

Ibn Shmuel, Y. *Midreshei Geulah*. Jerusalem and Tel Aviv: Mosad Bialik, 1954.

James, M. R. *Apocrypha Anecdota*. Texts and Studies 2.3. Cambridge: Cambridge University, 1893.

———. *The Apocryphal New Testament*. Oxford: Oxford University, 1924.

———. *The Lost Apocrypha of the Old Testament*. London: SPCK, 1920.

———. "A New Text of the Apocalypse of Peter." *JTS* 12(1910–11):36–54, 157, 362–83, 573–83.

———. "The Rainer Fragment of the Apocalypse of Peter." *JTS* 32(1931):270–79.

———. "The Recovery of the Apocalypse of Peter." *Church Quarterly Review* 159(1915):1–36.

———. *The Testament of Abraham*. Texts and Studies 2.2. Cambridge: Cambridge University, 1892.

James, M. R., and Robinson, J. A. *The Gospel According to Peter and the Revelation of Peter.* London: C. J. Clay & Sons, 1892.

Jellinek, A. *Bet ha-Midrasch.* Reprint ed. Jerusalem: Wahrmann, 1967. 1st ed. 1853–78.

Jensen, J. "Does *Porneia* Mean Fornication? A Critique of Bruce Malina." *Novum Testamentum* 20(1978) : 161–84.

Jeremias, J. "γέεννα." *TDNT* 1(1964) : 657–58.

Jonge, M. de. "Notes on the Testament of Levi II–VII." In de Jonge, ed., *Studies on the Testaments of the Twelve Patriarchs.* SVTP 3. Leiden: Brill, 1975.

Joüon, P. "Respondit et dixit." *Biblica* 13(1932) : 309–14.

Kadushin, M. *The Theology of Seder Eliahu.* New York, Bloch, 1932.

Kedar, B. "Netherworld: In the Aggadah." *EJ.*

Klijn, A. F. J. *The Acts of Thomas.* Novum Testamentum Supplements 5. Leiden: Brill, 1962.

Knibb, M. A. *The Ethiopic Book of Enoch: A New Edition in the Light of the Aramaic Dead Sea Fragments.* In consultation with E. Ullendorf. Oxford: Oxford University, 1978.

Kraft, R. A. "'Ezra' Materials in Judaism and Christianity." *Aufstieg und Niedergang der römischen Welt* II.19.1.

———. "The Pseudepigrapha in Christianity." Paper read at Studiorum Novi Testamenti Societas meeting at Duke University, August 1978.

———. "Reassessing the 'Recensional Problem' in the Testament of Abraham." In G. W. E. Nickelsburg, ed., *Studies on the Testament of Abraham.* SCS 6. Missoula, Mont.: Scholars Press, 1976.

Kuhn, K. G. *Konkordanz zu den Qumran-texten.* Göttingen: Vandenhoeck & Ruprecht, 1966.

Kuhn, K. H. "An English Translation of the Sahidic Version of the Testament of Isaac." *JTS* n.s. 18(1967) : 325–36.

———. "The Sahidic Version of the Testament of Isaac." *JTS* n.s. 8(1957) : 225–39.

Lacau, P. "Remarques sur le manuscrit akhmimique des apocalypses de Sophonie et d'Elie." *Journal asiatique* 254(1966) : 169–95.

Lang, F. "πῦρ." *TDNT* 6(1968) : 928–48.

Le Blant, E. *Les persécuteurs et les martyrs aux premiers siècles de notre ère.* Paris: E. Leroux, 1893.

Leclerq, H. "Catasta." *Dictionnaire d'archéologie chrétienne et de liturgie.* Paris: Letouzey & Ané, 1907–53.

Lefort, L. T. *Les vies coptes de Saint Pachôme et de ses premiers successeurs.* Bibliothèque de *Muséon* 16. Louvain: *Muséon,* 1943.

Leslau, W. *Falasha Anthology.* Yale Judaica Series 6. New Haven: Yale University, 1951.

Levenson, J. D. *Theology of the Program of Restoration of Ezekiel 40–48.* Harvard Semitic Monographs 10. Missoula, Mont.: Scholars Press, 1976.

Lévi, I. "Le repos sabbatique des âmes damnées." *Revue des études juives* 25(1892) : 1–32.

Lévy, I. *La légende de Pythagore de Grèce en Palestine.* Bibliothèque de l'École des Hautes Études, Sciences Historiques et Philologiques 250. Champion: Paris, 1927.

Lieberman, S. "On Sins and Their Punishments." In *Texts and Studies.* New York: KTAV, 1974. (English translation of "On Sins and Their Punishments" [Hebr.] in *Louis Ginzberg Jubilee Volume,* Hebrew section. New York: American Academy of Jewish Research, 1945.)

————. "Roman Legal Institutions in Early Rabbinics and in the Acta Martyrum." In *Texts and Studies.* New York: KTAV, 1974. (First printed in *Jewish Quarterly Review* 35[1944] : 1–55.)

————. *Shkiin.* 2d ed. Jerusalem: Wahrmann, 1970.

————. "Some Aspects of After Life in Early Rabbinic Literature." In *Harry Austryn Wolfson Jubilee Volume,* English section. Jerusalem: American Academy of Jewish Research, 1965.

Linforth, I. M. *The Arts of Orpheus.* Berkeley and Los Angeles: University of California, 1941.

Maier, J. "Das Gefärdungsmotiv bei der Himmelreise in der jüdischen Apokalyptik und 'Gnosis.'" *Kairos* 5(1963) : 18–40.

Mann, J. "Genizah Studies." *American Journal of Semitic Languages and Literature* 46(1930) : 267–68.

Marmelstein, B. Review of L. Ginzberg, *Ginze Schechter. Kiryat Sefer* 6(1929–30) : 324.

Marmorstein, A. "Jüdische Parallelen zur Petrus Apokalypse." *Zeitschrift für die neutestamentliche Wissenschaft* 10(1909) : 297–300.

Mendelsohn, S. "Capital Punishment." *JE.*

Mercati, G. "Anecdota apocrypha latina. Una 'Visio' ed una 'Revelatio' d'Esdra con un decreto di Clemente Romano." In *Note di letteratura biblica e christiana antica.* Studi e Testi 5. Rome: Vatican, 1901.

Milik, J. T. *The Books of Enoch: Aramaic Fragments of Qumrân Cave 4.* In collaboration with M. Black. Oxford: Oxford University, 1976.

————. "Le Testament de Lévi en araméen: Fragment de la grotte 4 de Qumrân." *Revue biblique* 62(1955) : 398–406.

Monbeck, M. E. *The Meaning of Blindness: Attitudes Toward Blindness and Blind People.* Bloomington, Ind., and London: Indiana University, 1973.

Mueller, J. R. and Robbins, G. E. "Vision of Ezra." In J. H. Charlesworth, ed., *The Old Testament Pseudepigrapha.* Garden City, N.Y.: Doubleday, in press.

Müller, U. "Die griechische Esra-Apokalypse." In *Jüdische Schriften aus hellenistisch-römischen Zeit.* V. Gütersloh: Gerd Mohn, 1976.

Nagel, P. "Zur sahidischen Version des Testaments Isaaks." *Wissenschaftliche Zeitschrift der Martin-Luther-Universität Halle-Wittenberg* 12(1963) : 259–63.

Nickelsburg, G. W. E. "Enoch, Levi, and Peter: Recipients of Revelation in Upper Galilee." *Journal of Biblical Literature* 100(1981) : 575–600.

————. "Eschatology in the Testament of Abraham." In Nickelsburg, ed., *Studies on the Testament of Abraham.* SCS 6. Missoula, Mont.: Scholars Press, 1976.

————. *Jewish Literature Between the Bible and the Mishnah.* Philadelphia: Fortress, 1981.

Nilsson, M. P. *Geschichte der griechischen Religion.* Handbuch der Altertums Wissenschaft. Munich: C. H. Beck, 1941.

Noonan, J. T., Jr. *Contraception: A History of Its Treatment by the Catholic Theologians and Canonists.* Cambridge, Mass.: Harvard University, Belknap, 1965.

Odeberg, H. *3 Enoch or the Hebrew Book of Enoch.* Cambridge: Cambridge University, 1928. Reprinted with a prolegomenon by J. C. Greenfield. New York: KTAV, 1973.

Olivieri, A., ed. *Lamellae Aureae Orphicae.* Kleine Texte für Vorlesungen und Übungen. Bonn: A. Marcus & E. Weber, 1915.

Pelikan, J. *The Christian Tradition: A History of the Development of Doctrine.* 3 vols. to date. Chicago and London: University of Chicago, 1971–.

Peter the Venerable. *Tractatus Contra Judaeos. Patrologia Latina* 189, 631–43.

Phillips, A. *Deuteronomy.* Cambridge Bible Commentary. Cambridge: Cambridge University, 1973.

Picard, J.-C. "Observations sur l'Apocalypse grecque de Baruch." *Semitica* 20 (1970): 77–103.

Pietersma, A., and Comstock, S. T. With H. A. Attridge. *The Apocalypse of Elijah.* Texts and Translations 9; Pseudepigrapha Series 19. Chico, Calif.: Scholars Press, 1981.

Pomeroy, S. B. *Goddesses, Whores, Wives, and Slaves: Women in Classical Antiquity.* New York: Schocken, 1975.

Pritchard, J., ed. *Ancient Near Eastern Texts Relating to the Old Testament.* 2d ed. Princeton: Princeton University, 1955.

Prümm, K. "De Genuino Apocalypsis Petri Textu." *Biblica* 10 (1929): 62–80.

Rad, G. von. *Deuteronomy: A Commentary.* Old Testament Library. London: SCM, 1966.

Riessler, P. *Altjüdisches Schrifttum ausserhalb der Bibel.* Augsburg: B. Filser, 1928.

Rosenstiehl, J.-M. *L'Apocalypse d'Élie.* Textes et études pour servir à l'histoire du Judaisme intertestamentaire 1. Paris: P. Geuthner, 1972.

Russell, D. S. *The Method and Message of Jewish Apocalyptic.* Philadelphia: Westminster, 1964.

Scheuer, W. "Tantalos." *Ausführliches Lexicon der griechischen und römischen Mythologie.* Leipzig: Teubner, 1889–1937.

Schmidt, C. Review of A. Dieterich, *Nekyia. Theologische Literaturzeitung,* 1894, 56–65.

Scholem, G. *Jewish Gnosticism, Merkavah Mysticism, and Talmudic Tradition.* 2d ed. New York: Jewish Theological Seminary, 1965.

————. "Kabbalah." *EJ.*

————. *Major Trends in Jewish Mysticism.* 3d ed. New York: Schocken, 1954.

————. "The Paradisic Garb of Souls and the Origin of the Concept of *Haluka de Rabbanan*" (Hebr.). *Tarbiz* 24(1955): 290–306.

Schwarzbaum, H. "The Prophet Elijah and R. Joshua b. Levi" (Hebr.). *Yeda'-'am* 7(1960): 22–31.

Schwenn. "Tantalos." PW.

Segal, A. F. *Two Powers in Heaven.* Leiden: Brill, 1977.

Segal, M. Z. *Sefer ben Sirah haShalem.* 2d ed. Jerusalem: Mosad Bialik, 1958.

Seymour, St. J. *Irish Visions of the Other World.* London: SPCK, 1930.

Shore, A. F., ed. *Joshua I–VI and Other Passages in Coptic Edited from a Fourth-Century Sahidic Codex in the Chester Beatty Library in Dublin.* Chester Beatty Monograph Series 9. Dublin: Hodges Figgis, 1963.

Silverstein, T. "Dante and the Legend of the *Mi'rāj*: The Problem of Islamic Influence on the Christian Literature of the Other World." *Journal of Near Eastern Studies* 11(1952): 89–110, 187–97.

———. "The Vision of St. Paul: New Links and Patterns in the Western Tradition." *Archives d'histoire doctrinale et littéraire du moyen âge* 34(1959): 199–248.

———. *Visio Sancti Pauli.* Studies and Documents 4. London: Christophers, 1935.

Smith, J. Z. "Wisdom and Apocalyptic." In B. A. Pearson, ed., *Religious Syncretism in Antiquity: Essays in Conversation with Geo Widengren.* Missoula, Mont.: Scholars Press, 1975.

Spitta, F. "Die Petrusapokalypse und der zweite Petrusbrief." *Zeitschrift für die neutestamentaliche Wissenschaft* 12(1911): 237–42.

Steindorff, G. *Die Apokalypse des Elias, eine unbekannte Apokalypse und Bruchstücke der Sophonias-Apokalypse.* TU n.s. 2.3a. Leipzig: J. C. Hinrichs, 1899.

Stern, L. "Die koptische Apokalypse des Sophonias." *Zeitschrift für ägyptische Sprache und Altertumskunde* 24(1886): 115–35.

Stone, M. E. "The Book of Enoch and Judaism in the Third Century B.C.E." *Catholic Biblical Quarterly* 40(1978): 479–92.

———. "Lists of Revealed Things in Apocalyptic Literature." In F. M. Cross, W. Lemke, P. D. Miller, eds., *Magnalia Dei: The Mighty Acts of God (Essays on the Bible and Archeology in Memory of G. Ernest Wright).* Garden City, N.Y.: Doubleday, 1976.

———. "The Metamorphosis of Ezra: Jewish Apocalypse and Medieval Vision." *JTS* n.s. 33(1982): 1–18.

Stone, M. E., and Strugnell, J. *The Books of Elijah, Parts 1 and 2.* Texts and Translations 18; Pseudepigrapha Series 8. Missoula, Mont.: Scholars Press, 1979.

Strack, H. L. *Introduction to the Talmud and Midrash.* Philadelphia: Jewish Publication Society, 1931.

Talmon, S., and Fishbane, M. "The Structuring of Biblical Books: Studies in the Book of Ezekiel." *Annual of the Swedish Theological Institute* 10(1975–76): 129–53.

Thomson, G. *Aeschylus and Athens.* 2d ed., 1946. Reprint ed., New York: Haskell House, 1972.

Timbie, J. "Dualism and the Concept of Orthodoxy in the Thought of the Monks of Upper Egypt." Ph.D. dissertation, University of Pennsylvania, 1979.

Tromp, N. J. *Primitive Conceptions of Death and the Nether World in the Old Testament.* Rome: Pontifical Biblical Institute, 1969.

Turcan, R. "La catabase orphique du papyrus de Bologne." *Revue de l'histoire des religions* 150(1956): 136–72.

Ullendorf, E. *Ethiopia and the Bible.* London: British Academy, 1968.

Vaillant, A. *Le livre des secrets d'Hénoch*. Paris: Institut d'Études slaves, 1952.

Veilleux, A. *La liturgie dans le cénobitisme pachômien au quatrième siècle*. Studia Anselmiana 57. Rome: Pontifical Institute of St. Anselm, 1968.

Vermes, G. *The Dead Sea Scrolls: Qumran in Perspective*. Cleveland: William Collins & World, 1978.

Violet, B. *Die Esra-Apokalypse*. GCS 18. Leipzig: J. C. Hinrichs, 1910.

Wernberg-Møller, P. *The Manual of Discipline*. Leiden: Brill, 1957.

Wertheimer, S. A. *Batei Midrashot*. 2d ed. Jerusalem: Mosad ha-Rav Cook, 1954.

Wahl, O. *Apocalypsis Esdrae. Apocalypsis Sedrach. Visio Beati Esdrae*. PVTG 4. Leiden: Brill, 1977.

————. "Vier neue Textzeugen der 'Visio Beati Esdrae.'" *Salesianum* 40(1978): 583–89.

Wibbing, S. *Die Tugend- und Lasterkataloge im Neuen Testament und ihre Traditionsgeschichte unter besonderer Berücksichtigung der Qumran-Texte*. Berlin: A. Töpelman, 1959.

Wurmbrand, M. "Falashas." *EJ*.

Wüst, E. "Erinys." PW suppl. 8.

Zandee, J. *Death as an Enemy*. Leiden: Brill, 1960.

Ziegler, J. *Septuaginta 14: Isaias*. Göttingen: Vandenhoeck & Ruprecht, 1939.

Zunz, L., and Albeck, H. *HaDerashot b'Yisrael*. Jerusalem: Mosad Bialik, 1947.

INDEX

Abaddon, 110n.24

Abdemerouchos, 168

Abortion, 69–72, 74–75. *See also* Abortion/infanticide, punishment for; Infanticide

Abortion/infanticide, punishment for, 6, 39n.96, 96–103, 141–43, 146–47, 161–62, 165–67

Abraham, Apocalypse of, 61, 65

Abraham, Testament of, 27, 61–63, 172

Abtelmolouchos, 168

Abysses. *See* Pits

Accuser, 148–49, 151, 155

Acherusia, 10, 17

Acts (of the Apostles), 113n.45

Acts of the Martyrs, 85, 119–20. *See also* Martyrs

Adultery, 38n.96, 69–71, 73–74, 87, 89, 91, 96, 132, 134–35, 145, 163, 167. *See also* Fornication

Aeneas, 49–50

Aeneid. *See* Virgil

Aeschylus, 76

Aftemelouchos, 102–3, 168. *See also* Angels, caretaking; Temelouchos

Aḥer, 154, 155

Alberic, Vision of, 25, 38–39n.96

Amélineau, E., 100

Amente, 14, 79–80, 149, 152

Amos, 58, 108nn. 15, 16

Angelology, 64–66, 158

Angels: caretaking, 97, 168 (*see also* Temelouchos); good, 148–49; of Tartarus, 102; of torment, 117, 120–21, 148, 161, 163–65

Antichrist, 22, 25, 34, 100, 163

Apocalypses, 58, 65–66n.83, 68; ascent, 37, 155, 172–73; genre, 2, 60, 158; historical, 59–60, 67; Jewish, 44–45; medieval, 134; Muslim, 134–35; tour, 2–3, 60, 66–67, 169–70, 172–73

Apocrypha, 34, 37, 71

Aqiba, 154

Arda Viraf, 47–48

Aristophanes, 42, 111, 116, 120n.52

Aristotle, 75n.21, 76

Asceticism, 17–19. *See also* Celibacy; Monasticism

Asín Palacios, M., 39–40, 47–48

'Avot d'Rabbi Natan, 93

b. Azai, 153–54

Azbuga, 156–57

Babylonian Talmud, 31n.71, 32, 170. *See also* Munich MS; Venice first edition; *names of individual tractates*

Balaam, 78

Bar Hebraeus, 18

2 Baruch, 59, 151, 167n.77

3 Baruch, 61–63, 143, 167n.77, 172

Baruch, Ethiopic Apocalypse of, 21–23, 35, 70, 72n.9, 74, 83, 92–93, 96, 100–101, 103–4, 114–15, 117, 119–26, 158–59, 161, 170–71

Beasts, 10, 17, 34, 116–17, 119–20, 146–47, 161

Becker, E. J., 38–39n.96

Berger, K., 134

Bible. *See* Greek Bible; Hebrew Bible; New